Inefficiency in Industry

The European Initiative

Series Editor: PROFESSOR DAVID G. MAYES
National Institute of Economic and Social Research, London, and
Co-ordinator of the Economic and Social Research Council (ESRC)
research project *The European Initiative.*

The late 1980s and early 1990s have produced major events and changes
in Europe which are set to produce fundamental shifts in the economic,
political and social changes throughout the continent. The European
Community's Single Market Programme due for completion at the end
of 1992 and the sweeping political reforms and revolution in Eastern
Europe have been the catalysts. This new series of books has been
established to publish the best research and scholarship on European
issues and to make an important contribution to the advancement of
knowledge on European issues.

Professor Mayes is Co-ordinator of a major research initiative on
European issues by the Economic and Social Research Council. The Series,
in addition to publishing the leading contributions made by that initiative,
will also publish other titles drawn from all disciplines in the Social
Sciences, including Economics, Political Science and Sociology.

Titles in the Series:

The European Challenge: Industry's Response to the 1992 programme
edited by David G. Mayes

The External Implications of European Integration
edited by David G. Mayes

Inefficiency in Industry
by David G. Mayes, Christopher Harris and Melanie Lansbury

The New Europe: Changing Economic Relations between East and West
by Susan Senior Nello

Prospective Europeans: New Members for the European Union
edited by John Redmond

Inefficiency in Industry

David Mayes, Christopher Harris and
Melanie Lansbury

HARVESTER
WHEATSHEAF

New York · London · Toronto · Sydney · Tokyo · Singapore

First published 1994 by
Harvester Wheatsheaf
Campus 400, Maylands Avenue
Hemel Hempstead
Hertfordshire, HP2 7EZ
A division of
Simon & Schuster International Group

Typeset in 10/12pt Times
by PPS Limited, 174 London Road, Amesbury, Wilts.

Printed and bound in Great Britain
by BPC Wheatons Ltd, Exeter

British Library Cataloguing in Publication Data

A catalogue record for this book is available from
the British Library

ISBN 0-7450-0867-4

1 2 3 4 5   98 97 96 95 94

Contents

Preface

This book is a joint effort in many respects. It was born out of a concern in several countries to explain the variety in performance of firms in manufacturing industry. Its immediate origins stretch back to the mid-1970s. The National Economic Development Office (NEDO) in London, which was set up in 1962, had the job of trying to increase the rate of economic growth in the UK and to improve the efficiency of British industry. It employed many routes for this, beginning with a grand design in the National Plan of 1965, but on the whole worked most effectively at the sectoral level (Middlemas, 1983). An important facet of the task was the selection of sectors on which to focus. The Labour government of 1974–9 felt that it needed a comprehensive strategy to cover the whole of industry. As part of that strategy it was decided to identify the weakest parts of the UK economy as *prima facie* targets for action. This identification focused on competitive performance in international markets and productivity performance.

It was quickly clear that focusing on averages covered up much of the problem. Not all the firms in each industry were poor performers. An industry where performance was generally weak might require a different policy approach from one where there were some good firms but pockets of poorer behaviour. The government was interested both in measures to improve industrial competitiveness in general and to target specific problems, for example, small firms, lack of finance and unfair competition. Performance is not just a within-industry question but an international one. NEDO based its main comparisons in this period on the UK and Germany.

Largely fortuitously, it discovered that Professor Richard Caves at Harvard was working on a similar problem and wanted to extend his own productivity comparisons (Davies and Caves, 1987) to a more detailed level. While NEDO had been collecting descriptive statistics from the Business Statistics Office in Newport, based on the individual responses to the *Annual Census of Production* during the 1970s, Caves had decided to explore a more sophisticated approach, involving the estimation of stochastic frontier production functions, using similar US data collected by the US Department of Commerce.

Caves and NEDO soon came to an agreement to advance the research jointly. The work on NEDO's data, undertaken by Caves' colleague Sheryl Bailey Dow, has recently been published in Caves (1992b), along with an extension of the study to Australia, Canada, Japan and South Korea. Caves' own work on the US is published in Caves and Barton (1990b). Work in the UK proceeded more slowly. First, it took some time to arrange access to the confidential data in the *Annual Census of Production*. In order to adhere to the strict terms of the Statistics of Trade Act, the analysis was undertaken by Bernard Mitchell and his colleagues at the Business Statistics Office. Second, it was necessary to raise finance for the analysis of the information. NEDO's own resources extended only to financing the estimation and the presentation of those results – largely undertaken by Michael Bramson and Anne Hickling.

The Economic and Social Research Council (ESRC) eventually provided a most welcome grant for the analysis (no. R000231195) and the main work was undertaken at the University of Exeter by David Mayes and Alison Green. This forms the large part of the basis of this book. Because the work took over a decade to complete, others were able to move much more swiftly. In particular, the Bureau of Industry Economics (BIE) in Australia not only joined the team but undertook a far more thorough initial estimation than any other country, largely completing it as early as 1984. This work, led by Chris Harris, forms the basis of the theoretical sections of our book. Harris's early work, covering problems with data, specification and estimation, was invaluable in the detailed design of the UK study. Indeed, unlike many international comparisons, this particular project has been characterised by the complementary treatment of different problems. This has enabled each participant to feed from the others, rather than the more common experience of conflicting treatment of the same problem, which makes comparison difficult. (The Japanese, for example, were worried by the high rate of failure to obtain satisfactory estimates of inefficiency in the US and demonstrated, by means of a Monte Carlo study (Torii and Caves, 1992), that larger numbers of failures were possible even when the underlying model was specified correctly, simply because of unfortunate random variation in the residual, inexplicable factors. This helped confirm that neither the Australian nor UK findings were implausibly failure-prone.)

We are most grateful to our fellow researchers for their comments during the course of the research, particularly to Richard Caves, who was tireless in his careful comments and frequent encouragement. The marriage of the UK and Australian experience, shown in this volume, exploits the complementarity of the research of the two groups but does not imply that they are incompatible with the other four studies. The BIE did not have the resources to complete the full analysis of the results (later tackled by Caves, 1992a, 1992b), while NEDO could not get adequate access to the data or resources to perform anything other than a pilot study followed by a single uniform approach to estimation. However, the constructive scepticism emanating from John Baldwin in Canada, and from Australia, after the diffficulties with estimation, led to the following of a very thorough research design and to an alertness to the possibilities of interesting results being the product of misspecification rather than to the behaviour which appeared to have been measured.

Although long in the making, this has been an exciting quest and one which is not yet over. The original study had three phases: first, the estimation of inefficiency, second, the explanation of inefficiency within each country and third, the comparison of inefficiency and its determinants across countries. Mayes and Lansbury are currently engaged on a further study, financed by the ESRC, to explain how efficiency changed during the 1980s in the UK. This is exploring not just how 'efficient' production and inefficiency compared with it has been changing over time, but the extent to which overall improvements in efficiency are due to the exit of the least efficient and the entry of more efficient plants rather than to the improvement in performance of those which survived throughout the period.

This latter study not only allows us to explore whether there was a 'Thatcher Revolution' in the 1980s, in the sense that much inefficiency was squeezed out of the system, but it also permits us to see whether absolute efficiency in the UK improved compared with its partners. It would be a second-order success to show that the spread of inefficiency within manufacturing in the UK had been reduced if at the same time the gap between the average efficiency in the UK and that in its major trading partners had widened. The answers to these exciting questions are still to come. What the current analysis described here has been able to reveal is answers to questions such as: Does greater concentration lead to less inefficiency? Does increased foreign competition improve efficiency? Does greater innovation lead to greater efficiency? Where is there the greatest variety in behaviour and the greatest apparent scope for improvement? These are quite significant enough for strong policy conclusions and we hope the results are as stimulating for the reader as the process of discovery was for the researchers.

1

Introduction

1.1 A UK perspective

Over the years there have been continuing complaints about the performance of British manufacturing industry. By comparison with the other main Organization for Economic Co-operation and Development (OECD) countries, UK output has been relatively slow to grow. Between 1965 and 1993, gross domestic product (GDP) of the major seven industrialised nations[1] increased by over 140 per cent, in 1980 prices – nearly twice as much as that of the UK over the same period. Furthermore, UK productivity has dropped down the OECD league table of GDP per capita from fifth in 1960 to thirteenth in 1990, according to OECD *Main Economic Indicators*. There is, however, no reason to think that the UK faces inherent difficulties which place it so far down the league table. Studies eager to analyse the causes of this slower growth, and to offer remedies, have looked at problems ranging from those relating to a lack of natural resources, distance from major markets and a distorted capital stock after the war (Prais, 1981b; Muellbauer, 1986; Davies and Caves, 1987; Rowthorn and Wells, 1987; Crafts, 1988; Porter, 1990). Such factors could perhaps explain why the UK has not been top of the league but not why it is so far down it.

It is not that the UK has no excellent companies. It has the world leaders in many areas, such as pharmaceuticals, aerospace and clothing, and continues to provide a flow of innovations which indicate no diminution in the ability to maintain a leading position. However, despite this, UK industry's export share over the period 1950–80 has fallen by around a third. There can be two general explanations of this apparent contradiction. The first is that the UK has chosen to specialise in a set of industries, sectors and markets where growth has been below average (Panic and Rajan, 1971). However, a second explanation is that the UK

1

has a long 'tail' of relatively inefficient companies that bring down average performance.

This book focuses on that inefficiency. It seeks to establish the extent of inefficiency in manufacturing in the UK and to explore the conditions that seem to let it persist. Many routes have been followed in the past to investigate this problem. Some have explored particular factors, like the absence of an adequate skills base (Prais *et al.*, 1990). Others have examined the structure of particular industries (Mayes, 1983; Daly *et al.*, 1985; Steedman and Wagner, 1989), have investigated a sample of firms in detail (Grinyer *et al.*, 1988) or have focused on the whole economy at a relatively aggregate level (Roy, 1982; Oulton, 1987, 1988). All of these routes have drawbacks: either they do not cover all determinants, or all sectors, or all firms; or they do not have sufficient detail to explore the nature of inefficiency. Here we fill in a different dimension to the analysis by examining the performance of nearly 20,000 individual establishments drawn from the whole of manufacturing industry. These 20,000 establishments include all large plants with more than 200 employees, half of those with 100–200 employees and a quarter of those with between 20 and 100. Conclusions drawn from it really will be representative of the economy as a whole, as it represents the large majority of activity in all industries. Of course this approach also has its drawbacks, which we discuss in detail. The major one is simply that in order to generalise we have to assume a regularity in what constitutes efficient behaviour. As a result this may confuse other sources of diversity, such as product variety, and inefficiency.

1.2   An Australian perspective

Variety in behaviour in firms and plants is not unique to the UK, but other countries usually combine it with faster growth. Indeed, this study is part of a much wider research project that compares results on a similar basis for the US, Japan, Korea and Australia (Caves and Barton, 1990b; Caves, 1992b). Canada has also participated in the research but with a somewhat different methodology, while work is at an earlier stage in Norway.[2] Chapter 6 provides an explicit comparison with these other countries.

Here we also focus on the experience of Australia. In some respects Australia is not an ideal comparator for the UK. It has a much smaller population spread around the fringes of a land mass bigger than Europe. It is not part of the largest regional market in the world (Europe) but isolated and, although closer to many Asian markets than even Japan, Taiwan or Korea, it is a long way from the major markets in Japan, North America, Europe and East Asia (Mayes, 1990; Bollard and Mayes, 1992). It has a long history of heavy protection for manufacturing industry and hence, until recently, a very closed market. However, in other respects its experience is very valuable. It has a very similar tradition of industrial organisation as a result of a long period of emigration from the UK and substantial investment by UK companies. It has a persistent balance of payments deficit and is approaching a solution by means that have many parallels in UK policy in the period since the late 1970s (Stanford, 1992).

The high level of protection has had important effects on the structure of Australian manufacturing. It encouraged inward investment from overseas, particularly from the UK (Corden, 1974, p. 330). As a result, overseas multinational companies tend to dominate much of tradeable manufacturing, aided by their access to best practice technology and management practices and the advantage from being the 'first mover'. However, these multinationals were interested in producing for the Australian domestic market, rather than using Australia as a base for exports (Committee for Review of Export Market Development Assistance, 1989), leading to plants that were often on a rather small scale. Parry (1977, p. 16), for example, suggests that in the early 1970s Australian chemical plants were typically only 10–50 per cent of the size required for effective world competition in terms of unit costs. Caves (1984, p. 346), writing about the structure of Australian industry as it was in 1977–8, the year of our study, concludes that 'Small market size and isolation do constrain both the overall productivity and the scale efficiency of Australian manufacturing industries. High levels of tariff protection impose an economic cost that consists mainly of making sub-optimal scale production feasible.' Protection reduced the incentive to resist the wage and work practice demands from the strong trade unions and to search for new and innovative ways of motivating employees and hence reduced efficiency relative to best practice elsewhere in the world (Plowman, 1992).

Focusing directly on Australian industry in this manner is more appropriate than looking at measures of output per head on a wider basis because simple comparisons of output per head generally do not allow for exchange rate variations from equilibrium levels or for effects on prices of tariffs and restrictions on trade (see Haig, 1987, for example). Haig shows that using price indices for the relevant industries Australia had an average per capita labour productivity 17 per cent higher than the UK in 1977, and 31 per cent higher in manufacturing. On a per hour basis the discrepancy in manufacturing is larger (32 per cent in 1974 and 44 per cent in 1983; 1977 figures are not available). Figures for the disparity in labour productivity rates within manufacturing are only available for 1983 and these suggest a very uneven spread of performance:

Ratio of Australian to British labour productivity in 1983
Food 0.99   Chemicals 1.60   Textiles 1.02   Metals 1.58   Other 1.31

These average figures themselves disguise the spread of productivity.

We should, therefore, expect to see a pattern of inefficiency that reflects the cushion between Australian costs and those prevailing in world markets. The smaller scale of Australian industry may explain why average productivity is lower than in the US but does not entail that plants are inefficient just because they are small. While the scope for inefficiency may be potentially much larger in Australia, in this study we look at it not just by comparison with the UK but in comparison with what appears to constitute 'efficiency' in an Australian context. We can thus see whether there is more variety of performance in Australia than in the UK. Caves (1992b) shows very clearly that despite the very different absolute levels of efficiency between the US, UK and Japan there is considerable similarity in the extent of inefficiency. The comparison is more tenuous at the industry level.

Comparisons are a two-way activity and although this book has two UK authors to the one Australian, the balance of relevance is largely even. Australian industrial policy has converged very firmly on the view that international competitiveness is the key to success, although special problems are presented by the 'sensitive' industries of motor vehicles and clothing, textiles and footwear (Stanford, 1992). Prior to this, there had been a widespread view that the discrimination against Australia's agricultural (and coal) exports in many of the major markets of the world and Australia's particular geographical difficulties required a programme of protection and support for manufacturing to redress the balance. The current solution (Stanford, 1992) involves combining what is known as 'micro-economic reform' – to a large extent a programme of internal and external liberalisation – and trade-related investment measures (TRIMs). These TRIMs include 'export facilitation', such as the opportunity for Australian motor vehicle and parts manufacturers to import automotive parts free of duty in return for automotive exports; 'Partnerships for Development' in information technology (IT), which require firms with substantial sales to the government to agree to achieve exports equal to over 50 per cent of imports within seven years; research and development (R & D) expenditure equal to at least 5 per cent of local turnover and a local content of 70 per cent for exports; and the 'Factor f', the pharmaceutical industry development programme, which tries to encourage similar actions by taking progress in achieving them into account when setting the administered prices for drugs purchased by the public sector.[3]

There is some debate over which factors/actors led to the changes in policy. Prime candidates include the Industries Assistance Commission (now Industry Commission) and more recently the National Farmers Federation, which pointed out the static (deadweight) effects, the adverse influences on other industries through exchange rate and input cost effects and the adverse dynamic effects. In addition, there was a wider perception (which included ministers) that the infant industries that were being afforded protection showed few signs of growing up. Trade union leaders came to realise that a focus on wealth creation rather than just on distribution would be necessary to improve employment prospects after the wage-growth-inspired recession of the early 1980s. Some of the elements for a new strategy have been put forward by the Australian Manufacturing Council (1990), which contain representatives from both the employers and trade unions.

Some of the evidence for changing past policy came from the Bureau of Industry Economics in Canberra, which undertook the parallel study of nearly 20,000 plants in Australian industry (Harris, 1988, 1992), although results only became widely available relatively late in the day. Particularly instructive were the BIE's (1990, 1991a) studies of plants located in different countries but performing the same processes in the same firm – in photographic paper and domestic water heaters. Here, even when all the main sources of difference were taken into account, Australia still came out of the comparison rather badly. Clearly inefficiency in the use of the factors of production is a problem in these plants. With the same skills, technologies and production levels, Australia seems to get less output from the same amounts of input. A comparison of two firms is scarcely economy-wide evidence but it is clearly suggestive. Some of the causes of difference were very specific. Productivity performance in the Sydney plant described in BIE (1991a) was handicapped by poor work and management practices, reflecting a history of adverse management–labour relations (a familiar story in parts of UK industry in the 1970s). The Melbourne plant in BIE (1990) was handicapped by low utilisation rates, which not surprisingly raised costs. If the number of productive hours could have been increased relative to those paid for, and if restrictive practices could have been reduced (particularly those relating to demarcation, which reduced multiskilling and inhibited machine setup and maintenance performance, and restrictions on the employment of temporary workers) substantial improvements in performance would have been possible. This scope for reform in the labour market has been relatively slow to come, in part reflecting no doubt the relationship between the Labor government and the Australian Council of Trade Unions since 1983 (Harris, 1991).

What the current study does is provide evidence at the other end of the scale. Here we consider the whole of Australian manufacturing industry, beginning with a basic dataset of some 26,000 establishments employing four or more people. Thus, despite the smaller economy there are actually more data points for Australia, achieved by including smaller scale outfits and not requiring the sampling of small scale plants used in the UK.

1.3 The nature of the research and the structure of the book

Up till now we have rather airily used the terms 'efficiency' and 'inefficiency' as if everybody knew what they meant. In practice this is far from true. 'Efficiency' is a dynamic concept that involves a firm being able to operate with the minimum level of resources necessary to produce its output and yet remain highly competitive over an extended period of time. Thus a firm that cuts its costs to the bone in the short term by avoiding investment in equipment, new technologies and skills may appear efficient for a while but will face higher costs – if it remains in business at all – in the longer term as it tries to make good for the lost time. The position is further complicated by the fact that both economies are open, so that changes in general competitiveness can occur through shifts in the exchange rate or fortuitous shocks to productivity in other countries, which bear no relation to the relative efficiency of a firm in a particular part of manufacturing (or any other specific industry for that matter).

'Inefficiency' is clearly operating below that efficient level. We therefore begin our discussion, in Chapter 2, by exploring what efficiency and inefficiency are. In particular it is necessary to distinguish between the variety that characterises any normally functioning market and discrepancies, where improvements could readily be made. Much micro-economic analysis is based on theoretical markets peopled by firms of a similar size producing identical products with a common technology and inputs of capital, labour and materials, which all have a common consistent quality. With some trivial exceptions this theoretical model does not describe any Australian or British manufacturing industries. Our approach does assume that a division into approximately 150 industries within manufacturing permits the use of single industry production functions. Ideally, if time and money were no object, it would be possible to use a variety of diagnostic procedures to improve the models (Harris, 1992), including tests for incorrect functional form (Anscombe, 1961; Ramsey, 1969), heteroscedasticity (Breusch and Pagan, 1979) and parameter stability (Chow, 1960). In particular it would have been of considerable interest to assess whether the same frontier was appropriate for small as well as large plants and hence whether technical inefficiency varied for the two groups (see Caves and Barton, 1990b, for an example). The obtaining of information on the extent of returns to scale and on the degree to which inputs are substitutable for or complementary to each other must remain for later study.

Chapter 3, therefore, explores the different routes that are available to estimate inefficiency and examines the results that are available from existing studies. Much of this existing work relates to the level of productivity rather than its distribution within industries. Other studies of firm level inefficiency include Battese and Coelli (1988), Bravo-Ureta and Rieger (1990), Grabowski *et al.* (1990), Kalirajan (1990) for agriculture, and Barla and Perelman (1989) for airlines.

Our methodology, which is developed in Chapter 4, gets round this problem of multiple sources of variation among firms by deliberately assuming that there is a stochastic element to productive behaviour, which represents all the varieties in individual establishments' behaviour within a particular industry, thus separating variation due to noise from variation due to inefficiency. Nevertheless, it is still necessary to provide some estimate of what represents efficient behaviour. In our case, regularity within the industry is represented by an augmented translog production function, which itself allows for a fairly flexible relation between the factors of production and output. This function, augmented by a stochastic component, is treated as an efficient frontier and inefficiency is measured by distinguishing a separate, unexplained part of the residual which lies within it.

This has its own drawbacks, efficiency is defined by practice, not by some theoretically attainable standard. This feature automatically limits the extent of possible inefficiency and also defines it in national terms. If Australian or British efficient performance lies well inside that of other countries for a particular industry, that discrepancy is not immediately accounted for. For this reason we also compare international performance in Chapter 6. Second, our approach assumes that each of the 140–150 industries used can reasonably be represented by a single production function. A single statistical category for an industry may in fact be an amalgam of rather different components, mass-production and craft work, for example. Third, the need to assume a shape for the distribution of inefficiency may result in patterns well removed from reality. In Chapter 3, we therefore contrast our chosen methodology with the other approaches available, as our results clearly contribute to the picture rather than constituting the full picture themselves. This discussion of other possible approaches also draws on previous work of the National Institute and of the Bureau of Industry Economics.

Although the simple results for inefficiency according to industry presented in Chapter 4 are themselves interesting, it is Chapter 5, which explains the determinants of inefficiency, that forms the heart of the book. In an ideal world it would be even more valuable if we could explore the results at the level of the individual establishment or firm. This would enable us to pinpoint the individual firms where action could best be taken. An exposition of this detailed approach is given by Tulkens (1989) for the Belgian Post Office, where the performance of every Post Office is estimated and compared with the most efficient. Local and central management can therefore see at a glance which branches can do with improvement.

Unfortunately, two factors hold us back from following this desirable approach. The first is the Statistics of Trade Act (1979) and its Australian equivalent, the Census and Statistics Act (1905), which prevent any analysis which might reveal details about an individual enterprise, as the data are provided to the statistical authorities in confidence. This in itself also imposes constraints on the process of estimation, as it is not possible for the researchers to examine any individual observations when unusual results are observed (naturally we employed strict data cleansing processes to avoid rogue observations entering the data set in the first place). This restraint is not as important as it might appear because the second problem is a lack of suitable information on the same establishment basis to use to explain inter-establishment, rather than inter-industry, variations in efficiency. The *Annual Census of Production* does collect a considerable volume of information on output, inputs and expenditure, but it does not provide the sorts of detail about product composition, working methods, skills, etc. that we would normally want to use. Some of these variables are available for the firm as a whole from company reports and other published statistics, but these would be difficult to allocate across establishments and any dataset that was not on a directly comparable basis would present an impossible logistical problem when dealing with 20,000 observations.

In dealing with the explanation of inefficiency, therefore, we have to look at differences in the characteristics of the industries themselves. There is a well-known literature (Averch and Johnson, 1962; Williamson, 1963; Leibenstein, 1966; Stigler, 1976), which has explored the interrelation between structure, conduct and performance across industries and it is this that provides our starting point. We would expect that the more competition in an industry appears to be impeded, the greater the chance that inefficiency can survive. The most simple impediments come from difficulty of entry and exit, a lack of exposure to foreign competition and the existence of monopoly. Industries open to foreign competition do indeed seem to show less inefficiency, but the effect of increasing monopoly is more complex. As in other countries a curvilinear relation is observed. In the US and Japan this showed that increasing monopoly only reduced efficiency up to a point and beyond that even more monopoly was associated with decreased measured inefficiency. In part this might reflect the greater ability of large firms to innovate, if we believe in a Schumpeterian approach to change, or it might imply that when there are large firms about, the more inefficient are unable to compete because of the exercise of market power.

Inefficiency can also appear when industries are changing rapidly. Under these circumstances the old can co-exist with the new when we are only looking at a single year, even though they will be shaken out later on. In a rapidly growing market there is room for inefficient players. It is for the obverse of this finding that we observed a concentration of companies, that decided they needed to change their performance markedly during recessions, in the course of our 'Sharpbenders' study (Grinyer *et al.*, 1988).

Segmentation of the market can also occur on a spatial basis, either because of high transport costs or because of variations in local tastes. This again allows firms to operate with different levels of efficiency and production scale. Differences in the organisation of the industry also have an impact with differences between industries characterised by multiplant firms and those that operate primarily from a single site. However, industries can also be subject to variation in performance for reasons not directly describable as inefficiency, such as product differentiation.

Taken together, these various explanations of inefficiency account for about half of the variation across industries. Although this is a high proportion by comparison with many cross-section studies, this nevertheless omits most of what one might regard as the archetypal form of inefficiency, i.e. X-inefficiency (Leibenstein, 1966, 1969, 1973, 1975, 1977, 1978), which is the part due to the individual organisational, effort and skill-related factors which are so significant in the comparison of individual plants. The reason the term X-efficiency is used is precisely because the features are so difficult to pin down and measure. As a result they usually form part of the unexplained residual (both in within-industry and cross-industry regressions). This is unsatisfactory for two reasons. First, because a residual catches all the remaining sources of error in the estimation process: measurement errors, misspecification and exceptional events (such as fires causing a loss of output) and bundles them in with the 'X'. Thus we have no idea whether the residual is an underestimate, overestimate, etc. The other sources of error would have been removed in the estimation process if we had been able to detect them. Second, if we cannot attribute to the residual specific factors, then it is impossible to decide which factors need to be changed to improve performance. Not surprisingly this provides a justification for the very detailed case study comparisons that we and others have done of matched plants (Mayes, 1983; BIE, 1990, 1991a; Prais *et al.*, 1990).

In order to put these results in context and draw conclusions for UK and Australian industry, our final chapter contrasts our findings with those of the other four countries in the full study.

1.4   Importance of the research

In many respects the results in this book confirm findings found elsewhere. Variation in efficiency is a characteristic of successful economies like Japan, as well as of less successful ones like Australia and the UK. A structural shift towards successful industries does not necessarily reduce inefficiency within industries but it does place the economy as a whole at a higher level of performance and is likely to increase the prospects for economic growth. Economic policy aimed at increasing the flexibility of industry improves the chances of achieving that change. Most work on flexibility has focused on the labour market. McCalman (1992), for example, has shown that although there are similarities at the macro-economic level with both centralised and decentralised wage determination being able to produce the required real wage decline in Australia following on adverse economic shock, significant differences emerge for employment by occupation and industry which favour the decentralised regime. Similar results have been produced for the UK (see Metcalf, 1993, for example). However, in Bollard *et al.* (1993) we have extended this analysis to product markets.

It is clear that protected industries in general seem to be associated with higher inefficiency, so the policies of both Australia and the UK in seeking to lower international barriers appear well placed. The continuing push towards the Single European Market takes this even further. Tariff barriers for much of UK manufacturing are already low and lack of import penetration in some sectors reflects more effective non-tariff barriers that the Single Market is designed to reduce. This reduction in artificial barriers emphasises the relative importance of policies to reduce the effectiveness of 'natural' protection, through reducing transport costs and removing the impediments to competition (see, for example, the BIE's work on benchmarking (BIE, 1992a, b, c, d, 1993) and the labour market (Harris, 1991, section 5.4).

Australia faces a more difficult course of action, as much barrier reduction has to be unilateral, particularly if the GATT negotiations fail to achieve much. The closer economic relations with New Zealand, although important for some industries, nevertheless represents only a small proportion of output. However, estimates by BIE (1989) suggest that overall gains could be as much as 22 per cent of the value of the additional trade due to the liberalisation. While Australia stood to increase its welfare by some $650 million annually, New Zealand could gain by nearer $1.1 billion (about eight times as much in per capita terms). Progress towards any other regional trade grouping is likely to be slow (despite Asia–Pacific Economic Council (APEC) and the importance assigned to Asia–Pacific relations in the recent election) and will in any case not come close to rivalling the importance of the European Community (EC) and the European Economic Area. Emphasis has been placed on continuing the strategy of reducing external barriers, encouraging micro-economic reform and improving macro-economic policy through reduced deficits, low inflation and low interest rates (Mayes, 1993).

Continuing the emphasis on supply-side improvements, or micro-economic reform, as it tends to be referred to in Australia, is expected to result in an increase in absolute efficiency compared with other countries. The pressures of the 1980s resulted in the closure of many of the weakest firms in manufacturing. The results in this book provide the basis for an analysis of these more recent years – a task on which we are currently embarked.

Notes

1. US, Japan, Germany, France, UK, Italy and Canada.
2. Further studies are expected in France and Belgium.
3. Such programmes tend to lack transparency and are difficult to evaluate empirically. In the only evaluation to date (Factor f) the BIE (1991b) considered it highly unlikely that the scheme enhanced Australia's economic welfare.

2

What is inefficiency?

The term efficiency, as used in economics, indicates the success with which resources are utilised; it expresses the extent to which firms are best utilising their available inputs to produce the maximum potential output. Efficiency is therefore a relative concept and its measurement requires a standard of performance against which the success of economic units is assessed (Førsund and Hjalmarsson, 1974). This could be either the best actual performance in an industry or a theoretical maximum. In this chapter we discuss the definition of inefficiency, considering both what constitutes firms' potential and five reasons as to why they should fall short:

1. Technology.
2. Quality of inputs.
3. Scale of production.
4. Allocation of resources.
5. Managerial, i.e. how the firm is run.

Failure to achieve efficiency is in part a problem of dynamic adjustment but also a problem of lack of market pressures, which permits inefficiency to persist. Beyond this there are reasons for variation among firms which reflect heterogeneity rather than pure inefficiency, e.g. product variation, transport costs, etc.

2.1 Why does inefficiency occur?

Fully efficient behaviour for the economy as a whole would require that each individual firm operated up to its potential. Indeed, 'efficiency' for the whole economy also involves an optimal distribution across the whole run of firms as well. Even if firms were capable of such fully efficient behaviour, economies are subject to external shocks (demand shocks, changes in technology, etc.) and they take some time to react. The optimum would therefore never be realised in practice. Nevertheless, for analytical clarity, economic analysis traditionally uses this optimum as a baseline against which to judge actual behaviour.

Starting with the performance of the economy as a whole, the central economic problem is how an economy should allocate resources efficiently given individuals' preferences and available technology. If a firm's main objective is assumed to be maximisation of profits, under perfectly competitive conditions the firm will produce at the most efficient point that satisfies this aim. That is to say, in an industry containing a large number of identical firms, firms are assumed to be price-takers, as no firm alone is large enough to deviate from the prices set by the market. With no barriers to entry or exit and full information on market and production conditions, each firm will be concerned with choosing the optimal levels of inputs and outputs which satisfy their profit-maximising objective, hence all firms will produce the same output using the same allocation of inputs. This same ease of entry and exit enables firms to respond rapidly to differences in the balance of demand and supply among markets as revealed by profit opportunity.

Under these conditions inefficiency is a short-term phenomenon, due to random shocks, and in the long term profit-maximising behaviour by firms will eliminate it (Stigler, 1976). Thus, over time, it is the speed of adjustment that affects efficiency. We should then ask whether efficiency is a static or a dynamic concept; later in this chapter we discuss this question in some detail. For the large part, explanations of efficiency take it as a static concept. They consider a snapshot and take the position at that particular time as the general picture of efficiency in the industry. This may be misleading but the great advantage of these simplifications is that an explanation of efficiency can be divided into two separate questions (Farrell, 1957). First, are resources allocated efficiently, and second, given their allocation, are they used efficiently?

This can be shown with the help of a simple diagram. Figure 2.1 represents a firm employing two factors of production, capital (K) and labour (L), in the production of a single output, Y. For simplicity constant returns to scale are assumed in order to avoid frontiers at each level of output. With a price ratio shown by DE for these two factors, a firm can have any combination of labour and capital along this line for the same total cost. The most efficient point of production, i.e. where the most output can be produced with these inputs, is C. Along curve II all input combinations give exactly one unit of Y, this curve is convex, entailing that as the firm continues to substitute capital for labour (or vice versa),

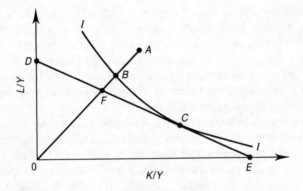

Figure 2.1 Farrell's measure of efficiency.

the amount of capital required to replace each lost unit of labour will become increasingly larger, in order to continue to produce the same unit of output. A firm would show *allocative inefficiency* if it chose a different combination of L and K – say B. At this point it requires BF extra resources to produce the output. However, given this factor ratio, the firm is also *technically inefficient* if it requires even more input to produce the goods, e.g. at point A. Thus the firm at point A is technically inefficient relative to the firm at point B due to its use of extra resources (shown as the distance BA). Firm A is allocatively inefficient as well, due to its excessive labour intensity and costs (shown as the distance BF) relative to the firm at point C. As proportions, the technical inefficiency of firm A is BA/OA, its allocative inefficiency is FB/OB, and its overall inefficiency is FA/OA.

Technical inefficiency therefore refers to the extent to which firms either use excessive inputs to produce their output with a given input mix, or underproduce output given their inputs and a given input mix. Farrell was referring to management's ability to manage and organise the firm. If, for example, we were to observe two identical firms with the same scale of operation, using the same technology and same combination of inputs to produce a homogeneous product, then differences in output produced could only be explained by differences in the way the two firms were operated, i.e. managed and organised. This source of inefficiency is also accounted for in X-inefficiency (Leibenstein, 1966). X-inefficiency explains non-optimal behaviour by firms, i.e. firms producing at a scale where costs are not minimised and profits not maximised. X-efficiency should be distinguished from technical efficiency, in Leibenstein's own words:

> The concept of T.E. (technical efficiency) suggests that the problem is a technical one and has to do with the techniques of an input called management. Under

X.E. (X-efficiency) the basic problem is *intrinsic* to the nature of human organization, both organization within the firm and organization outside of the firm. (Leibenstein, 1977, p. 312)

However, Martin and Page (1983) argue that X-inefficiency, if it exists, involves firms failing to produce at the outer bound of their production surface, and that this failure is related to the allocation of effort. On this basis, X-inefficiency is one component of Farrell's technical inefficiency.

In the following chapters we use the term 'technical inefficiency' to embrace all reasons for actual performance with given inputs falling short of that attainable. This reflects not only Farrell's technical inefficiency and Leibenstein's X-inefficiency but other factors as well, for example different technologies, input heterogeneity and output heterogeneity. Typically these are not of normative significance and should be allowed for in the analysis of the determinants of inefficiency. 'Inefficiency' in this sense can occur because of factors within the firm, the structure of the market, the regulatory system governing firm behaviour and a long list of other factors which we explore in detail in Chapter 5.

In reality we are dealing with snapshots of overlapping processes within the framework of optimisation. Firms are simultaneously doing the best they can with current resources and trying to move to a better basis through improving the factors of production, their allocation and the technology available. Some firms may therefore never reach their optimal point with respect to current resources if, for example, the process of change moves at a faster rate than their reactions to changing conditions or their rate of learning. Firms may find that new technology has been adopted by their competitors before they can reach optimal production using their existing technology. Trying to become fully efficient can therefore be a very expensive process, as changing capital and retraining labour before it has earned its full return is costly. Indeed, a firm that has an inappropriate allocation may be unable to change because its costs will be higher and hence profits lower, making it more difficult to raise the finance for the necessary investment from either internal or external sources. Efficiency therefore involves an optimal stance in this dynamic world, having the resources not just to achieve change but to generate it, as this is the principal source of competitive advantage (Nelson, 1991).

2.2 In what ways is the simple model misleading?

The simple model is only useful in so far as it clarifies analysis and acts as an aid to understanding. We must, of course, explain the full complexity of reality. There are several obvious reservations.

2.2.1 *The rate of adjustment*

First of all the forces for eliminating inefficiency may be weaker than is suggested. Although much of economics has been based on ideas of maximisation there is strong evidence that many firms operate on a basis that might be better described as 'satisficing', i.e. doing the best that is necessary to survive comfortably (Simon, 1959). Small shop-keepers, for example, are likely to have different growth objectives. Some may have no wish to expand outside their existing premises, which are also their home, others may value their health and their leisure more highly and hence not be prepared to push to the limit on every occasion. One of the clearest examples of this behaviour is set out by Political and Economic Planning (1965), where two clear groups of firms are distinguished – 'thrusters' and 'sleepers'. Providing market shares are not eroded, returns to shareholders are adequate and confidence within the firm is high, some firms are content to operate with only limited pressure for change and do not pursue all opportunities with vigour – the 'sleepers'. Other firms are willing to take risks in return for potential high returns ('thrusters'), that is not to say they will be more successful than sleepers; thrusting describes a form of behaviour – it may or may not deliver success, because of the risk. Those which succeed adjust faster, those who get it wrong may adjust more slowly than the satisficers because they have to pay the costs of failure.

The thrusters and sleepers dichotomy is obviously too strong as all intermediate steps are possible. The observation of the authors was that there was a very clear group of thrusters, whose behaviour differentiated them from the rest. This difference between firms is not just a matter of simple static inefficiency, it reflects the costs and risks of change. To a large extent the propensity for risk-taking depends on the abilities of firms' managers, their attitude to change and the risks involved. Between them these determine how the firm is run. Of course, everyone differs in their level of aversion to risk, some people are natural gamblers and others not, but the risks and potential costs will also depend on the structure and organisation of the individual firm, flexibility of resources, etc. The risks of change are likely to be higher for small firms which are unlikely to have any other sources of funds on which to fall back.

Strong stimuli are often required before firms will indulge in major appraisal and change. On the whole these stem from immediate and very real threats, for example loss of a major customer, cyclical downturns, or new competition or technology, rather than merely new opportunities enabling the firm to improve its efficiency. Grinyer *et al.* (1988) investigate in detail a group of firms that have been in relative decline with respect to their industry and have then managed a process of sharp and sustained recovery. These they label 'sharpbenders'. Initially the firm's performance

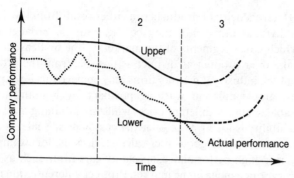

Figure 2.2 Range of satisfactory performance.

may fluctuate within satisfactory margins (Figure 2.2, period 1). A form of satisficing is therefore occurring and there is little incentive for the firm to change its behaviour. As time passes (period 2), however, the margins of satisfactory performance themselves tend to get revised downwards if there is persistent underperformance. This is a simple case of experience leading to revision of expectations. However, at some point in this downward process actual behaviour will fall below even the lowest acceptable levels (period 3). This can be the trigger that may shake the firm out of satisficing. The firm can react in one of two ways – it can make a firm attempt to address its problems, becoming more of a 'thruster' perhaps, in which case it must revise ideas and change behaviour markedly; or it can take steps that are insufficient to get out of the malaise and it will ultimately go out of business.

One other facet of the adjustment process is that the future is not known with certainty. One can adjust to eliminate observed inefficiency but the appropriateness of the adjustment depends on the forecast of where the market will be when the adjustment is complete. This involves forecasts of product innovation, technology change, tastes and the reaction of competitors. Not surprisingly, managers often get this wrong. Strategic approaches accept this risk of error and try to minimise its cost, while nevertheless chasing the opportunities.

2.2.2 *Heterogeneity*

Except in certain limited circumstances, such as commodity markets or plants within the same firm, industries are normally characterised by a variety of products. Indeed, it is this variety that helps drive the process of competition, each firm hoping to develop a product with an edge over the others. Heterogeneity of products can either result from the deliberate action of individual firms or it may be the result of broader industry headings, which cover segments of the market. In the first case firms may strive to make their product as distinct as possible from the products of other firms in the industry. One way firms may achieve this is to use brand names, for example different washing powders, by building up brand loyalty, are able to charge different prices whilst maintaining market share. Another possibility is for firms to offer the customer special facilities and accessories, or to provide good after-sales services as, for example, with cars. By offering high performance, speciality cars firms such as Morgan are able to carve out a niche in the market. Product differentiation therefore reduces the bite of competition and allows firms to be more inefficient and yet still survive.

Second, industry headings may be so broad that they contain a number of different activities. For example, in the car industry specialised firms produce high-performance cars on a small scale (e.g. Aston Martin, Morgan, Lamborghini), while other firms mass produce standard cars (e.g. Ford, Vauxhall, Rover). Hence what we observe is a collection of different activities with different levels of output for given inputs (or inputs for a given level of output), each of which may be efficient in its own sector. It may appear that this industry has a large spread of inefficiency; the small, specialised firms' output would tend to be low compared with its inputs when measured against the total industry's potential output if a high proportion of this industry was made up of large mass producing firms. As efficiency (and hence inefficiency) is a relative term it should ideally be measured using homogeneous firms, which employ similar technology and similar input mixes and levels, to produce similar outputs. Thus measuring inefficiency while treating differing activities as if they were homogeneous will give inaccurate results. Even quite small differences in specification may permit substantial differences in technology. The methodology employed in this work is outlined in Chapter 3.

2.2.3   *Heterogeneity of inputs*

Simplified theories also treat the factors of production – labour, capital and materials – as if they were homogeneous, but this is patently untrue (Prais *et al.*, 1990). Labour, in particular, is enormously variable. Individuals have their own skills and capabilities. Some of these can be substantially transformed by the firm itself through a programme of training. Moreover, the firm has the ability to hire and, to some extent, fire, so the quality of the labour force in one firm relative to another is a matter of choice for the firm concerned. For example Rolls-Royce employs panel-beating craftsmen whereas Rover uses robots and quality inspectors. However, the quality of the labour force cannot be changed instantaneously (Mayes and Ogiwara, 1992). Thus if an industry is struck by an external shock that affects some firms more than others, we can expect to observe different responses; in firms where the workforce is better qualified and trained it is likely to be more flexible, and thus the rate of change will be faster. This would only be 'inefficient', in one sense of the word, if the firm did not change as fast as it could. In another, one might argue that preparedness for the shock was part of efficiency. Although labour is heterogeneous, this is often corrected for (at least approximately) by weighting the number of employees in different classes by their wages relative to a suitable standard (BIE, 1988).

Of the other two factors – capital and materials – material inputs tend to be the more flexible, except where they are covered by long-term contracts or monopoly suppliers, for example utilities. Again, therefore, use of poorer quality or expensive inputs is, to a large extent, a matter of choice for the firm and shocks should be absorbed quite quickly, nevertheless much will depend on location. To correct for these differences in capital, empiricists add the insurance values of capital within different classes, while weighting classes by their user cost of capital relative to a standard (BIE, 1991a). This approach, although typically imperfect, is thought to reduce the biases associated with input heterogeneity. Physical capital is at the other end of the spectrum, change may be very expensive. Land is the most extreme case. One can improve the infrastructure (transport, telecommunications, etc.) but ultimately a firm has to uproot altogether to change location, with loss of capital, sunk costs, labour, suppliers, local customers, etc. On the other hand, in some cases machines can be reprogrammed or production lines reorganised to use capital more efficiently. Similarly, existing building space and structures can be better utilised. Some machines can be retrofitted to incorporate new technologies, for example by substituting new controllers, but in general the nature of the capital stock is largely determined when it is bought. Technology is embodied in the particular machine and can only be changed markedly by scrapping the machine and buying another. Technology changes over time so, to some extent, the nature of a firm's capital can be described by its age structure (vintage) of machinery. A firm is thus 'inefficient' to the extent to which it does not utilise its capital to its best effect *given* its structure and the quality and relative prices of the other more variable factors.

In practice, though, a technically efficient plant is not one where capacity of each and every resource is exactly balanced with demand from the market, but one that balances the flow of products through the plant with demand from the market. A plant should not run every capital item it owns flat out (subject to proper repair and maintenance), even though

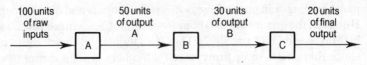

Figure 2.3 Steps in the manufacturing process.

one might think this should produce the maximum potential output. A more efficient strategy is to operate at a capacity that allows for 'statistical fluctuations' (random external shocks) and 'dependent events' within the production process. First, if a firm is better prepared for unexpected events then it can react faster than its competitors and gain a competitive advantage. Second, to produce any output there is a series of dependent events which occur during the transformation of the inputs into the finished good, the efficiency with which any one of these operations is completed is dependent on the efficiency with which its neighbouring operation is carried out.

This is illustrated in Figure 2.3, which shows a production line in which there are three processes that must be completed to transform the 100 units of input into 20 units of the final output. Within the production line the efficiency with which each process can produce its semi-output is dependent on the other processes. For example, if process A is inefficient and only produces 40 units of output A then even if process B is fully efficient it will only be able to produce 24 units of output B. Similarly process C will only be able to produce 16 units of the final product. This interdependency implies that the efficiency of a plant can only be as efficient as the least efficient operation, even if all the other operations are producing at their optimum. If the least efficient operations are not producing to the same level they will slow down the whole production process. Hence to increase overall output it is necessary to concentrate on improving the efficiency of these, rather than all, operations. In this way a plant may be able to increase output simply by utilising its existing capital better. This is highlighted by the optimised production technology (OPT) system (Goldratt, 1993) and optimisation techniques (Bowen, 1991).

A firm that has just set up a new factory can be expected to use the more advanced technologies, although not necessarily the most advanced, as these may be relatively untried or be inappropriate for the scale of production or particular type of products being made. However, there are still gains for such a factory to exploit because there is a strong element of learning in most production processes. Integrated circuits, for example, involve wastage of most of the units produced in the early stages as the fine tuning required to provide fault-free products is very difficult to achieve.

2.2.4 *Geographical location*

We have discussed differences in products and inputs: labour, capital and materials. Inputs can vary in quality, price and availability and many of these differences are generated by geographical location. Raw materials may be naturally concentrated in a certain area, and industries that use these materials may find it advantageous to locate themselves close by, if, for example, quality of materials decays rapidly, as with agricultural products, or transportation costs are a high proportion of total costs, e.g. coal inputs in the steel industry. On the other hand, areas may become 'honey-pots' e.g. the City of London. These areas attract particular skills, provide necessary auxiliary services, offer proximity to competitors, etc. and location away from these areas may be seriously disadvantageous to firms. Such locations are often encouraged by government policy as in the creation of 'technopoles' in France (Cohen, 1992).

2.2.5 *Scale of operations*

A firm's scale of operation or plant size is often a factor in determining efficiency. A firm's costs per unit of output often fall with scale, usually down to a minimum. The optimum scale of production is where costs are minimised, i.e. at the minimum efficient scale of production (Pratten, 1988), departures away from this result in *scale inefficiency*. Returning to Farrell's theoretical analysis of efficiency, if we relax the assumption of constant returns to scale, it is possible for a firm to be both allocatively and technically efficient, but if production is at a scale either too large or too small to minimise costs, the firm will suffer from scale inefficiency. On the one hand, in practice, this tends to occur if a plant is too small to be able to utilise its resources efficiently. Alternatively, the often complex hierarchy system that operates in many large firms can, in many cases, be a major source of inefficiency. A high level of bureaucracy can result in slow and/or conservative reactions to the process of change. Relations between managers and the labour forces can be weakened with an increasing hierarchical structure, thus reducing effort levels put in by the work force and a management out of touch with the problems of the factory floor. Finally small-scale activities may be more likely to attract persons with higher entrepreneurial skills and give these managers fewer constraints in implementing their ideas. Inefficiency due to plants of suboptimal scale, although potentially important, is not picked up by our average levels of industry inefficiency. This is because plants in an industry are counted as inefficient only to the extent that they fall short of what is estimated to be the output attainable in plants of their own factor proportions and scale.

2.2.6   *Scope and external economies*

The simple model of the firm that we discussed earlier assumes a single product that is produced in isolation, yet differences in efficiency of production can occur due to cost-saving externalites. Scope economies are achieved by firms undertaking related activities, for example the production of good A reduces the production cost of good B. In other words economies of scope are cost-saving externalities between production lines. External economies result from the presence of relevant facilities in other firms and public infrastructure, for example a bee keeper will benefit from a neighbouring orchard, or a firm would benefit from the building of a new motorway. Firms that benefit from such factors will tend to increase the estimated frontier and to increase measured average levels of inefficiency if the number of such firms in the industry is relatively small.

2.2.7   *Managerial control*

Finally, once competitive conditions, product differentiation, input heterogeneity, geographical location, rate of change and technology have all been accounted for, any remaining differences in the output of firms are then due to managerial and organisational influences and other human characteristics such as effort. Different managers have different ideas on how to organise a firm, different capabilities, different bargaining skills, etc. By managerial and organisational factors we are referring to technical inefficiency, that is the degree of ineffectiveness in utilising inputs. This can be due not only to factors reflecting the skills and capabilities of managers but also to factors beyond the control of those attempting to manage, such as the effort and willingness to work of the employees. For example, in an Australian plant-level study (BIE, 1991a) the productivity performance of the Sydney plant was handicapped relative to the Melbourne plant by poor work and management practices, reflecting a history of adverse management–labour relations. In particular, its performance was reduced by labour inflexibility, overmanning, limited job rotation, industrial disputes and unproductive work time, and by past management decisions in areas such as plant layout and excessive capital stock.

2.3   How should we view efficiency?

We have explained why, in reality, we observe vastly differing levels of productivity amongst firms within an industry and the existence of that diversity in the long, as well as in the short, term. We now move on to discuss how efficiency should be viewed, as this has major implications on the methods used for its measurement. In Chapter 3 our main concern is with the measurement of relative efficiency defined as a static concept, because this was how efficiency was viewed in Phases 1 and 2 of our international research programme. However, this was partly due to simplicity and the available resources; in addition our aim was to replicate, as far as possible, the US study.

2.3.1 Efficiency: A dynamic or static concept?

Inefficiency is a dynamic rather than a static concept. At any point in time a firm may appear to be inefficient in comparison to others in the industry if its productivity, using identical resources, is below its competitors. At any particular moment some firms will be more, or less, efficient than others, but this ranking will vary over time. External shocks within an industry will affect firms in different ways; firms will differ in their adjustment to shocks and they will differ in their speed of reaction to and preparation for shocks. Hence, looking at a snapshot of efficiency in an industry, a firm may appear to be inefficient relative to its competitors. However, if by not producing at maximum capacity it is more flexible and can adapt more quickly to external shocks in the economy then, over time, *it* will be more efficient. Efficiency as a dynamic concept reflects the speed of adjustment; a firm that does not react to shocks as quickly as it is able *and* is not using its resources in the best way is an inefficient firm. For an example, one can look at the television set industry. In the US, consumers demanded large 'furniture' sets, however, in Japan, where homes and per capita income were smaller, compact/portable sets were required. While the American firms were content with just satisfying home demand, in Japan the market saturated sooner and firms competed fiercely, spending much of their effort on designing smaller and better sets at lower prices. This type of product was a much better reflection of world demand and, by the end of the 1980s, the Japanese had dominated the television market. However, too much chopping and changing in response to short-term fluctuations can make costs excessive. A balance has to be struck.

If efficiency is a dynamic concept then ideally it should not be measured at just one point in time but rather over a period of time (Yoo, 1992b), one would then be able to estimate the stability of (in)efficiency. Despite this, in the past, measurement of inefficiency has generally been treated as a static concept. We continued this tradition in Phase 1, in part to ensure comparability with the studies of efficiency in the other countries in the project but mainly because a much more extensive dataset is required to adopt a dynamic approach involving information for several consecutive years. We are currently extending our analysis to measure inefficiency over time in the UK, using the period 1979–89, which helps introduce a more dynamic approach, but in the present study we only have data for the one year – 1977.

2.3.2 Efficiency: A relative or absolute concept?

Technical inefficiency tends to be measured as a relative concept. In a highly homogeneous industry differences in the productivity of firms can only be explained by inefficiency or 'noise', due to random events such as weather conditions and luck. The usual method of measurement is to establish a standard of performance with which economic units can be compared. This could be the best actual performance in an industry, or a theoretical potential. Firms in an industry will either be on this standard, in which case they are fully efficient, or below it due to inefficiency or noise; they cannot be above it (except possibly a fully efficient firm benefiting temporarily from a favourable combination of events or, for short periods of time, during peak capacity utilisation in an economic cycle or crisis). Although this is the common method a few attempts have been made to measure absolute inefficiency (Button, 1992). Absolute efficiency compares performance not with the best that is achieved but with what could be achieved in a manner comparable across industries. Hence some measure of this potential has to be obtainable from sources other than actual performance. Possibilities are behaviour in other countries or the specifications of the machinery used in production.[1] Button uses 'soft modelling' techniques to measure levels of X-inefficiency amongst industries, i.e. he uses indication rather than parametric estimation. This means that the approach does not require the specification of a production, or any other, function to act as a standard of performance. Instead it looks at the sensitivity of different industries to factors that are thought to influence levels of X-inefficiency.[2] Measures of absolute inefficiency have the advantage of allowing one to compare different industries directly, i.e. to say that one is more or less efficient than another. However, doubts can be raised as to its robustness, particularly when subjective measures are used. In addition, because it defines efficiency differently from the bulk of research in this area, absolute inefficiency (inefficiency amongst industries) as opposed to relative inefficiency (inefficiency within industries), comparison is difficult. Nevertheless, as we show in Chapter 4, this is a worthwhile exercise as one reason why an industry may show relatively little inefficiency is because there is substantial implicit or explicit collusion among the principal firms, each being able to maintain market share providing it aligns its cost structures fairly closely with its competitors. An example is given by Rees (1993) from the salt industry, where the pricing structure of the market apparently follows the cost structure of the smaller of the two firms in what is effectively an oligopoly.

2.4 Conclusion

By definition, the optimal position for any firm is at full efficiency as this maximises profits and, in theory, given perfect competition, this will be the firm's long-term position, although short-term shocks may drive it away from the optimum from time to time. In reality, perfectly competitive conditions are far from the norm and, within an industry, we observe a diverse range of productivity levels from any given level of inputs. Many of these differences in productivity can be explained by straightforward differences in the products, inputs and structures of firms as, in practice, there is considerable heterogeneity in all industries. One wishes to 'correct' measured inefficiency for such structural factors so that one is left with a corrected variable that has some normative significance, reflecting factors such as the degree of competition, public control and managerial/employee slack. Empirical evidence suggests that inefficiency is an important factor (Daly *et al.*, 1985; BIE, 1990, 1991a) and that therefore by reducing it firms could improve their productivity without even altering the quantity, type, or combination of factors of production.

Although in this chapter we covered various types of inefficiency, the remainder of this book will concentrate on technical inefficiency – the extent to which firms produce less than they could with their existing allocation of resources. We leave to future research the degree to which a better allocation and dynamic adjustment could be achieved. We are currently examining the so-called 'Thatcher miracle' in the 1980s, when productivity in UK manufacturing increased by 57 per cent.[3] In what follows we shall be examining the degree to which firms could improve productivity by simply utilising their existing resources more effectively.

Evidence indicates that technical inefficiency is a significant factor in explaining the underperformance of firms. Daly *et al.* (1985) suggested that the major discrepancy between UK and German plants is not a lack of capital, in the form of plant and machinery, but an inability to exploit that capital due to poor skill of both operatives and management. Before we present our new evidence of the existence of inefficiency in UK and Australian manufacturing we shall review the previous evidence and discuss alternative methods of measuring efficiency with the information we have available.

Notes

1. To a degree, plant-level studies (BIE, 1990, 1991a) are an attempt to examine absolute efficiencies, as are the bench-marking projects (BIE, 1992a–d, 1993).
2. The main factors used by Button (1992) were the five firm concentration ratios; inputs as a percentage of total outputs; export levels as a percentage of total

Inefficiency in industry

output; number of enterprises; average output; and percentage of the labour force who are manual workers.
3. The increase in output per person employed in manufacturing industries between 1980 and 1989 (CSO, *Economic Trends*, Annual Supplement 1992).

3

Means of estimating inefficiency

We have shown that inefficiency occurs for many reasons and hence it is the norm rather than the exception. It is an unusual company that, during the interval of observation, can exploit its resources to the full. Most are in a process of transition or subject to external fluctuations which reduce their performance below its technical maximum. With this in mind, we now explain what the distribution of technical efficiency might look like and how it can be measured.

We can describe technical efficiency in two ways. First, it can be some concept of 'technical potential', in which case each individual firm could either be realising that potential or, more likely, falling short of it. The obvious problem here is that these levels of productivity may be technically possible but unrealistic in practice. Moreover, if we never observe the technically feasible limit it is difficult to know how to calculate it. It is not usually just a matter of achieving the technical capacity of various machines but a much more complex process involving the organisation of production, marketing, human motivation, etc. We could perhaps infer it from the technical limits of the process. In the short term that technical potential is specific to the individual firm, reflecting its particular set of equipment, location, technology, stock of knowledge and products. Hence assessing technical efficiency on this basis could be a very detailed exercise.[1]

Second, we could describe efficiency as the best behaviour actually achieved by a firm in the industry. Thus firms would be compared with an observed best and not some yardstick that may not necessarily be achievable in practice. The more we move away from what is technically possible to what is actually achieved then one problem is replaced by another, as there are bound to be many sources of fluctuating 'actual' practice around the general level of 'best' performance. Hence one could overshoot the normal maximum performance – either because there are exceptional conditions, for example breakdowns are exceptionally low, the weather is exceptionally favourable; or, because the particular firm is very unusual and not representative of the industry at large. Bunching of outputs and inputs may result in the value added recorded in a period being greater than that technically feasible. While the excess would be picked up by a shortfall in surrounding years, this would not be reflected in a single period study. Of course, the longer the period of measurement the less important this problem is likely to be.

As soon as we start using actual behaviour, comparing performance across time or countries becomes very different. If the best actual performance in one year is low compared with potential then we might observe very little 'inefficiency' in an industry. If the performance of the large majority of firms was the same, but that of the best was markedly better, then inefficiency in the industry would appear to be worse. Comparing across countries it would be necessary to develop a common reference point because actual performance involves all the large number of different factors we have described.

3.1 The level of comparison

Over the years, variations in productivity have led to increasing interest in the efficiency of firms. Most past research, relating to either the whole economy or the whole of manufacturing, has been based on data aggregated to the level of individual industries, primarily due to the difficulties associated with the alternatives. If data at the level of the establishment are to be used this involves handling a huge dataset and confidentiality normally restricts access when dealing with detailed data on parts of firms, to say nothing of the difficulties for the outside researcher in gaining permission to use data collected for statistical purposes in the first place. These aggregative studies have primarily looked at productivity over time and space. For example, the productivity slowdown in the 1970s (Wenban-Smith, 1981; Roy, 1982) and the more extensive work (both in detail and scope) of Oulton and O'Mahony (Oulton, 1990; O'Mahony, 1992); comparisons of productivity by industry between the UK and its major competitors: Davies and Caves (1987) for the US; van Ark (1990a, 1990b) for the Netherlands and France and O'Mahony (1992) for Germany and comparisons between Australia and its competitors (Haig, 1987).

No study of productivity is without difficulty. The use of industry level data has clear problems. Across time, these studies are dependent on movements in average levels of productivity and therefore cannot easily take account of changes in the composition of individual industries. When making industry comparisons across countries it is very difficult to know whether like is being compared with like. There are considerable variations of product within even narrowly defined industries, and even where the product is almost identical there can be major differences in quality of material inputs and variations that relate to the location of the plant, all of which make it impossible to isolate the various sources of the variation in measured productivity with any great accuracy (Steedman and Wagner, 1987, 1989).

This means in practice that the most accurate comparisons of efficiency are undertaken at a highly detailed level (Mayes, 1983; BIE, 1990; Prais *et al.*, 1990). Use of establishment data alleviates those problems associated with that aggregated at the individual industry level, as here all the differences in the quality and vintage of capital, skills and training of the workforce, types of material inputs, are accounted for in firms (plants) producing products which are as near as possible identical. Two methods commonly used are matched plants and matched samples.

The matched plants technique attempts to eliminate sources of noise by comparing like with like at a detailed level (Daly *et al.*, 1985; Krafcik and MacDuffie, 1989; Steedman and Wagner, 1989; Prais *et al.*, 1989). Plants are chosen because of their similarity, the remaining sources of difference from the nature of the products, inputs and location are then taken into account to isolate differences due to efficiency. An extreme example is to look at the same process in different plants owned by the same company (BIE, 1990, 1991a). These results can then be extended to the industry as a whole but the great cost means that the samples must always be small compared with the size of the industry, except for one or two very concentrated industries like steel.

The idea behind the alternative method – matched samples – is to compare samples typical of each country. Here problems arise through differences in quality of outputs, for example in comparisons of British and German kitchen furniture manufacturers it was noted that the German industry is highly customised and the UK primarily high volume flat packs (Steedman and Wagner, 1987). Needless to say these detailed studies are enormously expensive even when looking only at one industry. Therefore simpler methods are needed if a widespread comparison is required.

Even more problems are encountered when considering monopolies or service industries. In the first case there is the lack of yardstick. Regulators are reduced to setting targets for technical performance and for cost reduction. In such industries it is possible to measure various characteristics of performance, for example, examination results for education, crime and clear-up rates for police services (Levitt and Joyce, 1986). This provides what is known as a data envelope in which to compare the one firm or industry with those similar to it.

Even if we had a set of firms which were fully efficient, if these represented all sorts of different products then we would get a very discontinuous reflection of what constituted efficiency. This can be illustrated diagrammatically. Figure 3.1 shows an industry containing six firms (A to F) all

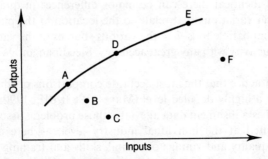

Figure 3.1 Multiproduct industry.

producing different products. It is rare for a plant in manufacturing industry to produce a single product, still rarer for plants from different firms to produce the same product. BIE (1990) gets over this by looking at different plants in the same firm and by concentrating on specific products which vary little, for example photographic paper. However, this is the exception not the rule. These firms are all fully efficient in the production of their product but considering efficiency of the whole industry gives a very disjointed picture (Figure 3.1). We are thus considering a multiproduct industry, and so it cannot be inferred that A is more efficient than B, B more than C, or E more than F just because they produce more output with less input. One way of handling this is to weight the output and inputs to account for these differences in firms (Tulkens, 1989) as we explain in more detail later. However, it is all too common merely to add these activities, which may be quite heterogeneous, together. Worse than this, individual plants in practice are classified to industries according to their principal product although a considerable proportion of their output may actually lie in a different industry altogether, only detailed studies can get round this.

3.2 Non-parametric programming

Non-parametric programming is probably the simplest way of looking at inefficiency. This generally compares the productivity of individual firms with the best actual performing firms within the industry (Figure 3.2). For each level of input a range of outputs is achieved by different firms. As firms are unlikely to be identical we will only observe a discrete series of points. In order to determine how efficient any particular production point

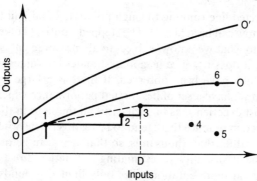

Figure 3.2 Single dimension diagram.

is one has to have a standard with which to compare, i.e. we have to explain what constitutes 'efficient' production at this level of inputs. The most commonly chosen route is to use best performances actually achieved in the industry as the standard from which to compare the efficiency of the other firms in the industry. A linear programming technique is normally used to estimate the hull of such performances, linking up the highest points, although there is no reason why a quadratic or some other appropriate form could not be used.

In Figure 3.2 we have reduced the problem to a single dimension to make the issue clearer, at this level there is a hierarchy of possible ways in which one can look at inefficiency:

1. Observations.
2. Stepped frontier.
3. Linear interpolation.
4. Linking of extreme points.
5. Non-linear approaches.

First, looking at observations, firms 1, 2 and 3 represent the best performance attained with their use of inputs. Firms 4 and 5 are clearly inefficient, compared with the other firms they produce less with more inputs. However, unless one can hypothesise what is achievable for their particular input combination we clearly have a problem in measuring how inefficient they are and hence deriving a sensible basis for comparison of inefficiency. We might have a better idea of inefficiency if we had a further point, such as 6, which is at least using the same scale of inputs as firm 5. As it stands, we can measure inefficiency only in terms of the excess in use of resources compared with the level shown by D, we cannot do it compared with 6. In Chapter 4 we explore this in more detail.

Second, the faceted line running through points 1, 2 and 3 in the figure shows what we know can be achieved. The stepped frontier (Tulkens, 1989) restricts analysis to what we 'know' subject to all measurement issues that have been raised, it does not give us good estimates for values which are not near ones which have been observed. If there is a large number of observations then we have a set of best actual performance which, we can say, describes most experience as in such cases all the steps in the frontier are small. However, in practice there tend to be relatively few observations, tens or hundreds rather than thousands, so that steps can be quite large. This increases the desirability of estimating a frontier direct, as non-parametric statistical representation gives only limited grounds for generalising to other behaviour what is the observed economic production function.

It would also be reasonable to assume that, provided inputs and outputs are sufficiently divisible, intermediate points are also achievable. A frontier could be formed by a straight line linking together observations. This opens up two possibilities. First, linking adjacent observations – linear interpolation – would include a point such as 2 in the frontier. Alternatively, one could link the extreme points 1 and 3 and assume that points along it are technically possible but have not been achieved in practice. In this case point 2 lies inside the frontier. That is, we might argue that the point on the line linking 1 and 3 at point 2's level of inputs could be feasible.

Finally the actual possibilities might lie on a curve (OO) linking extreme points thus admitting even better performance. Indeed 1 and 3 themselves may be well inside the feasible, O'O' instead of OO. We have drawn this curve concave although parts of the line could be noticeably convex.

Although a straight line is likely to be a better representation than the stepped one it may still be inaccurate, particularly if the gap between observations is substantial. Clearly, therefore, there is enormous scope for variation of opinion, although in practice firms cannot add inputs in the simple manner assumed in this diagram because they are likely to be restricted, for example, by financial constraints. Furthermore, to reflect reality one must look at increasing the dimension to consider multiple inputs and outputs. Thus we have a complex multivariate problem which we discuss later.

3.2.1 *Cost minimisation*

It is possible to look at the question of inefficiency from another or 'dual' point of view – in terms of cost minimisation for a given output rather than output maximisation for given inputs (Hammond, 1986). In a single dimension the problem is clearly symmetric, one is just measuring at 90° of the other.

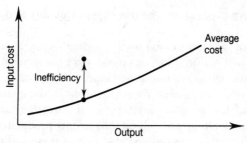

Figure 3.3   Cost minimisation.

3.2.2 *Multidimensionality*

Single output, several inputs

This method assumes a degree of homogeneity and similarity between establishments in the same industry, which is likely to be rather greater than that which actually applies. A single dimension discussion, assuming one output and one input, is helpful in setting the groundwork but gives a poor reflection of reality. Firms have a far more complex structure of production than the diagrams we have used suggest and those within an industry will differ in the inputs they use in producing a single output. Therefore, one must extend the model to include the use of multiple inputs. By this we not only mean different inputs, such as labour, capital and raw materials, but that these inputs themselves are heterogeneous, for example labour can be skilled or unskilled, full-time or part-time, involved in production or non-production, each of which is part of the actual production process. Furthermore, capital could be hired or owned and raw materials, such as energy, differ.

Multiple output, single inputs

The accuracy of this method does depend largely on having a single activity (homogeneous) industry. For example, within an industrial classification that consists effectively of two distinct industries, if one were to measure inefficiency assuming homogeneity we could have a position as shown in Figure 3.1. This illustrates an industry containing six firms, A to F. A frontier of efficiency has been drawn by linking up the best-performing establishments. Relative to this frontier the other establishments appear to be highly inefficient. This will not reflect the true situation in this industry accurately if plants A, D and E, the highest performers, are different from the others. For example, they may use different technologies, or produce a different product, maybe one of lower quality and sold at a lower price.

In reality there are very few (if any) single product industries where the firms or establishments within it can be considered homogeneous. Industries traditionally assumed to be homogeneous are those in the agricultural sector (Farrell, 1957) although even there variations in the quality of the land, machinery and labour, and variations in the weather, distort the simple picture. If one could identify all establishments producing a single output (e.g. oil seed rape[2]) one would be able to plot these and construct a standard of performance from the highest performing establishments, in the same manner as Figure 3.2. All other establishments are below the standard because of either inefficiency or the large number of relatively small factors that affect each producer differently, such as soil quality and exposure to wind and frost. However, even many seemingly single activities do in fact produce a collection of differing products, for example the different processes involved in the dairy industry (Førsund and Hjalmarsson, 1979). Identifying just one process – say, bottling – this may appear homogeneous because all plants are using identical inputs to produce a single homogeneous product. In fact, over recent years milk bottling plants have increasingly become more diverse, producing differing types of milk: skimmed, semi-skimmed and homogenised. Indeed, while the traditional milk bottle may have been interchangeable among plants, containers now vary and most are disposable or require recycling before re-use so the cleaning of returned bottles is no longer part of the process.

Multiple outputs, multiple inputs

The most realistic model involves both multiple outputs and multiple inputs.

3.2.3 Linear programming

These three multidimensionality concepts can be modelled similarly using linear programming, as an example we take the first case, single output, several inputs. Introducing multi-inputs one then gets a surface (Farrell, 1957). For simplicity assume a single output is produced using two inputs, capital (K) and labour (L). For any point in one dimension one gets a marginal trade-off for the other. In Figure 3.4 we fix K at some point K^*. Returns to labour are diminishing, because beyond the optimal combination of inputs, adding further labour cannot further increase output without additional capital. For example, if a sewing machine in a clothing factory is operated by just one machinist, once all the machines are occupied further labour will be surplus to requirement and will add nothing more to output.

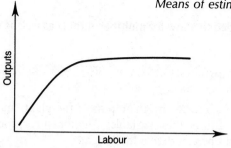

Capital held fixed at some level K*

Figure 3.4 Multidimensionality – two input, single output case.

In Figure 3.4, any point under the curve is inefficient because, given the inputs, actual output is below that which can be achieved. We can repeat this for all combinations, thus giving a surface. Inefficiency can be measured relative to the surface or with respect to each factor. This can be extended to gross output with as many dimensions as one likes. However, at some stage weighting of the inputs is required, which is where the concept of price usually emerges.

3.2.4 *Using weights*

Where it is not possible to break industries up into their distinct activities, weights can be used to combine multiple inputs/outputs into a single measure. There are various methods by which weights have been used in non-parametric programming.

Taking the simple case of a single output and two inputs, the idea of linear programming is to maximise Y subject to $\Sigma C_i X_i$, where Y is the output and X_i the inputs of the plant and C_i the input costs. Thus one has a series of points in three dimensions.

Y_1, X_{11}, X_{21} or, if $X_1 = K$ and $X_2 = L$

Y_1, K_1, L_1

Y_2, K_2, L_2

How, then, does one know what is inefficient? One technique is to use the total factor productivity ratio, which enables the use of weights. In the two input case these weights could be W_1 and W_2, and are most likely to reflect the input costs. Thus the ratio would be given by:

$$Y/(W_1 X_1 + W_2 X_2)$$

This can then be extended to allow for multiple outputs as well as multiple inputs. In this case:

$$\sum_{j=1}^{t} V_j Y_j \Bigg/ \sum_{i=1}^{m} W_i X_i \qquad (3.1)$$

where Y_j are the outputs and X_i are the inputs of the plant, and V_j and W_i are the respective weights on these variables. This measures productivity across plants, provided one can derive the weights.

This method does pose the problem of weights. One might be able to find some industry-wide measure. In the private sector prices could be used. However in the public sector, where factors and products are not traded, weights must be implicitly generated (Ganley and Cubbin, 1992).

Given a sufficient number of plants in the sample, linear programming readily accommodates multiple outputs and inputs, without the need to aggregate them. Each plant is compared with the other plants in the sample. A plant is regarded as technically efficient if the ratio of its weighted outputs to its weighted inputs is no less than similar ratios for all other plants, subject to certain constraints. The constraints include that weights are non-negative and that no producing unit can be more than 100 per cent efficient with the same weights. Each plant's 'objective' is to choose the set of weights that maximise its efficiency, subject to these constraints. Thus, the weights are not determined *a priori*.

3.2.5 *Measuring changes in productivity*

Measuring changes in productivity introduces the concept of time. In this case there is not only the problem of weights but also that of index numbers, should one use base weights or current weights, or, in the case of the Tornquist index, a combination of the two, for example Gathon and Perelman's (1989) study on railway lines.

The Tornquist index takes the two steps together, i.e. it involves both weights and it considers changes in productivity over time. It is given by:

$$\Delta g_t = \sum_{i}^{m} [(gy_{it} + gy_{it-1})/2] \ln (Y_{it}/Y_{it-1})$$

$$- \sum_{i}^{n} [(gx_{it} + gx_{it-1})/2] \ln (X_{it}/X_{it-1}) \qquad (3.2)$$

where the Y_{it} are outputs, the X_{it} inputs and gy and gx are the elasticities of cost with respect to Y and X; g is thus the partial derivative of total cost. Here, the first line is the increase in weighted output and the second is the increase in weighted inputs with gy and gx providing the weights. The difference is a dynamic performance measure.

3.2.6 *The drawbacks of linear programming*

There are a number of drawbacks to this linear programming technique. The first is that it concentrates on actual achievement rather than on the potential achievable. Ideally we would like a 'production frontier', which has some technically describable properties, for example a clear mathematical form. For a given technology, the production frontier is the theoretical limit to the level of output that can be achieved using each of the possible combinations of inputs. The form of function can be quite complex as is the case with ten parameter (translog) frontier we use later (Chapter 4). In practice, many firms will operate inside the frontier because of the existence of some form of inefficiency. Once again no such exact function is possible if we are dealing with a variety of different products and processes under a single industry description.[3]

The second drawback is simply that it does not translate readily to the context of economic decision-making by the firm.[4] On the one hand non-parametric linear programming techniques do not involve any explicit parametric explanation of behaviour. That is to say the non-parametric work has no model of behaviour to support it and we cannot explain the process firms are following, i.e. how the inputs are transformed into outputs. On the other hand, it does not go beyond the information available. This problem can be overcome by using production functions. Production functions represent general tendencies among the data if estimated from them. These can be imposed on the basis of extraneous information.

While input- and output-based measures of efficiency are readily calculated and decomposed, the estimated frontier and derived efficiency measures are susceptible to outliers and measurement error (Førsund and Hjalmarsson, 1974), particularly when dealing with establishment level data (Tyler, 1979).

3.3 Parametric programming

The non-parametric model does not give any functional form to suggest the maximum (efficient) output that can be obtained from any feasible combination of inputs. Parametric programming specifies a production function which describes the way in which establishments can produce outputs most efficiently from their factors of production. The parametric model is of the form $y = f(x)$, but in the case of a production function, $y = f(x, \beta)$, where x is the vector of inputs and β the vector of parameters. The model in general form for the ith unit in an industry can be written:

$$\ln (y_i) = \ln f(x_i; \beta) - v_i \quad v_i \geqslant 0 \ (i = 1, \ldots, n) \tag{3.3}$$

where y_i is the output obtained by unit i from x_i, a vector of nonstochastic inputs, and β is the unknown parameter vector. The one-sided error term (v) ensures that all observations lie on or beneath the deterministic frontier $\ln f(x_i; \beta)$, which is the maximum output that can be obtained given inputs specified by x_i (Forsund and Jansen, 1977). The inefficiency of production units is assumed to be reflected in the magnitude of the v_i.

Aigner and Chu (1968) suggested that β be estimated by minimisation of:

$$\sum_{i=1}^{n} |\ln (y_i) - \ln f(x_i; \beta)| \tag{3.4}$$

for the n units in the industry, subject to $\ln (y_i) \leqslant \ln f(x_i; \beta)$. This is a linear programming problem if $\ln f(x_i; \beta)$ is linear in β. The alternative is to minimise:

$$\sum_{i=1}^{n} [\ln (y_i) - \ln f(x_i; \beta)]^2 \tag{3.5}$$

subject to $\ln (y_i) \leqslant \ln f(x_i; \beta)$, which is a quadratic programming problem if $\ln f(x_i; \beta)$ is linear in β. Schmidt (1976) established that the linear and quadratic programming estimates of β are maximum likelihood (ML) where the one-sided error term is distributed as an exponential and half-normal respectively.

The advantages and disadvantages can be summarised as follows:

1. The principal advantages are:
   (a) the technology is parametric and smooth, whereas that derived by non-parametric programming is piecewise and linear;
   (b) non-constant returns to scale can be allowed for via the functional form selected for $\ln f(x_i; \beta)$;
   (c) it is straightforward to derive measures of technical inefficiency for each unit in the industry, via the estimated ε_i.
2. The principal disadvantages are:
   (a) the functional form selected to represent the technology could be overly restrictive, leading to errors in the computed efficiencies (Fare *et al.*, 1985);
   (b) the estimated parameters have indeterminate statistical properties, because no assumptions are made explicitly about the distribution of the one-sided error term (Schmidt and Lovell, 1979);
   (c) the estimated frontier and derived measures of inefficiency remain susceptible to extreme observations and measurement error, because the model does not allow for random shocks in the production process that are outside the control of the units in the sample (Pitt and Lee, 1981);

(d) a limit may be imposed implicitly on the number of units in the sample that are efficient (Førsund and Hjalmarsson, 1979; Førsund *et al.*, 1980).

It is, of course, difficult to get sufficient information about individual plants to estimate production functions for each of them and this problem applies whether we are using parametric programming or other forms of estimation. This would require a series of observations where technology is unchanged but demand, output and inputs vary. However, it is difficult to vary some inputs in the short run. Physical capital in particular can only be increased as the result of investment, which may require planning permission. Similarly, some capital may be specific to the particular process and hence its disposal will incur a 'sunk cost' – an irrecoverable investment – which will discourage firms. In addition, there are redundancy and training costs for changing the numbers employed. Hence observations will combine short-term and long-term responses. In the short term the main response to a change in market conditions will be to vary the labour input rather than capital, as shown by ST_1 in Figure 3.5. However, in the longer term the whole scale of operation can be changed, as indicated by LT, enabling the firm to move to a new short-term set of options, ST_2. Thus observations across different time periods could reflect short run efficiency and imply a totally implausible production function connecting them if the long-term and short-term functions cannot be distinguished.

3.4   Parametrical statistical estimation

The parametric programming model can be made statistical by assuming a distribution for v and estimating (3.3) via maximum likelihood (ML).

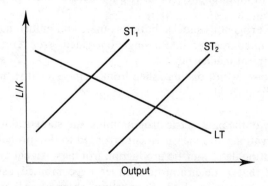

Figure 3.5   Short-term versus long-term functions.

Afriat (1972) suggested a two-parameter beta distribution for exp[$-v$], which corresponds to a gamma distribution for v (Richmond, 1974). Other possible distributions for v include the exponential and half-normal (Schmidt, 1976). However, different distributions for v lead to different estimates for β, and there are no good *a priori* arguments for any particular distribution (Lee, 1983).

A further problem in this case, due to the on- or below-the-frontier constraint, is that the ML estimators are consistent and asymptotically efficient only if the density of v is zero at $v =$ zero, and if the derivative of the density of v with respect to its parameters approaches zero as v approaches zero (Greene, 1980). The gamma density function satisfies these conditions, but it is restrictive for statistical convenience to govern the assumption about the distribution of technical inefficiency.

An alternative method for the estimation is ordinary least squares (OLS). The assumptions of the classical regression model apply to the equation given the usual conditions, with the exception of the non-zero mean of the disturbances (v) (Schmidt, 1976). The method of OLS therefore provides a best linear unbiased and consistent estimate of the parameter vector, except for the intercept term. The conventionally computed standard error and the assumption of asymptotic normality are appropriate. The OLS residuals can be used to derive a consistent estimate of the intercept term, which is then shifted until all residuals except for one or more support points have the correct sign.

The parametric statistical models attribute all variation in firm performance to variation in firm efficiencies relative to the common production frontier. These models are difficult to justify for the following reasons:

1. The possibility that the performance of a firm could be affected by factors entirely outside its control (such as bad weather, unpredictable variations in machine or labour performance, variable input quality, breakdowns in input supply) as well as by factors under its control, is ignored.
2. The effects of exogenous shocks (both fortunate and unfortunate) and inefficiency are aggregated into a single one-sided error term that is labelled 'technical inefficiency'.
3. Statistical 'noise' is not distinguished from inefficiency (the 'noise' is assumed to be one-sided).

The susceptibility of the parametric programming and statistical methods to extreme observations and measurement error led to the 'probabilistic' method of estimating deterministic production frontiers. Aigner and Chu (1968) suggested that a deterministic frontier be computed using the parametric programming method. Supporting observations are then discarded and a new deterministic frontier is computed. The process continues until the computed frontier stabilises and the outlier problem is 'solved' (Timmer, 1971).

However, the placement of outliers above the final frontier is not easily reconciled in economic or statistical terms with the concept of the frontier as a maximum possible output. Moreover, as a 'probabilistic' frontier is a deterministic frontier computed from a subset of the original data, hypothesis testing on the 'estimators' is not possible.

An alternative method that allows one to measure inefficiency of industries as a whole and overcome more of the problems discused above is the stochastic production frontier model. The stochastic production function gives a clear basis in economic theory for the chosen behaviour and yet, by separating the residual into a 'white noise' and an efficiency component, admits of variation for various particular and largely random, as well as identifiable, reasons. This enables us to avoid defining the best as some unusual outlier and permits the determination of a frontier of efficient behaviour which is attainable in practice.

The stochastic production frontier model, popularised by Aigner, *et al.* (1977), and Meeusen and van den Broeck (1977), combines two ideas. The first assumes that if there is a *reasonably* similar set of firms in an industry it is possible to identify a production function. Of course, in the extreme case of perfectly competitive markets there is only one observation and hence this method would be inappropriate (Hart and Shipman, 1991). However, in practice even in close approximation to competitive markets, as in agricultural production, observations tend to differ because of differing locations, fertilities, weather, pests, experience, etc. The second idea is that there is variation in behaviour due to a variety of factors best described as random variation when taken together. Hence we are able to estimate a stochastic production function, which is based on the standard specification, $\ln(y_i) = \ln f(x_i; \beta)$; where y_i is a measure of output obtained by unit i from x_i, a vector of non-stochastic inputs, and β is the unknown parameter vector; f is the functional form. Including the residual, e, gives:

$$\ln(y_i) = \ln f(x_i; \beta) + e_i \tag{3.6}$$

In justifying shifting the function outwards to form the frontier the assumption in the case of the parametric programming and statistical frontiers was that the value of $\ln y_i$ with the largest positive residual, e_i, represents the maximum attainable, if the whole of e_i is related to inefficiency. However, this gives a distribution (*viz* the normal) that is subject to question, as there may also be sources of variation, other than 'white noise', that are firm-specific and unlikely to be distributed across all firms in such a symmetric way, i.e. non-normally distributed. Thus the heterogeneity of firms within an industry may well appear in the inefficiency component of the residual.

However, a number of alternative methods have been suggested in the literature. Zvi Griliches suggested we should run the regression through an upper quantile of firms, thus assuming the quantile represents frontier behaviour. This method avoids the shift, although again it is virtually a variant on the probabilistic frontier approach. Another method is to shift the function outwards by adding, say, twice the standard error of the regression estimate at the mean, i.e. this assumes that there may be a small residual caused by special factors and avoids dominance by outliers (in logarithmic form the errors will be proportionate). In a large sample it is implied that roughly 2.5 per cent of observations would lie outside this frontier. However, this decision is rather arbitrary and a more accurate procedure could be used if the distribution of inefficiency is known. Unfortunately there is relatively little empirical evidence so the tendency has been to proceed by simple assumption.

If behaviour is random then the appropriate assumption would be the normal, as in Figure 3.6(a). However, it seems unlikely that this and similar symmetric assumptions are plausible as they imply that greater and lesser efficiency around the norm is equally likely. A more realistic assumption about the shape is that it might be skewed, implying a tail of inefficiency (Figure 3.6(b)). A plausible form for such a skewed distribution might be the log-normal (Hart, 1980). This accepts that attaining the frontier is unlikely, although most firms are not a long way from it, and there is a considerable 'tail' of those with lower inefficiency.

There are a number of ways of deriving the residual distribution from a more practical standpoint. One is to assume that the residual has two components – one reflecting largely random variation which follows the common assumption about the shape of error distribution, $N(0, \sigma_u^2)$, and the other reflecting inefficiency. Thus $e_i = u_i - v_i$, where u_i is a random symmetric component and v_i an asymmetric component that represents technical inefficiency; u and v are independent by assumption.

3.4.1 *The random component*

The component u represents both positive and negative effects on the production process, $u \gtreqless 0$. A variety of contributory factors has been suggested by past researchers to explain the sources of the stochastic variation. Zellner *et al.* (1966) claimed that this random component reflects 'factors such as weather, unpredictable variations in machine or labour performance, and so on'. Aigner and Chu (1968) explain it by 'pure random shocks in the production process that might be due to careless handling and defective or damaged output'. Such random movements can occur in any firm depending largely on the luck of the producer, although certain industries will be more prone to stochastic fluctuations than others, for

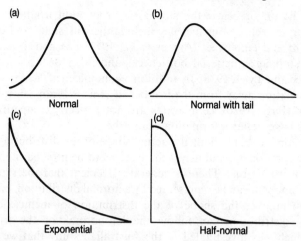

Figure 3.6 Functional distributions.

example in agriculture, where productivity of farms is highly sensitive to climate, soil type and topography. The random component can also represent problems of methodology, for example measurement, observation and reporting errors by the economic units on the levels of output (Aigner *et al.*, 1977) and 'unimportant' variables omitted from the functional form $f(x_i; \beta)$ (Corbo and de Melo, 1983).

If the variables are mismeasured in a random manner then this merely reduces the efficiency of the estimators and could introduce heteroscedasticity into the residuals. However, if the error is related to the X variables then biases will result. Similarly if important variables have been omitted the resultant OLS estimation of the remaining parameters will be both biased and inconsistent (Johnston, 1984).

Measurement, observation and reporting error are particular problems when attempting to measure capital stock. In the UK and Australia estimates of capital stock do not exist for individual establishments and proxies have to be used (Chapter 4 and Appendix 1). Where countries do collect capital stock data this is often inaccurate leading to biased and inconsistent estimations (Tybout, 1990).

3.4.2 *The inefficiency component*

The component v represents technical inefficiency. The inefficiency component is an asymmetrically distributed, negative error term that means that firms lie on or below the stochastic production frontier. Factors contributing to technical inefficiency include the will, skills, and effort of management and employees (Aigner *et al.*, 1977; Lee and Tyler, 1978), and work stoppages, material bottlenecks and other disruption to production (Lee and Tyler, 1978). In addition 'economic inefficiency' will also result in deviation away from the frontier. By this is meant 'firm-specific knowledge' (Page, 1980), i.e. markets are not perfectly competitive and some firms have better information than others.

There is some debate about the actual shape of the distribution of the inefficiency component, and as yet there seems to be little hard empirical evidence to resolve this. There is general agreement that the symmetric random component can be represented by a normal distribution, but much less agreement over the shape of the distribution of inefficiency. The inefficiency distribution can follow the log-normal, or the truncated normal, which was investigated in the Australian study that we discuss in Chapter 4. However, although many shapes are believable, in practice the assumed shape has been exponential (Meeusen and van den Broeck, 1977) or half-normal (Aigner *et al.*, 1977), these are shown in Figure 3.6(c) and (d) respectively. These functional forms imply that firms cluster near efficiency and that their frequency diminishes monotonically as inefficiency increases. It is, however, relatively difficult to produce strong arguments for particular shapes. However, Stevenson (1980) suggested that characteristics such as extent of education or training, intelligence, persuasiveness, and other factors relating to managerial effectiveness are unlikely to be distributed over the population with such a monotonically decreasing distribution. He proposed the possibility of a non-zero mode for the density of v and generalised the half-normal and exponential specification for the dual cost function. The generalisation permits a non-zero mode for the density function of v (a truncated-normal distribution), the appropriate truncation point being estimated, along with the production frontier, by maximum likelihood (see pages 46–7) and enables the relevance of the special case of a zero mode to be tested as explored in the Australian study.

The stochastic production frontier model does have a number of potential disadvantages. First, because the method is parametric, the results for measured technical efficiency and inefficiency are sensitive to the functional form selected (Corbo and de Melo, 1983). Therefore the functional forms must be specified for both $f(x_i; \beta)$ and the components of the error term. Second, it is assumed generally that the selected functional form is valid over the complete range of the observations, whereas it is preferable that the restrictions imposed by this assumption are tested. The findings of Huang and Bagi (1984) indicate that a misspecification of the functional form can lead to error, which is incorrectly considered to be a component of measured technical inefficiency. The reason for this is that the evidence of technical inefficiency is negative skewness of the regression error term, and such skewness can reflect both inefficiency and misspecification of the functional form. Finally, there can be another statistical problem. Schmidt and Sickles (1984) noted that if a firm knew its level of technical inefficiency, for example, this should affect its input choices. It would then be invalid to assume that inefficiency was independent of the regressors. There can also be the more usual problem of simultaneity bias, which occurs if the levels of certain inputs are correlated with the overall error term.

3.5 Specification of the production function

In addition to the functional forms assumed for the two components of the residual, final estimates of inefficiency will largely depend upon the choice of specification for the production frontier itself.

The most widely used functional forms are those of Cobb–Douglas, constant elasticity of substitution (CES) and the transcendental logarithmic (translog) form, however, no function is ideal as each has its drawbacks. Assuming just two factors of production, labour (L) and capital (K) the CES production function has the form:

$$Y = (a_0 + a_1 L^p + a_2 K^p)^{1/p} + e \qquad (3.7)$$

where if $a_0 = 0$ the function exhibits constant returns to scale. The two best known special cases of the CES function are the linear production function ($p = 1$), given by:

$$Y = a_0 + a_1 L + a_2 K + e \qquad (3.8)$$

and the Cobb–Douglas production function ($p = 0$), given by:

$$Y = AL^{\alpha}K^{\beta} + e \qquad (3.9)$$

where e is an error term $\alpha + \beta$ is often restricted to equal unity as this imposes constant returns to scale. The Cobb-Douglas is a convenient form to use because it is linear in logarithms:

$$\ln Y = \ln A + \alpha \ln L + \beta \ln K + \ln e \qquad (3.10)$$

Both the CES and the Cobb–Douglas functions have drawbacks in that they both assume that the returns to scale are fixed, which results in the long run average cost curve (LRAC) being either constantly rising (decreasing returns), horizontal (constant returns), or constantly falling (increasing returns). Thus the LRAC cannot take on the 'U' shape so often assumed in the theory of the firm. However, the translog function allows the elasticity of scale to change with output and/or factor proportions. The homogeneous Cobb–Douglas function restricts the elasticity of substitution between capital and labour to unity, the CES (as its name implies) to a constant while the translog permits variability.

The translog function originated in work by Christensen *et al.* (1971). In its most general form, imposing only the assumption of symmetry (the effect on output of substituting labour for capital is the mirror image of the effect of substituting capital for labour) it is specified as:

$$\ln Y = a_0 + a_1 \ln L + a_2 \ln K + a_3 (\ln L)^2/2 + a_4 (\ln K)^2/2$$

$$+ a_5 (\ln L \ln K) + \Sigma_i a_{i+5} X_i + e \tag{3.11}$$

where $e = u - v$, with u and v defined in Section 3.4 and the X_i variables are other influences. As the translog function, in this form, imposes no homogeneity restrictions, it allows for convenient treatment of economies of scale and for the optimum scale to be determined. It also permits the investigation of non-homotheticity (large and small plants using inputs in different proportions) (Caves, 1982).[5]

Given its general form, unlike the Cobb–Douglas, the translog does not impose prior restrictions on the underlying production structure. This reduces the probability that a misspecification of the functional form could lead to error that is incorrectly considered to be inefficiency.

3.6 Estimating production functions

The stochastic frontier model can be estimated by maximum likelihood or, in some circumstances, by corrected ordinary least squares. As this is the model we use, we explore the possible methods of estimation of it and the difficulties this poses in some detail. We show that although the model can be estimated by maximum likelihood it is also possible to use ordinary least squares with some manipulation of the calculated residuals. Unfortunately there are three cases where such estimates are not obtainable. In part this is a problem with the method but it also shows that there are cases where the assumptions about the distribution of efficiency are not borne out by the data.

The basic structure of the stochastic production frontier model takes the form:

$$y_i = \beta x_i + e_i \tag{3.12}$$

where y_i is a measure of output (in logarithms), x_i the vector of inputs (in logarithms) and other conditioning variables β the vector of parameters and e_i a residual which can be decomposed into a stochastic component, u_i, and an inefficiency component, v_i. Thus:

$$e_i = u_i - v_i \tag{3.13}$$

Assuming the inefficiency component is truncated normal, we can show that the density function for v is:

$$g(v) = \frac{1}{\sqrt{(2\pi)} \; \sigma_v F(\mu/\sigma_v)} \exp\left[\frac{-(v - \mu^2)}{2\sigma_v^2}\right] \quad v \geqslant 0 \tag{3.14}$$

where μ is the mode of v and $F(.)$ the distribution function of the standard normal. Assume that u is distributed as a normal random variable zero mean and variance σ_u^2. If u and v are independent their joint density function is:

$$[h(v, u)] = \frac{1}{2\pi\sigma_v\sigma_u F(\mu/\sigma_v)} \exp\left\{\frac{-[u^2/\sigma_u^2 + (v - \mu)^2/\sigma_v^2]}{2}\right\} \quad v \geqslant 0 \tag{3.15}$$

and after substituting for u from (3.13) we get:

$$[h(v, e)] = \frac{1}{2\pi\sigma_v\sigma_u F(\mu/\sigma_v)} \exp\left\{\frac{-[(e + v)^2/\sigma_u^2 + (v - \mu)^2/\sigma_v^2]}{2}\right\} \tag{3.16}$$

Hence the marginal density function for e can be obtained by integrating (3.16) over the range of v:

$$[h(e)] = \frac{1}{\sqrt{(2\pi)}\sigma F(\mu/\sigma_v)} \exp\left[\frac{-(e - \mu)\sigma^2}{2\sigma^2}\right] F\left(\frac{\mu - e\lambda^2}{\sigma\lambda}\right) \tag{3.17}$$

where $\sigma^2 = \sigma_v^2 + \sigma_u^2$ and $\lambda = \sigma_v/\sigma_u$. Clearly these can be simplified in the half-normal case where $\mu = 0$ to the forms shown by Aigner *et al.* (1977).

On this basis we can derive the maximum likelihood (ML) estimates of β, λ, σ^2 and μ from the first-order conditions for a maximum of the log-likelihood function which is given by:

$$\begin{aligned}
\ln L(y, x; \beta, \lambda, \sigma^2, \mu) = &-(n\ln 2\pi)/2 - (n\ln\sigma^2)/2 \\
&- (1/\sigma^2)\Sigma_{i=1}^{n} (y_i - \beta x_i + \mu)^2/2 \\
&- n\ln F\{\mu^2[(1 + 1/\lambda^2)/\sigma^2]^{1/2}\} \\
&+ \Sigma_{i=1}^{n} \ln(F\{(1/\sigma^2)^{1/2}[\mu/\lambda - \lambda(y_i - \beta x_i)]\})
\end{aligned} \tag{3.18}$$

where n is the size of the sample, as $\sigma_v = \dfrac{\sigma}{\sqrt{(1 + 1/\lambda^2)}}$

This derivation requires a non-linear algorithm for optimisation (Aigner *et al.*, 1977). The resulting estimates are consistent and asymptotically efficient but with unknown finite sample properties (Olson *et al.*, 1980).

The alternative estimation method uses ordinary least squares (Richmond, 1974). OLS gives a best linear unbiased and consistent estimate of β except for the constant term:

$$y_i = E(e_i) + \beta x_i + [e_i - E(e_i)] \tag{3.19}$$

where E is the expectations operator and the error term $e_i - E(e_i)$ has zero mean. $E(e_i)$ is thus the bias of the constant term and the method used to correct for this is hence called corrected OLS (COLS). It can be shown that COLS performs as well as ML for sample sizes below 400 and $\sigma_v^2/\sigma_u^2 < 10$ (Olson *et al.*, 1980).

As our error term is specified by three parameters $(\sigma_v, \sigma_u, \mu)$ it is insufficient to calculate only the variance. We must therefore calculate the third and fourth moments of the regression residuals, these measure the degree of skewness and kurtosis, respectively.[6] The third moment tells us whether we are correct in assuming an asymmetric residual.

The parameters of the error term can be computed from the moments as:

$$\text{var}(e) = \sigma^2 - \frac{\mu \sigma_v f(\mu/\sigma_v)}{F(\mu/\sigma_v)} - \frac{\sigma_v^2 f^2(\mu/\sigma_v)}{F^2(\mu/\sigma_v)} \tag{3.20}$$

$$= \sigma_v^2(1 - 2/\pi) + \sigma_u^2, \quad \text{if } \mu = 0, \tag{3.21}$$

where $f(.)$ is the density of the standard normal.

The derivation of the third and fourth moments is more complex giving:

$$E\{[e - E(e)]^3\} = \frac{\sigma_v(\sigma_v^2 - \mu^2)f(\mu/\sigma_v)}{F(\mu/\sigma_v)} - \frac{3\mu\sigma_v^2 f^2(\mu/\sigma_v)}{F^2(\mu/\sigma_v)}$$

$$- \frac{2\sigma_v^3 f^3(\mu/\sigma_v)}{F^3(\mu/\sigma_v)} \tag{3.22}$$

$$= \sigma_v^3 \sqrt{(2\pi)}(1 - 4/\pi) \quad \text{when } \mu = 0 \tag{3.23}$$

$$E\{[e - E(e)]^4\} = 3\sigma^4 - \mu\sigma_v(\mu^2 + 3\sigma^2 + 3\sigma_u^2)f(\mu/\sigma_v)/[F(\mu/\sigma_v)]$$

$$- 2\sigma_v^2(2\mu^2 + \sigma^2 + 2\sigma_u^2)f^2(\mu/\sigma_v)/[F^2(\mu/\sigma_v)]$$

$$- 6\mu\sigma_v^3 f^3(\mu/\sigma_v)/[F^3(\mu/\sigma_v)]$$

$$- 3\sigma_v^4 f^4(\mu/\sigma_v)/[F^4(\mu/\sigma_v)] \tag{3.24}$$

$$= 3\sigma_u^4 + 6(1 - 2/\pi)\sigma_v^2\sigma_u^2 + (3 - 4/\pi - 12/\pi^2)\sigma_v^4 \tag{3.25}$$

when $\mu = 0$, as shown by Olson *et al.* (1980).

As these three moments are non-linear functions of σ_u, σ_v and μ they must be solved using an iterative routine.[7]

There are two cases in which the COLS estimator of the generalised error term parameters does not exist in a meaningful form. The first arises in data for which the estimated σ_v is negative. It occurs frequently for industries with a positive third moment of the residuals – that is, in cases for which the results are skewed in the 'wrong' direction for a stochastic production frontier – case (1) failures.

The second problem with the COLS method and the generalised error specification arises in cases for which the value of $\hat{\mu}/\hat{\sigma}_v$ selected by the iterative routine is persistently less than minus five. In such cases the magnitude of $F(\hat{\mu}/\hat{\sigma}_v)$ tends to zero and the magnitudes of the calculated second, third and fourth moments of the residuals become unbounded – case (3) failure.

When the half-normal/normal error structure is adopted – equations (3.21), (3.23) and (3.25) – the equation system is linear and the standard error parameter of the normal error term is estimated consistently by:

$$\hat{\sigma}_u^2 = \hat{\mu}_2 - (\pi - 2)\hat{\mu}_3^{2/3}2^{-1/3}(\pi - 4)^{-2/3} \quad \text{if } \hat{\mu}_3 \leqslant 0$$

$$\hat{\mu}_2 \qquad\qquad\qquad\qquad\qquad \text{if } \hat{\mu}_3 > 0 \qquad (3.26)$$

A case (2) failure occurs if the estimated value of σ_u^2 implied by (3.26) is negative. (3.17) can be rearranged to show that such failures occur if:

$$\hat{s} = \frac{\hat{\mu}_3}{\hat{\mu}_2^{3/2}} < (\pi - 4)\sqrt{2(\pi - 2)^{-3}} = -0.9953 \qquad (3.27)$$

where $\hat{s}$ is the skewness of the OLS residuals. From (3.23) $\hat{\sigma}_v$ can be estimated consistently in the half-normal/normal case by $\hat{\sigma}_v = \hat{\mu}_3^{1/3}\pi^{1/2}2^{-1/6}(\pi - 4)^{-1/3}$. If ML is used, Olson *et al.* (1980) reported that finite maxima always appear to exist for $\hat{\lambda}$ and $\hat{\sigma}^2$ and hence the calculated $\hat{\sigma}_v$ and $\hat{\sigma}_u$ have the correct, positive signs. Such results reflect the way in which the likelihood function is parameterised.

3.7 Estimating inefficiency

As noted above, theory provides little guidance on picking a distribution for v. It follows that the choice and evaluation of particular distributions are based on statistical methods. Two approaches have been suggested in the literature.

The first approach follows from the notion that the stochastic frontier model is a generalisation of the standard ordinary least squares (OLS) model, with the additional feature of a one-sided error component, v. It follows that a test for the existence of a frontier can be based on the OLS residuals, noting that the null hypothesis is that the errors are independently and identically normally distributed.

Schmidt and Lin (1984) suggested that the test be based on the sample skewness of the residuals, given that the most obvious difference between a normal and the sum of a normal and a one-sided error is the skewness of the latter. This test is defined as:

$$\sqrt{b_1} = \hat{\mu}_3/\hat{\mu}_2^{3/2} \qquad (3.28)$$

where $\hat{\mu}_2$ and $\hat{\mu}_3$ are, respectively, the second and third moments of the residuals. Two means of performing the $\sqrt{b_1}$ test were outlined. The first was based on the 5 per cent and 1 per cent critical values for skewness.[8] The second means was to transform the skewness variable to a form that is approximately standard normal. The corrected ordinary least squares (COLS) estimate of σ_v in the half-normal/normal error structure is a simple function of μ_3, so for large samples the skewness test is equivalent to testing whether the COLS estimate of σ_v is significantly different from zero.

A more general test for normality than those based solely on the skewness of the OLS residuals is that suggested by Jarque and Bera (1980). This asymptotic test makes use of information on both the skewness and kurtosis of the OLS residuals, just as COLS estimation of the truncated-normal/normal error structure employs data on the second, third and fourth sample moments of the residuals.

The second approach to the choice and evaluation of particular distributions employs asymptotic Lagrange multiplier tests based on the Pearson family of truncated distributions (Lee, 1983). Tests can be derived explicitly for the half-normal and truncated-normal distributions but it is necessary to have sample moments of the residuals for individual establishments.

Unfortunately the decomposition of the residuals can only be made when the data conform sufficiently closely to the required pattern. The previous section discussed three circumstances when the parameters of u and v cannot be calculated. These can be summarised as follows:

Case 1. In this instance the skewness of the overall residuals is positive, meaning that the tail of the distribution lies above rather than below the production frontier. This implies that some establishments in the industry are 'super efficient', rather than inefficient.

Case 2. The second failure occurs when the variance of v is greater than the variance of the residuals. In case (2), the implied inefficiency is so great that $\sigma_u^2 < 0$, which is infeasible by definition of a variance.

Case 3. This only occurs for $\mu \not\equiv 0$. In such a case with COLS estimation the magnitudes of the calculated second, third and fourth moments of the residuals become unbounded and the non-linear estimation routine aborts.

3.8 Measures of inefficiency

There are two ways of viewing inefficiency – from the point of view of the individual enterprise and from that of the industry as a whole. The former is simple in principle as it involves the ratio of the firm's actual performance to that it could have on the frontier. If there were no stochastic element involved this would be an easy requirement. As it is, even for the individual case the observed residual is a combination of technical inefficiency and all the other special factors affecting that specific firm.

In our study confidentiality meant that we were not able to identify individual firms or establishments so we restrict our discussion here to measures which relate to inefficiency and its distribution for the whole industry. Five measures of efficiency are commonly used by researchers in this type of analysis: σ_e, skewness, lambda, average technical efficiency (the Lee–Tyler measure; Lee and Tyler, 1978) and average technical inefficiency.

Clearly the simplest place to start is the standard error of the residuals from the regression themselves, σ_e. Their standard error can always be calculated and no assumption needs to be made about the shapes of the distributions of u and v. This gives a measure of the variation of behaviour of the industry, i.e. the spread of behaviour, but does not distinguish between that due to technical inefficiency and that due to noise. If the variations caused by the other omitted factors are indeed random noise, relatively small and common, either over time or across industries, we can attribute most of the difference in behaviour to inefficiency.

The second measure, skewness (s) of the overall residuals gives an indication of the extent of the tail; this can also always be calculated. However, the residuals can be skewed in the 'wrong', positive direction and it is a matter for debate whether these positive values should also be included in the analysis, as we discuss in Chapter 5.

The final three measures can only be calculated when the combined residual, e, can be successfully decomposed into the stochastic and inefficiency components, u and v. The simplest measure, lambda (λ), gives the relative importance of inefficiency to random variation (in the half-normal/normal case). It is measured by the ratio of the two standard deviations:

$$\lambda = \sigma_v/\sigma_u \tag{3.29}$$

This compares the inefficiency under the control of the management, to the external sources of variation in performance in the industry, and hence in effect gives a normalised measure of inefficiency.

The most helpful measure, if it can be calculated, is the direct ratio estimate of technical efficiency, TE. For the ith observation within a given industry it is:

$$TE_i = \frac{y_i}{f(x_i; \beta) \, \exp[u_i]} \tag{3.30}$$

where TE is the ratio of actual to potential output. The average technical efficiency (ATE) of the *industry* is given by:

$$ATE = E[\exp(-v)] = \int_0^\infty \exp(-v)g(v)\, dv$$

$$= \frac{\exp[\sigma_v^2/2 - \mu]F(\mu/\sigma_v - \sigma_v)}{F(\mu/\sigma_v)} \tag{3.31}$$

$$= 2\exp[\sigma_v^2/2]F(-\sigma_v) \text{ when } \mu = 0, \tag{3.32}$$

where $g(v)$ is the density function for v (Afriat, 1972). This provides a measure of the average of the ratio of actual output to the frontier (potential) output, i.e. it compares what is actually achieved with what could be. The ATE of the industry can be estimated consistently, but with an upward bias, by substituting the estimates of the parameters in (3.23).

The final measure of efficiency is the average of the distribution of the one-sided disturbance, v_i (Schmidt and Lovell, 1979):

$$v_i = u_i - \ln[y_i/f(x_i; \beta)] \tag{3.33}$$

The mean inefficiency is referred to as average technical inefficiency (ATI), the expected value of v. It is given by:

$$ATI = E[v] = \int_0^\infty vg(v)\, dv$$

$$= \mu + \frac{\sigma_v f(\mu/\sigma_v)}{F(\mu/\sigma_v)} \tag{3.34}$$

$$= (2/\pi)^{1/2}\sigma_v \text{ when } \mu = 0 \tag{3.35}$$

The ATI of the industry can also be estimated consistently, but with an upward bias, by substituting the estimates of the parameters in (3.34). The measure can be made independent of the level of factor inputs to the industry by dividing it by the mean of the dependent variable in the regression. With a log regression the residuals have a direct interpretation in terms of the percentage deviations from the fitted frontier. For example, if a residual were, in percentage terms, 10 per cent, this would imply a multiplier of 1.1, which gives a natural log of 0.095, close to 10 per cent. In other words the residuals can, to a certain level of approximation, be read directly as percentage deviations.

Finally, two features of these average measures should be noted. First, they provide no information on the level of allocative efficiency in the industry, or on the extent to which plants in the industry are of optimal scale. This is because a plant is counted as inefficient only to the extent that it falls short of what is estimated to be the output attainable in a plant of its own factor proportions and scale. Second, the measures are essentially an unweighted average of the technical efficiencies and inefficiencies of the production units.

3.9 Conclusion

In this chapter we have discussed the means of estimating relative inefficiency. Although inefficiency is more realistically a dynamic concept, here we concentrate on measurement at a snapshot in time.

Previous analyses, using establishment data, have used one of three techniques: non-parametric programming, parametric programming and parametrical statistical estimation. Although we have considered each of these, in order to lay sufficient groundwork for the chapters which follow, we have concentrated primarily on the stochastic production frontier model because it is the approach we have used in this study. The next chapter applies this to UK and Australian manufacturing industry and explores the resulting estimates of inefficiency.

Notes

1. Although we have characterised this discussion in terms of the 'firm' it is also debatable what the appropriate unit of measurement should be. Clearly, where firms cover more than one industry it should relate to the division of the firm which is involved, if not to the individual plant. Nevertheless, a large firm may optimise across plants, making the identification of individual parts of it misleading. There are some grounds for arguing that the measurement unit should be the decision-making unit, so that the result can be matched against the intention and the responsibility. In what follows the word 'firm' is normally used to denote the appropriate branch or plant, which may or may not, in fact, be a complete firm.
2. Even in the case of oil seed rape, although a field may be used for the one product on a specific occasion, it can be used for other purposes and the capital and labour skills will reflect that.
3. This disadvantage is the converse of the main advantage of non-parametric programming, namely that it does not require the specification of any explicit frontier.
4. A complaint that can be made about most of the methods we discuss.
5. A production function is *homogeneous* of degree n if multiplying all inputs by factor s causes output to increase by s^n, i.e. if $f(sz_1, sz_2) = s^n \cdot f(z_1, z_2) = s^n \cdot y$. If $n = 1$ then f is linear homogeneous.

    A function is *homothetic* if it is a monotonic transform of a homogeneous function, i.e. a homothetic function $f(\mathbf{x})$ can be written as $f(\mathbf{x}) = g[h(\mathbf{x})]$ where g is monotonic and h is homogeneous.
6. Skewness is defined as $\mu_3/\mu_2^{3/2}$, where μ_2 and μ_3 are, respectively, the second and third moments of the regression residuals. Kurtosis, μ_4/μ_2^2, equals 3 for the normal distribution where μ_4 is the fourth moment of the regression residual. Deviations from 3 by this ratio of moments reflect kurtosis different

from that of the normal distribution. Positive deviation is used to indicate that a density is more peaked around its mean than the density of a normal curve, whereas negative deviations indicate that a density is flatter around its mean than the density of a normal curve.

7. In the Australian study Harris used ZSYSTEM (International Mathematical and Statistical Libraries, 1980).

8. These are reported in the *Biometrika Tables for Statisticians*.

4

Estimates of industrial inefficiency in the UK and Australia

In this chapter we discuss the results of the UK and Australian studies, looking first at the production functions and second at the actual measurements of inefficiency for the industrial classifications.

4.1 UK and Australian data[1]

The unit of analysis in both studies was the manufacturing establishment, classified by four digit (A)SIC class.[2] Here, manufacturing broadly relates to the physical or chemical transformation of materials or components into new products, whether the work is performed by power-driven machines or by hand.

The UK study was based on data for 19,023 establishments in 151 industries. This was obtained from the *Annual Census of Production* for 1977. An establishment, as defined in the UK Standard Industrial Classification (SIC), is the smallest unit, at a single location, which can provide the information normally required for an economic census, e.g. employment, expenses, turnover and capital formation. In cases where a single business carries out largely integrated activities at different addresses these may be considered as a single establishment, although separate figures are obtained of employment and net capital expenditure at each unit. However, in order to ensure a comprehensive coverage of all activities, in certain cases two or more establishments under a common ownership or control are combined into an establishment. Information is collected from all manufacturing establishments with 20 or more employees. In 1977 the establishments covered in the census employed over 7.25 million workers and had a turnover of nearly £130,000 million (Census of Production, 1977; *Summary Tables*).

In compliance with the Statistics of Trade Act (1979), we were not ourselves allowed direct access to data relating to the individual establishments in order to preserve the confidentiality promised to the firms which supply the information. The Business Statistics Office (BSO) had to process the data on our behalf and we could only obtain output for our own use which was sufficiently aggregated that no individual establishment or firm could be identified. In effect this meant we were restricted to information at the level of the SIC industry.

The Australian study drew establishment data from the 1977–8 *Census of Manufacturing Establishments*, where establishments are as classified by the four-digit Australian Standard Industrial Classification (ASIC); this covered 166 industries. ASIC thus gives data at a similar level of disaggregation to SIC. Twenty-six industries were excluded from analysis as they each contained fewer than 20 observations. Unfortunately the actual divisions between industries are not in the main drawn identically in the two countries which complicates comparison.

In the ASIC, the establishment is similarly defined as in the UK, but it is not identical. It is in general a unit covering all the operations carried on under the ownership of one enterprise (business) at a single physical location. The exceptions relate to locations where the subsidiary activities exceeded $A2.4 million in terms of sales and transfers out of goods and services during the year. These locations are treated for statistical purposes as two or more establishments corresponding to the various kinds of activity carried on. The establishment statistics also include data relating to separately located administrative offices and ancillary units serving the establishments and forming part of the enterprise that owns and operates the establishments.

Only employment and wages and salaries data are collected from single establishment manufacturing enterprises with fewer than four persons employed. These small enterprises contribute only marginally to statistical aggregates other than the number of establishments, so they were excluded from subsequent analysis. The records for all other establishments numbered more than 26,000. These establishments had an average total employment of around 1.1 million persons and turnover in excess of $A48,000 million in 1977–8.

The Australian data were also subject to strict controls for confidentiality and had to be processed by the Australian Bureau of Statistics (ABS) so that although the analysis relates to individual establishments none of the resultant statistics, in any way, related to individual firms.

4.2 Choice of the production function

In view of the size of the datasets and the heterogeneity of industries involved in both the UK and Australian studies we opted for the transcendental logarithmic (translog) specification of the production function.

There is a debate among researchers as to whether output should be measured gross or net of material inputs in formulating the production function; total (also referred to as gross) output versus net output (or the very similar variable, value added). The translog approximation to the unknown gross output (GO) function can be written as:

$$\ln GO = a_0 + a_1 \ln K + a_2 \ln L + a_3 \ln M + a_4 (\ln K)^2/2 + a_5 (\ln L)^2/2$$

$$+ a_6 (\ln M)^2/2 + a_7 (\ln K \ln L) + a_8 (\ln K \ln M)$$

$$+ a_9 (\ln L \ln M) + \Sigma_i a_{i+9} X_i + e_1 \qquad (4.1)$$

where gross output depends on the flows of capital (K), labour (L), material (M) services and X_i other influences. The error term e_1, is defined as $e = u - v$, where u is the random residual and v is the asymmetric measure of inefficiency. Alternatively, if output is measured net we can use the translog value-added (VA) function[3]:

$$\ln VA = b_0 + b_1 \ln L + b_2 \ln K + b_3 (\ln K)^2/2 + b_4 (\ln L)^2/2$$

$$+ b_5 (\ln K \ln L) + \Sigma_i b_{i+5} X_i + e_2 \qquad (4.2)$$

where VA is defined as value added and all other variables defined as above. Both (4.1) and (4.2) were estimated for the Australian data but we had to exercise a choice in the case of the UK as our resources were limited. This choice was made in part on the basis of a detailed pilot study of a sample of six industries. We were also concerned that both material input and gross output are likely to be determined in the year in question, thus posing problems of simultaneity. These led us to adopt the value added specification.

The US and Japanese studies (Uekusa and Torii, 1985; Caves and Barton, 1990b) use Value Added (Net Output (NO)) *per head*, which restricts a wider comparison with our results:

$$\ln(NO/L) = \alpha_0 + \alpha_1 \ln L + \alpha_2 \ln(K/L) + \alpha_3 [\ln(K/L)]^2$$

$$+ \alpha_4 (\ln L)^2 + \alpha_5 [\ln(K/L)(\ln L)] + \Sigma_i \alpha_{i+5} X_i + e_3 \quad (4.3)$$

In addition to the input and output variables, X variables were included to allow for differences in the nature of inputs (labour, capital and materials) and outputs within a particular industry.[4] First, in relation to labour one could distinguish between different occupations (production versus non-production workers), differences in hours worked and differences in skills (as roughly reflected by the wage levels). One might expect that higher skilled workers would be more productive and that products requiring a greater input from non-production workers, such as those involved in research and development would have a higher unit value. Second, firms differ in the composition of their capital stock, as buildings, plant and machinery each play a different role in the production process. It is even more important to separate out stocks and work in progress, as these items of working capital are conceptually different. Stocks of the finished product are not an input in the normal sense of the word but are an output remaining unsold at the end of the production year. Ideally, one would also like to know what proportion of the capital stock is leased or hired as opposed to owned by the establishment, as the two categories were usually recorded differently in the accounts of the period and hence simple addition could value them inconsistently. Third, one would like to identify differences in the composition of material costs, i.e. the percentage used on fuels, the proportion for resale or recycling, as these do not require the same amount of transformation in their production. Finally, firms within an industry differ in the degree of product specialisation, the degree to which they export, etc. These explanatory variables should increase the robustness of the production frontiers by accounting for various differences in the factors used by different firms and establishments which influence their measured levels of output. Unfortunately, in practice the number of measures that can be included are restricted by the data available. The Australian study obtained data on the following eight variables:

X_1^a The weight accorded to the owned plant component of the capital input, as opposed to leased and hired.

X_2^a Proportion of non-production workers as a percentage of average total labour.

X_3^a The cost of goods purchased for resale as a percentage of material costs.

X_4^a The weight accorded to the electricity and fuels energy component of total material costs.

X_5^a The weight accorded to the inventories component of the capital input.

X_6^a The proportion of turnover that can be accounted for by other operating revenue, i.e. revenues accrued from activities outside the main industry activity.

X_7^a The proportion of total capital input that is accounted for by total rent, leasing and hiring expenses.

X_8^a The proportion of total material costs that is accounted for by payments for commissioned and subcontracted work.

Fifteen industries were employed for exploratory regressions. These were selected in an attempt to represent industries varying, to some degree, in the number of establishments and in the degree of product differentiation, thus enabling the model specification to be tested and simplified. These exploratory series of regressions used either gross output (4.1) or value added (4.2) as the dependent variable. The full set of additional variables were included in the GO regressions, whereas in the VA regressions additive variables that relate to GO or materials were excluded, thus only X_1^a, X_2^a, X_5^a and X_7^a were used. The X variables are all $0 \le X_i \le 1$ (or the percentage equivalent). They imply that the components of the input variables have a differential effect on output. Thus, for example, taking the production/non-production distinction in the labour input that $L = L_1 + L_2$ where 1 and 2 refer to production and non-production workers, respectively. If L_2 has a different effect, d, on output from L_1, just using the aggregate variable L will exclude this effect from the regression. The correct variable would be $L^* = L_1 + (1 + d)L_2$ or $L(1 + dX_1)$ where $X_1 = L_2/L$. The input variables in (4.1) and (4.2) are included in logarithmic form and Griliches (1987) shows that if X_1 is included in the regression as well as ln (L) then its co-efficient b_1 will approximate d. Higher order effects are neglected.[5]

In the full series of GO regressions X_1^a and X_4^a were retained. These co-efficients were significant in the regressions for six and seven industries, respectively, and with one exception they were positive. The findings indicate that the weights accorded to the owned plant component of the capital input and the electricity and fuels component of total purchases, transfers in and selected expenses tended to be understated in around 40 per cent of the exploratory industries. In the full series of VA regressions X_1^a and X_5^a were retained. These were positive and significant in the regressions for six and five industries, respectively.

The UK study included five X variables:

X_1 Proportion of plant and machinery in total capital stock.
X_2 Number of production workers as a percentage of total labour.
X_3 Cost of goods for resale as a percentage of total material costs.
X_4 Stocks as a percentage of capital stock.
X_5 Annual per capita income of non-production workers.

These have the same rationale as in the Australian case. The different specifications reflect the different data available for the two studies.

Although in the case of both Australia and the UK we were limited in the availability of explanatory data our aim was to attempt to replicate as far as possible the US analysis (Caves, 1985), which specified nine X variables:

X_1^{us} Proportion of plant and machinery in total capital stock.
X_2^{us} Number of production workers as a percentage of total employees.
X_3^{us} Cost of goods purchased for resale as a percentage of total material costs.
X_4^{us} Cost of fuel and electricity as a percentage of total material cost.

X_5^{us} Exports as a percentage of total deliveries.
X_6^{us} Stocks as a percentage of total capital stock.
X_7^{us} Degree of product specialisation.
X_8^{us} Annual hours worked per production worker.
X_9^{us} Annual income of non-production workers.

4.3 The UK pilot study

A pilot study was conducted in order to establish whether the methods used by Caves could be applied to the UK data successfully, and if so, to establish the form of the production frontier model to be applied in the full study.

A pilot study in this context has a special importance as it is not possible either to review the estimation process in detail as it takes place, or to run a variety of hypotheses and choose the optimal specification after the event. Thus the choice of a single procedure, which could be executed correctly at arms length by the statistical office, had to be decided upon at the outset.

The pilot study was carried out using establishment data from the 1977 *Annual Census of Production* (ACOP) for six industries:

MLH 213   Biscuits.
MLH 312   Steel tubes.
MLH 381.1   Motor vehicle manufacturing.
MLH 417.2   Warp knitting.
MLH 450   Footwear.
MLH 491   Rubber.

These industries were selected to give a range of large/small and labour/ capital intensive industries. A number of the variables specified in the US study were not available in the UK. The most important of these was capital stock, for which no direct estimates exist at the establishment level. The variable therefore had to be constructed.

Information available from ACOP includes acquisitions and disposals of capital items in the three groups of buildings, plant and machinery, and vehicles; and, for firms employing more than 100 people, expenditure on rent and leasing of equipment.

The net acquisition of capital was capitalised using estimates of average service lives of the assets concerned and assuming straightline depreciation. Land and buildings, plant and machinery and vehicles were each treated separately. Hired and rented assets were similarly capitalised from the expenditure on leasing and hiring after making allowance for the interest element included in the payments. The following life-lengths were assumed for the various assets:

l_1 (land and buildings)   50 years.
l_2 (plant and machinery)   12 years for MLH 381.1;
             19 years for MLH 312, 450, 491;
             20 years for MLH 213;
             21 years for MLH 417.2.
l_3 (vehicles)   7 years.
l_4 (leased plant and machinery) 12 years.
l_5 (rented buildings)   30 years.

These life-lengths were based on assumptions used by the Central Statistical Office (CSO) in the perpetual inventory method for estimating the capital stock, reduced by one-third in accordance with a widespread view that the CSO estimates of lives are too long.[6] An interest rate of 10 per cent was also assumed.

However, these estimates represent only very crude attempts to measure the capital stock of an establishment, being based on only a single year's investment data. A more reliable method would be to use a series of several years' data from ACOP. Although this would smooth out any lumpiness in investment expenditure it would also be a complex and expensive task.[7]

Table 4.1 Establishment size and the importance of leasing

Minimum List Heading	Total number of establishments	Number of establishments employing less than 100	Estimated percentage of leased capital in total capital stock
213	39	13	12
312	88	36	17
381.1	408	200	28
417.2	39	15	22
450	221	89	58
491	221	88	21

No information was available on hiring and leasing by firms with less than 100 employees. Although these small firms form a relatively small proportion of total employment and output in these industries, the number of these establishments is much more significant as can be seen from Table 4.1. Thus in about 40 per cent of cases, on average, no renting or leasing information was available and it was necessary to scale up the capital stock estimates for these smaller establishments by assuming that the ratio of the owned to the leased capital stock for each is the same as the average for all firms in the industry for which the information exists.

We also had no data on hours worked by establishment so, unlike Caves and Barton (1990b), the labour variable had to be restricted to numbers employed.

In order to test which would give the 'best' set of estimates of technical inefficiency, and whether the method used was robust to changes in the specification, the following variables were used as dependent variables in the equation: gross output, gross value added, gross output per head, gross value added per head and net output per head. Each equation was estimated both with and without the values assumed for leased assets in the capital stock.

4.3.1 Results of the pilot study

The aims of the pilot study were fivefold: (1) to discover whether the equations fitted well and produced co-efficients within a reasonable range; (2) whether an efficiency measure can be estimated in this way; (3) whether the efficiency measure was robust to changes in the dependent variable? (4) did the choice of measure of capital stock make a significant difference to the results? (5) whether or not the X variables played a significant role.

Fit of the equations

In most cases, using gross output or gross output per head as the dependent variable, the expected problems with multicollinearity occurred, leading to significant, wrong-signed co-efficients on the materials term and some of the higher-order terms. In some instances the model was clearly over-parameterised by inclusion of the higher order and X_i terms. When the materials terms were dropped and gross value added was used as a dependent variable, the equations became much more acceptable in general. However, there was a wrong-signed co-efficient on labour for MLH 312 (steel tubes) and no significant terms in the equation for MLH 417.2 (warp knitting). Using gross value added, the R^2 suggested a good fit, for most industries it was above 0.9, and the Durbin–Watson statistic was in the acceptable range.[8] When gross value added per head was used as the dependent variable all co-efficients were of the correct sign, although MLH 417.2 (warp knitting) again showed no significant terms. However, in this case the R^2 values were rather low, varying between 0.23 and 0.47 for the six industries. Very similar results were obtained using net output per head as the dependent variable.

Estimation of the efficiency measure

Table 4.2 shows the incidence of successful estimation of the efficiency measure for each industry. No estimates could be obtained using gross output per head and only one using gross output as the dependent variable.

In two industries, 381.1 (motor vehicle manufacturing) and 450 (footwear) no estimates of inefficiency could be obtained.

Table 4.2 Successful estimation of efficiency

Minimum List Heading	Dependent variable				
	Gross output	Gross value added	Gross output per head	Gross value added per head	Net output per head
213				×	
312		×		×	×
381.1					
417.2	×	×		×	×
450					
491		×		×	×

Robustness of efficiency measures

Using λ as the measure of inefficiency, a comparison can be made of the values of λ obtained using the various dependent variables. From these comparisons it was found that estimates of λ from the net output per head equations were noticeably lower than those from the gross value added and gross value added per head equations.

Capital stock

When the estimates of λ were compared using the two measures of capital stock, it was revealed that there was a clear relationship between the estimates obtained in each pair with, in nearly all cases, the estimate including leased assets giving a lower value for λ, i.e. a lower standard deviation of the technical inefficiency measure of the residuals relative to the random component. This would appear to be a plausible result, as the attempt to include the additional leased asset component of capital stock could have reduced both misspecification (picked up as inefficiency in the estimation) and the random error in the estimation. It gave a small improvement on the overall fit as indicated by R^2. However, the change in λ was not generally large and there was a strong correlation between the two sets of estimates of λ.

X variables

All the X variables took on significant co-efficients at some stage in the pilot study. However, those most frequently significant were:

X_2 Production workers as a percentage of total employees (negative co-efficient).

X_4 Stocks as a percentage of capital stock (positive co-efficient).
X_5 Annual per capita income of non-production workers (positive co-efficient).

This suggested that the inclusion of X_2, X_4 and X_5 in the final modelling could yield benefits in terms of better specified frontiers and more reliable efficiency measures.

4.3.2 *Conclusions from the pilot study*

Unfortunately, as only six industries were used, of which only three delivered more than one estimate of inefficiency, these results did not provide a clear indication on how to proceed. However, they did provide some pointers. It was concluded that the equations using gross output and gross output per head as the dependent variable were not so successful and these were discarded. In the remaining cases there was a high degree of variation in the various dependent variables and some of the equations fitted poorly.

The reasons as to why no estimates of inefficiency could be obtained for motor vehicle manufacturing and footwear were unclear. The former, a particularly large industry, may exhibit a very wide range of performance and it is possible that a single production function is inappropriate for the entire industry. In this case it may be argued that better results could be obtained by splitting the industry into large and small establishments in an attempt to pick up some of the variation in performance within the industry.

The production function and inefficiency estimation was fairly robust to the choice of capital stock measure, with similar results obtained using the estimates with and without leased and rented assets. Although the estimates of λ were generally higher when leased assets were excluded, there seemed to be no conclusive reason to prefer either estimate and therefore for simplicity it was proposed that the estimate of capital excluding leased assets be used as the assumptions used were rather sweeping.

Finally, it was clear that the inclusion of various of the X variables appeared to have considerable effects on the results.

4.4 The process of estimation

In general, conducting an exercise of this scale at a distance from the data itself presents many problems, both for those handling the data directly and those trying to interpret it from a distance. As the second group cannot have access to individual results it is not possible for them to follow normal statistical procedures, such as a visual inspection of the data or an examination of regression residuals. All the information that the second group can see has to relate to the data for each industry as a whole, and detailed procedures have to be laid down for how the statistical agency should deal with problems only recognisable from the data themselves.

The Australians were able to use data cleansing methods to make sure problems of outliers and errors were removed as far as it was possible. A number of approaches were possible when it came to choice of functional form. One procedure, trialled in the Australian study, was to follow a sequence of tests on the appropriateness of the functional form. The less elegant procedure in the UK case was to test down from the most general augmented translog specification.

In Australia, estimating using the COLS method (BIE, 1988), under the assumption of a half-normal/normal error structure, the residual could be satisfactorily decomposed initially for 79 of the 140 industries, a success rate of 56 per cent, with value added as the dependent variable. Of the other 61 industries, 37 and 24 were characterised by case (1) and case (2) failures, respectively. In Chapter 3 we defined a case (1) failure as one where the skewness of the overall residual is positive and a case (2) failure as one when the implied variance of v is greater than the variance of the total residual, e. A poorer success rate was achieved initially using gross output as the dependent variable; only 46 (33 per cent) of the full dataset (140) of four-digit ASIC categories. Of the other 94 industries, 92 (66 per cent) were characterised by a case (1) failure, and 2 (1 per cent) by a case (2) failure.

To exclude those establishments that were unsuitable for analysis, certain editing criteria were applied to the primary data before the stochastic production frontiers were estimated (BIE, 1988, Appendix 3). For example, establishments that reported zero values for the input or output variables were excluded, both because this suggested some peculiarities in their production activities and because it was required by the logarithmic formulation of the production frontier. In addition, establishments were excluded that reported data lying far enough from the industry mean to suggest errors in reporting.

However, the confidential nature of the census data for individual establishments precluded inspection by the Bureau of Industry Economics (BIE) of the actual observations within each industry. Hence there remained the possibility of measurement or reporting error. This would not only contribute to failure of residual decomposition but would also result in inconsistent parameter estimates (Johnston, 1984).

As an initial step to investigating this possibility, plots of residuals against observed values for the dependent variable of the regressions were examined. Many of the industries that were characterised by case (1) and case (2) failures contained a small number of outliers that could have strongly influenced the regression plane. However, the regression residuals alone are not a sufficient diagnostic tool for the identification of influential observations (Belsley *et al.*, 1980). This tool fails to show directly what the estimated model would be if a subset of the data were deleted, and the extent to which the presence of erroneous observations affects the estimated co-efficients, standard errors and test statistics.

Belsley *et al.* (1980) reported a number of techniques for diagnosing influential data points that avoid some of these weaknesses. In this study we used the studentised residuals (RSTUDENT), the covariance matrix (COVRATIO), the change in fit (DFFITS), and the hat matrix (HAT). In general, these statistics, respectively, indicate observations that are influential in the determination of large residuals, changes in the covariance matrix of the estimated co-efficients, changes in the fit to the dependent variable, and multivariate outliers.[9]

Having identified the highly influential observations, it was then necessary to investigate the possibility that measurement errors were present. To this end the raw data on the basic variables (gross output, value added, capital stock, persons employed and material inputs) for the individual establishments in question were inspected by officers of the ABS. It was found that one variable in particular frequently aroused suspicions of measurement error, namely the reported capital stocks. The next most frequent explanation for the finding that an observation was influential was that the figures had been imputed by the ABS in cases where an establishment had not supplied the relevant data.

As a result of this examination of the raw data, roughly half the highly influential observations were diagnosed as being most probably attributable to measurement error. The corrective action was to delete the offending observations. In all, 281 (1.3 per cent) of the total number of observations were deleted. The other influential observations were retained, so the information on potentially inefficient establishments in an industry was available for extraction by our analysis. Such thorough cleansing enabled the Australians to eliminate all case (2) failures.

The UK study did not have the opportunity to carry out such detailed cleansing. However, the data had already been cleansed in the sense that zero or implausible values had been corrected by BSO officials following up the relevant establishments.[10]

Implausible values are defined in terms of a studentised range of more than 3 and large growth rates from one year to the next in any variable. This, it must be stressed, was an operation on the data, not on the residuals. The negligible number of extreme residuals resulting were corrected for by elimination not follow up as used by the ABS.

In order to choose the functional form, the 'general to specific' method was applied to the UK regression model (Mizon, 1977; Hendry, 1979).

Starting with an equation as unrestricted as possible, the model was 'tested down' eliminating insignificant variables at each stage of the process, until the elimination of further variables would adversely affect the diagnostic statistics.

4.5 Choice of inefficiency distribution

In Chapter 3 we discussed the different assumptions on the distribution of the inefficiency component that can be adopted. In the context of the restrictions and the design of our study it is debatable as to whether one should use the half-normal/normal error or the truncated-normal/normal error structures. In the case of the Australian data it was possible to test the appropriateness of the methodology, first for skewness and second for the ATI measure of efficiency.

The descriptive statistics (Appendix 2: Tables 1 and 2) show that 91 (65 per cent) of the 140 Australian industries showed negative skewness with value added as the dependent variable (29 per cent for gross output). However, we can test whether the skewness observed appears to differ from the symmetric normal in any significant manner.

The first test used was based on the sample skewness of the residuals, given that the most obvious difference between a normal and the sum of a normal and a one-sided error is the skewness of the latter. With value added as the dependent variable, thirty-five of the 140 skewness values were significant at the 10 per cent level. Twenty-seven of these 35 values were negative. These results suggested that 27 (30 per cent) of the 91 non-zero values of ATI (with the half-normal/normal error specification) differed significantly from zero. Results with gross output as the dependent variable were very poor. Forty-one of the 140 skewness values were significant at the 10 per cent level (two-tailed test). However, just two of these values were for industries with the residuals skewed in the direction that is appropriate for a stochastic production frontier, i.e. negatively skewed. This is one of the reasons why we do not discuss these gross output results further. It remains a matter for further research to examine whether the blame for this unsatisfactory outcome should lie at the door of the data, the specification or the method as a whole.

The Jarque–Bera statistic is the more general test for normality because it makes use of information on both skewness and kurtosis of the OLS residuals. The sample values and significance level of the Jarque–Bera statistic are given in Appendix 2: Tables 1 and 2 for the gross output and value added regressions respectively.

Analysis of the value added data[11] indicated that the hypothesis of normality is rejected at the 10 per cent significance level for 64 of the 140 industries (this is replicated for gross output). This sample of 64 included

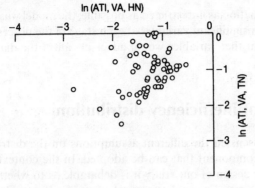

Figure 4.1 Relationship between the estimates for ln(ATI) derived with a generalised and half-normal error structure, value added frontiers (*source*: Harris, 1992).

30 of the 35 industries (39 of the 41 industries) selected by the skewness statistic, plus 34 (25) additional industries for which the deviation from normality was predominantly due to kurtosis rather than skewness. Thirty-four (15) industries in the sample had negative skewness values, so the results suggested that 37 per cent (38 per cent) of the non-zero values of ATI, with the half-normal/normal specification, differed significantly from zero. The number of significant estimates for ATI declined to 31 (11) with the truncated-normal/normal error specification, due to case (1) and case (3) failures.

These low proportions led the Australian team to have considerable reservations about the methodology. After all, we anticipate that there is some technical inefficiency in all industries. The rather weak specification of the capital variable in the UK case could readily feed through into distortion of the pattern of the residuals.

The Australian results suggested the degree of similarity between the half-normal (HN) and truncated-normal (TN) assumptions (Figure 4.1) was not substantial and the UK study opted for the assumption of a half-normal distribution in order to achieve conformity with the other countries in this international study. The resources for the truncated-normal estimation were not in any case available.

4.6   Choice of efficiency measure

In theory we could have estimated technical inefficiency for each individual establishment (Jondrow *et al.*, 1982), as the UK and Australian data related to individual establishments. This would not only have revealed to us the spread of inefficiency within an industry, but would have been of great interest to the managers of the individual firms. However, this was ruled out by the strict confidentiality of the information contained in the datasets. In Chapter 3 we discussed the five measures commonly used to measure technical (in)efficiency: ATI, ATE, λ, σ_e and skewness. A choice made between these alternatives and should be based on the data, using the theories of statistical decisions (McAleer, 1984; Sargan, 1984) given appropriate diagnostic checking (Pagan and Hall, 1983). However, we considered at this stage in the analysis that it would be more instructive to explore the full range of results.

In the UK all five measures were calculated (Appendix 2: Table 3). Skewness (SKEW) and σ_e (SIGMAE) could be calculated for all 151 industries. However, the others could only be measured for industries where the residuals were decomposed, 103 industries for ATI and ATE but only 72 for λ (*LAMBDA*).[12] Table 4.3 shows the correlation matrix between the various measures and also the number of establishments (n).

Table 4.3 Correlation matrix between measures of (in)efficiency and numbers of establishments

	n	LAMBDA	SKEW	ATI	ATE
LAMBDA	0.30				
SKEW	−0.15	−0.78			
ATI	0.03	0.48	−0.77		
ATE	−0.03	−0.47	0.77	−0.99	
SIGMAE	−0.11	0.02	−0.31	0.77	−0.77

Table 4.3 shows first that the signs of these measures are as one would expect. The highest correlations were those between ATI and ATE. This is expected because ATI can be shown to be directly functionally related to ATE. The lowest correlation was between SIGMAE and LAMBDA, which were virtually uncorrelated. This reflects the difference in their construction. LAMBDA depends strongly upon the assumptions about the shapes of the distributions of u and v, and its formation, as the ratio of the standard deviation parameters for v and u introduces ideas about the role of v, which are not present in the other measures. On the other hand, SIGMAE does not rely on assumptions about the shapes of distributions in the same way. It is a linear combination rather than a ratio of them. It is only a measure of the relative technical inefficiency of different industries in so far as the random influences (σ_u) are relatively unimportant.

The UK data also showed weak correlation between the (in)efficiency measures and the number of establishments in the industry, n. The highest correlation, 0.30, between LAMBDA and n, may be affected by outliers. Once they are removed the true correlation may well be nearer to zero.

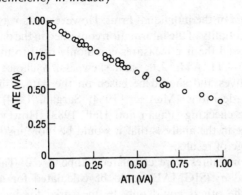

Figure 4.2 Relation between ATI and ATE (*source*: Harris, 1992).

If anything, we would expect industries with smaller numbers of firms to show greater measured inefficiency, as they may reflect more restricted competition, although the increasing imprecision with which technical inefficiency is measured as the number of observations declines could confound this. However, large industries may have a greater chance of including heterogeneous subindustries, which would also tend to increase measured variation. The main reason for this concern was that, in the US, Caves (1985) found strong correlation between the (in)efficiency measures and n (0.47 with ATE). This, he remarked, 'contradicts a great deal of economic theory and established empirical evidence'. It subsequently turned out (Caves and Barton, 1990a) that to a considerable extent this result was based on a computer error and no other country studies showed a strong correlation with number of firms.

In Australia ATI and ATE were the preferred measures. Figure 4.2 shows the relationship between the estimates for ATE and ATI, derived with the generalised error distribution, using value added as the dependent variable. As one would expect, given their method of calculation, there is a smooth relationship between them. ATE and ATI are bounded at values 1 and 0, respectively – the values that indicate the absence of inefficiency. In practice, for Australian manufacturing industries, ATE is bounded at 0.4 and ATI at 1. It is desirable that such characteristics be taken into account in any multivariate analysis of influences that might explain inter-industry differences in ATI or ATE, so that the estimates are not biased and inconsistent. *A priori*, there are few grounds for selecting either ATE or ATI as the single preferred measure of efficiency. One might also consider selecting the logarithmic transforms of these variables, which have different bounds to those of the untransformed variables (Green and Mayes, 1991).

4.7 Success in estimating efficiency measures

It is easy to be overwhelmed by the mass of information so the full results for the UK and Australia are presented in Appendix 2: Tables 1, 2 and 3. The most prominent feature of these results was the large number of cases for which the residuals could not be satisfactorily decomposed, due to case (1) or case (2) failures.

Of the 151 UK manufacturing industries, 48 (32 per cent) showed a positive skewness of the combined residual (case (1) failure). Such a situation is likely to occur for industries where most of the variance of the composed error is due to randomness (σ_u^2) rather than inefficiency (σ_v^2) (Olson *et al.*, 1980). As this in effect inverts the concept of a frontier, it might in fact be possible to calculate a measure of efficiency for these cases by deriving the inefficiency measures from the residual moments as if they applied to an estimated cost function. In the cases of 31 industries (20 per cent) the opposite was true; these showed a large negative (< -1.0) skewness of the combined residual (case (2) failure). This is most likely to occur when most of the error variance is due to inefficiency rather than randomness. In effect the residuals for the industries with either case (1) or case (2) failures are skewed too strongly overall in either the wrong or right direction respectively for a stochastic production frontier, due to one or more outlying observations that might reflect erroneous data. Thus, for the UK study, full results are available for 72 out of 151 industries (48 per cent).

After 'cleansing' the Australian data, with value added as the dependent variable, the success rate increased by 9 percentage points (91 out of the 140 industries). All the failures were case (1) failures – 35 per cent of industries. This experience of case (1) failures was very similar to that in the UK, where 32 per cent of industries showed positive skewness. However, with gross output as the dependent variable, the number of residuals successfully decomposed fell by 4 percentage points from that obtained before the deletion of erroneous observations. Once again all failures (100 out of 140) were case (1) failures.

Although it may seem that the removal of erroneous observations has little effect on the success rates, it is important to take into account that the observations removed were both erroneous and highly influential, so the previous estimates of the model parameters as well as the inefficiency measures would have been incorrect.

The elimination of all the case (2) failures from the Australian results was consistent with the notion that these can be due to measurement or reporting error. Another likely explanation for the UK's high levels of case (2) failures is that it is inappropriate to attempt to capture 'industry' behaviour using a single production function for many of our categories. For example, this may well explain the high number of case (2) failures in the Timber and Furniture group (MLH 4710–4790), five out of six industries show case (2) failures. Although it may be that the furniture industry is especially inefficient, a more likely explanation is that the industry possesses other characteristics that make the fitting of a single production function inappropriate – including mass production and craft work under the same heading, for example.

In an attempt to overcome this problem Caves (1988) has suggested that it may be more appropriate to divide industries into large and small establishments and to fit not one, but several different production functions. However, our data showed that neither the subgroup subject to case (1) failure nor that subject to case (2) failure contained a particularly high quantity of very large or very small firms. These seemed to be distributed fairly evenly thoughout the whole sample, rather than being concentrated in any particular one of the broader SIC industry classifications. In any case, the total number of establishments within an industry is often rather small, making further decomposition by size out of the question. Difference by size is not sufficient explanation alone, as in most cases Caves was able to estimate satisfactory measures of inefficiency using the whole set of establishments without disaggregation. He found that division into large and small establishments 'merely' improved the fit rather than changed the production function estimates.

However, such explanations should also apply to the Australian data, as ASIC is not strikingly different from the UK SIC in its approach. Quite possibly some of the problem can be put down to the unsatisfactory manner in which we were compelled to measure capital. Lack of observations prevents finer disaggregation in Australia or the UK. Microstudies of matched establishments within industries or closer analysis of the individual observations by the statistical authorities if, confidentiality permitted, might be ways forward.

The sheer number of these failures might lead one to question the validity of the methodology but such a result is to be expected from the estimation method. Uekusa and Torii (1985) in a Monte Carlo study have examined the expected numbers of case (1) and case (2) errors when $\lambda = \sigma_u = \sigma_v = 1$ for a variety of sample sizes.[13] For a sample of size 100, case (1) failures are to be expected on 29 per cent of occasions whereas for a sample of size 200 the expected number falls to 21 per cent. In the UK study the average sample size was 130 but the true value of λ was unknown. Therefore, on this limited evidence, our results appear to be consistent with experience, however, more evidence is required to make a more accurate assessment. Uekusa and Torii also showed that the expected number of case (2) failures is approximately zero at sample sizes of 100 and 200. Therefore in this respect there does seem to be a problem with the UK results, although the Australian experience indicates that the case (2) failures could possibly have been eliminated had we been able to cleanse the data thoroughly by closer inspection.

4.8 Measuring inefficiency – UK results

In order to simplify the results, Table 4.4 shows just two of the five measures of inefficiency, ATI and skewness, using 18 industry groups, although there are some industries for which ATI cannot be calculated because of a case (1) failure which are also shown in the table. On the other hand skewness can be measured for all industries.

The first obvious feature of these results is that many industries do not appear to show any great level of inefficiency, in fact about a third of all industries do not show variations in performance that can readily be described as 'inefficiency' rather than variation due to purely stochastic factors. Thus, efficiency in this sense is a relative term (Chapter 2), we are therefore measuring inefficiency by looking at the spread of inefficiency within an industry, i.e. the length of the tail in the functional form of the combined residual. Thus, we are not making any estimate of different levels of inefficiency amongst industries, i.e. of absolute inefficiency. Measuring absolute inefficiency would give very different results than our measurement of relative inefficiency (Button, 1992). Therefore, observing a low level of inefficiency means that the establishments in the industry do not differ much from each other in terms of efficiency – they are clustered. However, while this may mean that the firms have a common level of efficiency, that in itself does not entail that the industry has any particular level of efficiency relative to its competitors in other countries. On the contrary, on an international scale they could be highly inefficient.

Table 4.5 shows a summary of the inefficiency measures for the industry groups (SIC 2-digit).[14] Although there are 18 groups in total, only 16 are shown because two – coal & petroleum (26) and leather & fur (43) – were characterised solely by case (1) and (2) failures. Looking across all the measures we observe that, with few exceptions, the measures tend to agree, this is best at the extremes (most and least efficient groups).

The most efficient industry groups were clothing & footwear (44, 45) and building materials (46). Building materials have become increasingly traded, which may help to explain the relatively high level of efficiency within this industry. However, much of the industry is characterised by heavy, low value added items made from widely available raw materials, so that the distances over which they are distributed, even with scale economies, are relatively small. This industry group contains some of the most efficient industries – cement (4640) and other building materials (4692) – but also one of the most inefficient industries – glass (4630). The clothing & footwear grouping also contains a wide spread of efficiencies within it, footwear (4500) is an efficient industry whereas weatherproof outerwear (4410) is inefficient. The least efficient industry headings are food, drink & tobacco (21, 22, 23, 24), paper & printing (48) and timber & furniture (47). The food, drink & tobacco industry is heavily dependent

Table 4.4 Spread of inefficiency across industries by ATI and skewness, UK (%)

Standard Industrial Classification code	Industry heading	Number of industries included	Case (1) failure	ATI		Skewness		Case (2) failure
				below mean	above mean	above mean	below mean	
21,22,23, 24	Food, drink & tobacco	14	36	7	29	21	14	21
26	Coal and petroleum products	3	33	0	0	0	0	67
27	Chemicals	16	31	25	31	38	19	13
31	Iron & steel	3	0	33	33	67	0	33
32	Aluminium & other metals	3	0	67	33	67	33	0
33,34	Mechanical engineering	21	38	14	29	14	29	19
35	Instrument engineering	4	50	25	0	25	0	25
36	Electrical engineering	11	27	27	27	27	27	18
37	Shipbuilding	1	0	100	0	100	0	0
38	Vehicles	6	50	0	17	0	17	33
39	Metal goods n.e.s.	11	45	36	18	36	18	0
41,42	Textiles	16	19	31	31	31	31	19
43	Leather & fur	3	33	0	0	0	0	67
44,45	Clothing & footwear	9	56	11	11	11	11	22
46	Building materials	7	43	43	14	43	14	0
47	Timber & furniture	6	0	0	17	0	17	83
48	Paper & printing	8	13	25	50	25	50	12
49	Other manufactures	9	11	22	44	33	33	22
	All industries	151	32	22	26	25	22	20

mean ATI = 0.320; mean skewness = −0.427

Table 4.5 Summary of inefficiency

SIC code	Industry heading	SIGMAE	ATI	LAMBDA	ATE	SKEW
21,22,23, 24	Food, drink & tobacco	0.568 (16)	0.404 (16)	1.724 (5)	0.640 (15)	−0.364 (4)
27	Chemicals	0.483 (14)	0.350 (13)	6.038 (15)	0.683 (13)	−0.356 (3)
31	Iron & steel	0.444 (12)	0.341 (11)	1.711 (3)	0.689 (11)	−0.366 (5)
32	Aluminium & other metals	0.424 (10)	0.319 (6)	2.184 (8)	0.708 (5)	−0.419 (8)
33,34	Mechanical engineering	0.402 (8)	0.337 (10)	2.211 (9)	0.693 (10)	−0.488 (12)
35	Instrument engineering	0.274 (1)	0.231 (3)	1.738 (6)	0.783 (3)	−0.376 (7)
36	Electrical engineering	0.396 (3)	0.329 (7)	3.259 (13)	0.702 (7)	−0.508 (13)
37	Shipbuilding	0.400 (6)	0.317 (5)	1.720 (4)	0.708 (5)	−0.371 (6)
38	Vehicles	0.398 (4)	0.331 (8)	1.961 (7)	0.697 (9)	−0.442 (9)
39	Metal goods n.e.s.	0.425 (11)	0.332 (9)	3.919 (14)	0.699 (8)	−0.477 (11)
41,42	Textiles	0.418 (9)	0.316 (4)	2.825 (12)	0.710 (4)	−0.428 (10)
44,45	Clothing & footwear	0.294 (2)	0.211 (2)	1.551 (1)	0.802 (2)	−0.256 (1)
46	Building materials	0.470 (13)	0.210 (1)	1.664 (2)	0.803 (1)	−0.280 (2)
47	Timber & furniture	0.484 (15)	0.401 (15)	2.227 (10)	0.639 (16)	−0.513 (15)
48	Paper & printing	0.398 (4)	0.384 (14)	8.100 (16)	0.661 (14)	−0.826 (16)
49	Other manufactures	0.401 (7)	0.342 (12)	2.360 (11)	0.688 (12)	−0.512 (14)

Figures shown are weighted averages.[15]
Efficiency rankings for each measure are shown in parenthesis (1 = most efficient, 16 = least efficient).

on raw material from the agricultural sector, this may partly explain the apparent inefficiency. Not only are agricultural products heavily dependent on weather conditions, and hence supply and price cannot always be guaranteed, but these products tend to be based locally, due to climate, soil type, terrain, etc. and production facilities are spread right across the country, with regional products, such as apples from Kent. This geographical dispersion is likely to increase inefficiency. Considering the experiences of the paper, printing and publishing industries in the past it is not suprising to find this group amongst the least efficient. Over the last couple of decades the British printing industry has been losing its position in the international market, primarily to Germany and Japan. Between 1975 and 1985 the UK's printing industry's world export share fell from 9.2 per cent to 5.9 per cent (Porter, 1990). In addition, the industry has had severe problems with strong trade unions over this period. The final industry group, timber & furniture, contained only six industries, of which five were case (2) failures.

The importance of the difference between absolute and relative inefficiency, on the one hand, and coverage, on the other, is very clear from chemicals. Chemicals, particularly pharmaceuticals, is a star performer in terms of international competitiveness, containing some of the UK's best companies (Hart, 1993). In 1985, British petroleum/chemicals industry's exports accounted for 6.9 per cent of world exports (Porter, 1990). Yet within chemicals, companies have restructured substantially because it is difficult to compete at the bulk end of the market, for example. In some sectors there are opportunities for niche products, such as specialised organics, while in pharmaceuticals the scale can vary markedly. This will enable a wide range of performance to be maintained.

Clothing may appear an unlikely candidate to head the list until the strength of competition among suppliers within the industry is recalled. With strong purchaser power on the part of retailers, margins are squeezed and the threat of low price competition from overseas is considerable.

Disaggregating further, the ten most efficient, or least inefficient, industries are shown in Tables 4.6(a) and 4.6(b). For simplicity we have chosen to present only the ATI and skewness measures (Appendix Tables 4(a) and 4(b) show a complete ranking of all industries using these measures). Again these are only those industries which were neither case (1) nor case (2) failures, hence it may well be that other industries (case (1) failures) are as, or even more, efficient than some of these. Our measures indicate the level of relative (in)efficiency very different results are obtained, using the same data set, by attempts to measure absolute (in)efficiency (Button, 1992). Button's ten most and least efficient industries using soft modelling techniques to measure absolute efficiency are shown in Appendix 2 of this chapter. Comparing our results with those of Button the most stark difference is in the ranking of the cement industry. Using ATI, the cement industry is the most efficient industry, whereas using Button's soft modelling technique the cement industry is the least efficient industry. Such differences can be explained by the structure of the industry. The cement industry is one where in 1977 only seven suppliers had 100 per cent of the market (*Statistics of Production Concentration*), however, in practice, three firms dominated. A cartel came into existence in 1934 (Cement Makers' Federation Agreement), this involved market sharing, barriers to entry, etc. This was eventually broken up in 1987. The existence of a cartel explains the high relative efficiency in this industry. Members of a cartel will be similar with respect to output, inputs, size, etc. and hence the spread of efficiency will be small. However, internationally they may be very inefficient, as suggested by Button's analysis.

Table 4.6(a)   Ten most efficient industries using the ATI measure

MLH	Industry	ATI
4640	Cement	0.115
2770	Dyes & pigments	0.123
3995	Drop forgings	0.124
4692	Other building materials	0.130
4991	Musical instruments	0.134
2795	Printing ink	0.170
4500	Footwear	0.175
3395	Scales & weighing machinery	0.188
4130	Weaving	0.190
2791	Polishes	0.190

Table 4.6(b)   Ten most efficient industries using skewness

MLH	Industry	Skew
4692	Other building materials	−0.007
4991	Musical instruments	−0.026
3995	Drop forgings	−0.041
2770	Dyes & pigments	−0.042
4221	Household textiles	−0.057
4640	Cement	−0.058
2791	Polishes	−0.064
4130	Weaving	−0.099
3220	Copper, brass, etc.	−0.100
2391	Spirits & distilling	−0.122

One feature of Tables 4.6(a) and 4.6(b) is the variety of different industries included. It is interesting to look at the types of industries that are most efficient and some of their general characteristics. A comparison of Tables 4.6(a) and 4.6(b) tells us about the correlation between these two measures. There are seven industries that are common in both the lists: dyes & pigments, polishes, drop forgings, other building materials, cement, musical instruments and weaving.

Dyes & pigments (2770) and polishes (2791) are both part of the chemicals and petroleum products industry, printing ink (2795) is only in the top ten using the ATI measure. From our comments earlier it is not surprising that these industries appear on the list of most efficient industries. Here, there does seem to be a link between absolute and relative efficiency.

Weaving (4130) is classified under textiles. Although textiles are subject to protection through the multifibre arrangement there is fierce competition from low labour-cost countries, which tends to eliminate any low productivity plants. Success has tended to come at the higher quality, higher value added end of the market.

Table 4.7(a) Ten most inefficient industries using ATI

MLH	Industry	ATI
3652	Broadcast receiving equipment	0.606
2292	Starch & miscellaneous foods	0.499
2190	Animal & poultry feed	0.492
2730	Toilet preparations	0.492
3962	Jewellery & precious metals	0.457
3940	Wire & wire products	0.447
2310	Brewing & malting	0.435
3397	Food & drink processing machinery	0.426
3360	Earth-moving equipment	0.411
3210	Aluminium	0.405

Table 4.7(b) Ten most inefficient industries using skewness

MLH	Industry	Skew
4292	Other textiles	−0.981
4890	Other printing	−0.968
3940	Wire & wire products	−0.962
3680	Domestic electrical goods	−0.950
4810	Paper & board	−0.914
4230	Textile finishing	−0.873
4821	Cardboard boxes etc.	−0.826
4630	Glass	−0.811
4941	Toys & games	−0.801
4410	Weatherproof outerwear	−0.796

At the other end of the spectrum the most inefficient industries also show considerable heterogeneity (Tables 4.7(a) and 4.7(b)). As in the case of the top ten most efficient industries, it is necessary to recognise that these are only those industries for which the residuals could be satisfactorily decomposed. It may well be the case that there are other industries which are equally or more inefficient than these, in particular case (2) failures, industries that are highly (implausibly) inefficient.

The wire & wire products industry is the only one contained in both lists, which reflects the lack of correlation between ATI and skewness measures at the lower efficiency levels.

Due to the considerable heterogeneity of these industries it is, for the most part, easier to describe them individually than as a series of groups. In a similar manner to that above, the apparent inefficiency of some of these industries can be readily explained by looking generally at the structure of the industry.

Our estimates indicate that the broadcast receiving equipment industry (3652) is the most inefficient industry using the ATI measure. This is entirely consistent with the experiences of the last decade in the industry, with the loss of market share to foreign competitors, in particular to Japan, the US and Germany. Using the skewness measure other textiles (4292) are the most inefficient. This is one of two industries in the textile classification that are highly inefficient, the other being textile finishing (4230). In the UK the textile industry has in the past been very sensitive to labour costs and this may be reflected in the large spread of inefficiency within these industries. Here is an interesting contrast with weaving, which is among the more efficient industries. This may represent an industry that has responded to the high external pressures while the others have yet to react fully. This emphasises the need to explore the determinants of inefficiency in more detail, rather than relying on these descriptive measures, which is what we move on to in Chapter 5.

The inclusion of starch & miscellaneous food products (2292) may reflect the nature of the industry. It is clearly one containing a great deal of diversified products, for example, coffee, tea, nuts, glucose, and seasonings and stuffings; and is therefore poorly defined under just one heading. A single production function is most probably inappropriate for this industry.

The brewing & malting industry (2310) is another that is not a clearly defined single industry. Brewing is concentrated in six major firms, whereas malting consists of a large number of very small firms. Therefore fitting a single production function may not be suitable for this industry.

In general, therefore, we observe considerable variety in the results, some of it apparently counterintuitive. In part this reflects an intuition based on knowledge of absolute efficiency revealed through international competitiveness, which may reflect different factor prices among countries, not knowledge of the spread of behaviour within industries. The casual empiricism of the present section is therefore followed up in Chapter 5 by a detailed analysis of the determinants of relative efficiency as measured here.

4.9 Measures of inefficiency – Australian results

In the 1970s, the Australian economy was affected by the world-wide disturbances in exchange rates (with the breakdown of the pegged exchange rate system), large increases in oil prices from 1973, the subsequent boom in certain agricultural and mining commodities, and increasing competition from the manufactured exports of developing countries in the region. In addition, the economy was affected by Federal Government policies such as a move towards equal pay for women, an across-the-board tariff cut and a sharp rise in real wages (Industries Assistance Commission, 1978).

The effect of the recession on manufacturing in Australia was similar to that in other OECD countries. However, the subsequent recovery in activity was stronger in the OECD group as a whole than in Australia, and the rise in unemployment rates was relatively greater in Australia than in the OECD. Manufacturing activities in which Australia could be expected to have a comparative advantage, such as basic metals and processed primary products, tended to fare better during the recession in terms of activity and employment than more highly protected activities such as textiles, wearing apparel, footwear and leather, and the fabricated metal products, machinery and equipment industry (including motor vehicles) (Industries Assistance Commission, 1978).

The trade performance of Australian manufacturing industries during the late 1970s was quite different from that observed in many other industrialised countries. Reflecting Australia's area of comparative advantage, relatively high proportions of Australia's exports came from the rural and mining sectors. In contrast, relatively low proportions of exports came from the manufacturing sector, and the ratio of exports to gross product for that sector was quite low. The export performance of Australia's manufacturing sector at that time largely reflected exports by industries engaged in relatively simple processing of outputs from the rural and mining sectors (Industries Assistance Commission, 1977).

Australian manufacturing industries overall had relatively high tariff protection, and the share of imports in their domestic markets was low relative to countries such as Canada and Sweden – countries with broadly similar per capita incomes, population structures, demand patterns and domestic market sizes. High tariffs had encouraged domestic production in a wide range of import-competing industries, rather than in industries with a high export performance (Industries Assistance Commission, 1977). The overall outcomes for the performance of the manufacturing sector over the decade ending 1977–8 were a decline in its employment share from 25 to 19 per cent, in its share of GDP from 28 per cent to 22 per cent, and in its share of the domestic market from 83 per cent to 76 per cent (Industries Assistance Commission, 1979).

The major changes in protection against import competition over the decade ending 1977–8 were the general reduction of 25 per cent made in all tariffs in July 1973; the progressive introduction of temporary assistance, mainly in the form of quantitative restrictions on imports of certain manufactured goods (particularly textiles, clothing and footwear, and transport equipment); and the reductions in tariffs (in January 1977) which followed the devaluation of the Australian dollar in November 1976. The so-called temporary assistance measures substantially increased the effective rates of protection afforded to industries which were already the most highly assisted (Industries Assistance Commission, 1978). These measures tended to negate movements made during the decade towards a lower and more uniform structure of assistance to manufacturing.[16]

The spread of inefficiency across Australian industries was similar to that of the UK (Table 4.8). The overall mean value of ATI was 0.303 for Australia compared with 0.320 for the UK. In the Australian study, ATI

Table 4.8 Spread of inefficiency across industries by ATI, Australia (%)

ASIC code	Industry heading	Number of sub-industries	Case (1) failure	ATI		Case (2) failure
				below mean	above mean	
21	Food, beverages & tobacco	23	43	13	44	0
23	Textiles	9	44	33	23	0
24	Clothing & footwear	10	40	50	10	0
25	Wood, wood products & furniture	9	22	33	45	0
26	Paper, paper products, printing & publishing	9	22	45	33	0
27	Chemical, petroleum & coal products	10	50	30	20	0
28	Non-metallic mineral products	8	13	50	37	0
29	Basic metal products	8	38	50	12	0
31	Fabricated metal products	14	36	36	28	0
32	Transport equipment	8	50	13	37	0
33	Other machinery & equipment	19	21	68	11	0
34	Miscellaneous manufacturing	13	38	8	54	0
	All industries	140	35	35	30	0

Six industries were excluded from the analysis because the number of observations, etc. were unavailable for reasons of confidentiality.
mean ATI = 0.303

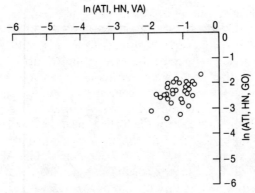

Figure 4.3   Relationship between the estimates for ln(ATI) derived with a half-normal error structure, gross output and value-added frontiers (*source*: Harris, 1992).

could be calculated for about 65 per cent of all industries (using value added and the half-normal distribution), of these, 58 per cent were below the average value of ATI, indicating that there was only a moderate skew to the distribution of inefficiency across manufacturing as as whole.

The most efficient two-digit subdivisions on average in Australian manufacturing, according to the ATI measure with gross output as the dependent variable, are non-metallic mineral products and transport equipment, as can be seen in Table 4.9. Basic metal products and food, beverages and tobacco have the highest mean levels of measured inefficiency.

The mean estimates of ATI with value added as the dependent variable are much larger than those obtained with the gross output set. The most efficient industry subdivision, according to the value added data, has a higher mean level of ATI than that of the most inefficient industry in the gross output data (note that the same industry subdivision is being referred to here, basic metal products). Thus it appears that the ATI estimates are very sensitive to the form of the dependent variable. The correlation co-efficient between the two sets of estimates of ATI is only 0.194 (BIE, 1988). The discussion in Harris (1992) suggests a limited linear and log-linear relation only with the half-normal error structure (see Figure 4.3).

The most efficient two-digit subdivisions on average, according to the ATI measure with value added as the dependent variable, are basic metal products and textiles. At the other end of the spectrum, miscellaneous manufacturing, transport equipment, and food, beverages and tobacco have the highest mean levels of measured inefficiency. Basic metal products, with an effective rate of assistance of 14 per cent, consists of relatively lightly assisted activity but the sector is highly concentrated. By contrast, textiles, with an effective rate of assistance of 57 per cent, receive well above the average level of assistance (26 per cent) provided to Australian manufacturing in 1977–8 (Industries Assistance Commission, 1979). However, this sector has quite a low degree of concentration (Madge *et al.*, 1989).

The casual observation of no simple relationship between measured technical efficiency and the degree of concentration or the assistance afforded Australian manufacturing industries is borne out also by the characteristics of the industries with the highest mean levels of technical inefficiency. Transport equipment (effective assistance rate of 61 per cent) was highly protected during 1977–8 and had quite a high degree of concentration, whereas miscellaneous manufacturing (effective assistance rate of 27 per cent, low concentration) and food, beverages and tobacco (effective assistance rate of 13 per cent, moderate concentration) received much less assistance from government. Of course, the diversity of activities undertaken within the miscellaneous manufacturing industries would tend to increase their measured levels of technical inefficiency.

Table 4.9 Mean and standard deviation of ATI estimates by two-digit ASIC subdivisions

ASIC code	Industry	Gross output		Value added	
		ATI	Number of observations	ATI	Number of observations
21	Food, beverages and tobacco	0.113 (0.066)	3	0.362 (0.121)	13
23	Textiles	0.085 (0.035)	4	0.239 (0.170)	5
24	Clothing & footwear	0.106 (0.021)	4	0.277 (0.046)	6
25	Wood, wood products, & furniture	0.099 (0.036)	3	0.330 (0.073)	7
26	Paper, paper products, printing, & publishing	0.105 (0.031)	3	0.271 (0.119)	7
27	Chemical, petroleum, & coal products	0.073 (0.018)	3	0.301 (0.153)	6
28	Non-metallic mineral products	0.038 (0.000)	1	0.301 (0.068)	7
29	Basic metal products	0.119 (0.029)	4	0.235 (0.042)	5
31	Fabricated metal products	0.108 (0.024)	4	0.296 (0.091)	9
32	Transport equipment	0.065 (0.048)	3	0.369 (0.121)	4
33	Other machinery & equipment	0.092 (0.034)	6	0.244 (0.056)	15
34	Miscellaneous manufacturing	0.096 (0.038)	2	0.391 (0.070)	7

Standard deviations are in parenthesis.

To examine these issues further, the ten most efficient and least efficient industries according to the ATI and skewness measures are shown in Tables 4.10(a) and 4.10(b), respectively. The set of industries from which these industries are drawn includes (for both measures) only those industries for which an ATI estimate could be derived using value added as the dependent variable and a half-normal/normal error structure. Ninety-one of the 140 industries met this criterion.

Table 4.10(a)   Ten most efficient industries using the ATI measure

ASIC Class	Industry	ATI
2347	Woollen yarns & fabrics	0.060
3369	Industrial machinery & equipment nec	0.103
2765	Soap & other detergents	0.114
2643	Paper stationery	0.132
2345	Cotton yarns & fabrics	0.142
3165	Non-ferrous steam, gas & water fittings	0.143
2117	Bacon, ham & small goods	0.148
2351	Household textiles	0.157
2766	Cosmetics & toilet preparations	0.161
2632	Paper bags (incl textile bags)	0.166

Table 4.10(b)   Ten most efficient industries using the skewness measure

ASIC Class	Industry	Skewness
2765	Soap & other detergents	−0.008
3369	Industrial machinery & equipment nec	−0.009
2347	Woollen yarns & fabrics	−0.013
2643	Paper stationery	−0.032
3351	Radio & TV receivers, audio equipment	−0.042
2351	Household textiles	−0.045
2766	Cosmetics & toilet preparations	−0.049
2117	Bacon, ham & small goods	−0.058
3165	Non-ferrous steam, gas & water fittings	−0.083
2861	Clay bricks	−0.093

As discussed above for the UK, there is a considerable overlap between the industries listed as the most efficient according to the ATI and skewness measures, with eight of the ten ASIC classes appearing on both lists (ASIC 2861 and 3351 do not appear in Table 4.10(a), whereas ASIC 2345 and 2632 do not appear in Table 4.10(b)). However, it appears from Figure 4.4 that the correlation between the ATI and skewness measures for the set of industries not subject to case (1) failure becomes weaker as the magnitude of skewness increases.

From Table 4.10(a), we see that ASIC classes 2345, 2347 and 2351 are classified as part of the (two-digit) textiles industry, which has a high technical efficiency (Table 4.9), despite its level of assistance, which suggests

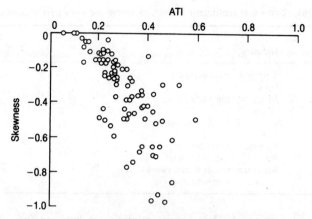

Figure 4.4 Relationship between the ATI and skewness derived with a half-normal error structure, value added frontiers.

a relatively low competitiveness in world markets. However, ASIC classes 2632 and 2643 are classified as part of the paper industry, which has a lower technical efficiency ranking, while ASIC classes 2765 and 2766 are classified as part of the chemical industry which has an intermediate technical efficiency ranking.

At the other end of the spectrum are the most inefficient industries according to the ATI and skewness measures (Tables 4.11(a) and 4.11(b)). There is some overlap between the industries listed as most inefficient according to the ATI and skewness measures, with five of the ten ASIC classes appearing on both lists (ASIC 2352, 3234, 3242, 3484 and 3485). The reduced overlap between the sets of most inefficient industries compared with the outcome for the most efficient industries is consistent

Table 4.11(a) Ten most inefficient industries using the ATI measure

ASIC Class	Industry	ATI
2188	Wine & brandy	0.591
2122	Butter	0.526
3471	Flexible packaging & abrasive papers	0.497
3242	Boats	0.494
2352	Textile floorcoverings	0.461
2175	Prepared animal & bird foods	0.458
2641	Publishing	0.455
3484	Signs & advertising displays	0.447
3234	Motor vehicle parts nec	0.435
3485	Sporting equipment	0.430

Table 4.11(b) Ten most inefficient industries using the skewness measure

ASIC Class	Industry	Skewness
2352	Textile floor coverings	−0.970
2767	Inks	−0.964
3234	Motor vehicle parts nec	−0.925
3242	Boats	−0.859
3161	Cutlery & hand tools nec	−0.771
2187	Malt	−0.743
3485	Sporting equipment	−0.710
2532	Resawn & dressed timber	−0.704
2451	Mens trousers & shorts (work)	−0.684
3484	Signs & advertising displays	−0.659

with the observation of a less precise relationship between the ATI and skewness measures as the magnitude of skewness increases (Figure 4.4).

From Table 4.11(a) we see that ASIC classes 3471, 3484 and 3485 are classified as part of the (two-digit) miscellaneous manufacturing, which has the highest technical inefficiency of the twelve two-digit ASIC subdivisions (Table 4.9). This outcome is consistent with the heterogeneous nature of the products manufactured by these ASIC classes, which would tend to increase their level of measured technical inefficiency. Moreover, each of these classes had average effective rates of assistance equal to (class 3471) or well above (classes 3484, 3485) the manufacturing average in 1977–8 (Industries Assistance Commission, 1983).

Also listed in Table 4.11(a), ASIC classes 2122, 2175 and 2188 are classified as part of the (two-digit) food, beverage and tobacco industry, which has the third highest technical inefficiency of the twelve two-digit ASIC subdivisions (Table 4.9). Whereas the butter class has a small number (36) of establishments and is quite highly concentrated, the wine and brandy class contains more than 100 establishments and is considerably less concentrated. What these classes have in common is levels of assistance which, at 37 and 96 per cent, are well above the manufacturing average of 23 per cent (Industries Assistance Commission, 1983). The prepared animal and bird foods class has different characteristics again. It is dominated by some large firms, contains more than 100 establishments Australia-wide, and received a negative (−5 per cent) rate of assistance in 1977–8.[17]

The remaining four ASIC classes listed in Table 4.11(a) appear to have a wide range of characteristics. However, motor vehicle parts and boats are classified to the two-digit transport equipment industry, and three of the four classes have above average rates of assistance (the exception is the diverse publishing class). Moreover, both motor vehicle parts and textile floorcoverings received substantial increases in their effective rates of assistance in the subsequent five years.

4.10   The UK and Australia compared

Using value added as the dependent variable and assuming a half-normal distribution of v, Table 4.12 summarises the estimates of ATI for those industries for which the residual could be successfully decomposed.

Table 4.12   Estimates of inefficiency for the UK and Australia

Country	Minimum ATI	Maximum ATI	Mean ATI	Standard deviation
Australia	0.060	0.591	0.303	0.103
UK	0.115	0.606	0.320	0.102

The mean values of ATI are very similar, and in both the UK and Australia about a third of all industries do not show variations in performance that can readily be described as inefficiency rather than variation due to purely stochastic factors. The range of inefficiency is also similar in the two countries, as are the standard deviations.

At the industry level the main problem involved in comparing the extent of inefficiency over countries is that different countries classify industries in different ways.[18] It is therefore necessary to match industries as closely as possible. Figure 4.5 compares inefficiency, using ATI, for 27 matched industries.

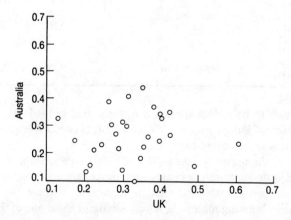

Figure 4.5   Relationship between the ATI estimates for matched Australian and UK industries, half-normal error structure, value added frontiers.

Table 4.13 Comparison of UK and Australian results

UK code	Australian code	Industry	UK ATI	Australian ATI
2120	2161	Bread	0.300	0.318
2730	2766	Toilet preparations	0.492	0.161
3110	2943	Steel	0.357	0.227
3120	2945	Steel tubes	0.269	0.307
3210	3142	Aluminium	0.405	0.333
3220 3230	2963 3143	Other metals	0.245	0.234
3333	3365	Compressors	0.225	0.214
3340 3350 3399	3369	Industrial machinery	0.331	0.103
3393 3680	3353	Refrigerators & household apliances	0.367	0.263
3640	3351	Audio, receivers, etc.	0.606	0.240
3652	3241 3242	Ships & boats	0.317	0.410
3950 3996	3151	Metal containers	0.282	0.274
4120 4130	2345	Cotton, weaving, etc.	0.298	0.142
4160 4292	2356	Textile products	0.382	0.375
4221	2351	Household textiles	0.215	0.157
4410	2452	Waterproofs	0.397	0.251
4500	2460	Footwear	0.175	0.245
4612	2861	Clay/non-refractory goods	0.290	0.220
3397	3368	Food & drink processing	0.426	0.271
4692	2872,4 2882,4	Building materials	0.130	0.324
4710	2531,2,5	Timber	0.401	0.347
4821	2634	Cardboard boxes	0.347	0.186
4830	2643	Stationery	0.204	0.132
4890	2641,2,4,5	Publishing	0.426	0.354
4910	3461	Rubber	0.312	0.305
4920 4960	3471 3474	Plastics	0.354	0.443
4941 4991	3484 3487	Miscellaneous	0.266	0.391

There appears to be a close similarity in the extent of inefficiency for a large proportion of industries, simple correlation between Australian and UK industries was estimated to be 0.53.

In all but seven industry classes (bread, steel tubes, ships & boats, footwear, building materials, plastics and miscellaneous) the extent of inefficiency in the UK exceeded that in Australia, of these the largest difference was in building materials, which we found to be one of the most efficient industries in the UK. Overall, the largest differences were in audio & receivers, toilet preparations, and industrial machinery, and the smallest in textiles, rubber and metal containers.

4.11 Summary and conclusion

The aim of Phase 1 of the research was to estimate frontier production functions for manufacturing industries, as defined by the Standard Industrial Classification, and hence measure their inefficiencies. The results obtained from this exercise for the UK revealed that for many industries it was not possible to decompose the residual satisfactorily into the inefficiency component and the stochastic component, and hence measure inefficiency accurately. In total this was the case for 52 per cent of the industries studied; 32 per cent were case (1) failures and 20 per cent were case (2) failures. This implies that those industries for which a case (1) failure occurred were either largely efficient, or the methodology of fitting a single production function to the industry was inappropriate. At this stage we can only speculate as to the possible causes for the case (1) failures, although the study by Uekusa and Torii (1985) indicated that the number of case (1) failures that we experienced may not be unusual. However, if it is because of inappropriate methodology this has important implications for the technique of frontier production function analysis. Case (2) failures may be due either to the methodology, or because the industries are very inefficient. The fact that in the Australian study Harris (1988) was able to eliminate all of the case (2) failures by removing erroneous observations may be an indicator that the screening methods used in the British study were insufficient.

We were able to calculate a measure of inefficiency for 48 per cent of industries in the UK and 65 per cent in Australia. On the basis of these data and the chosen estimation method we concluded that about a third of all industries do not show variations in performance that can be described as technical inefficiency rather than purely random factors using this particular methodology.

In this chapter we have relied primarily on descriptive statistics. In the next one we seek explanations of these variations in inefficiency, this is followed by a comparison of our results with those of others.

Notes

1. For a detailed explanation of the data used and definition of the variables see Appendix 1.
2. This level of disaggregation is in line with the suggestion of Meeusen and van den Broeck (1977) that two-digit industries are too heterogeneous and that at least three-digit, and preferably four-digit, observations are required.
3. There is a small technical difference between 'net output' and 'value added' in the U.K. statistics:

Net output is calculated by deducting from gross output the cost of purchases (adjusted for fluctuations of stocks of materials, etc. during the year) and the cost of industrial services received, and, where applicable, duties, etc.

Gross value added at factor cost is calculated by deducting from net output the cost of non-industrial services, e.g. rent of buildings, hire of plant, machinery and vehicles, advertising, rates, bank charges, etc.

4. The inclusion of compositional variables is discussed by Griliches and Ringstad (1971).
5. Experiments with them in the pilot study failed to produce significant estimates.
6. The perpetual inventory method for constructing the capital stock is described in Mayes and Young (1993) together with an assessment of the accuracy of the estimates in an attempt to suggest how the CSO methodology might be improved.
7. It is hoped that this will be possible if agreement is reached to set up the ACOP results for every year as a confidential longitudinal database as exists in the US and Canada.
8. The data were ordered by establishment size so that the DW statistic is a test of the appropriateness of the functional form in these circumstances.
9. For each industry regression the following critical values of the diagnostic measures were used to identify influential observations:

$$\text{RSTUDENT} > 2$$

$$1 + \frac{3p}{n} > \text{COVRATIO} > 1 - \frac{3p}{n}$$

$$\text{DFFITS} > 2\left(\frac{p}{n}\right)^{1/2}$$

$$\text{HAT} > \frac{2p}{n}$$

where p is the number of parameters in the regression model and n the number of observations. An observation was considered to be highly influential if it jointly exceeded at least three of the four criteria.

10. A more common problem for correction was due to different definitions of the units of measurement, e.g. thousands as opposed to millions.
11. Analysis of gross output data is shown in parentheses.
12. ATI and ATE can be calculated for case (2) failures whereas λ can only be calculated for those industries which are neither case (1) nor case (2) failures.
13. This work has been extended in Torii (1992a) where he shows how asymmetric bias to variables (such as capital) can make it difficult to compute σ_v, as the estimator of the third moment of the residuals is adversely affected.
14. Table 4.5 is limited to industries with negatively skewed residuals and excludes case (2) failures.
15. Inefficiency measures were weighted using net output (Census of Production, 1977).
16. The effective rate of assistance is defined as the proportional increase in an industry's value added to tradeable inputs due to assistance. The assistance estimates derived by the Industries Assistance Commission in Australia include the effects of tariffs, quantitative import restrictions, subsidies and bounties, local content schemes, export incentives and concessional duty provisions for imported materials.

17. The concentration ratios for the four largest enterprise groups on a value added basis in 1977–8 were respectively 0.49, 0.43 and 0.33 for ASIC classes 2122, 2175 and 2188 (Madge *et al.*, 1989).
18. For comparison ATI estimates must also be available for both countries. The number of matched industries is thus further reduced by the case (1) and case (2) failures.

Appendix 1

Sources of data and definition of variables – UK

Stochastic Production Frontier

The data were drawn from the 1977 *Annual Census of Production*, which is made each year by the Business Statistics Office (BSO), who also estimated the frontier production functions and efficiency measures for us to ensure compliance with the Statistics of Trade Act (1979).

Value added (VA)

Net output less the costs of non-industrial services such as rent of buildings and hire of machinery.

Capital input (K)

Acquisitions less disposals of the three categories: buildings, plant and machinery, and vehicles, each adjusted for average life lengths as estimated by the Central Statistical Office (CSO) and adjusted by the National Economic Development Office (NEDO), assuming straight-line depreciation. Estimates of leased capital employed were added to these estimates of owned capital. For firms of more than 100 employees data are available on expenditure on rent and leasing of equipment and of buildings. These values, again adjusted for expected lives were divided by the average interest rates prevailing over the year. For smaller companies it was assumed that the ratio of leased to owned capital was the same as for the average of the larger companies in the same industry.

Labour input (L)

Number of employees, adjusted for full-time equivalent of part-time staff plus working proprietors (outworkers were excluded).

Definition of variables – Australia

Gross output (GO)

GO was defined as turnover plus the change in inventories of finished goods. Individual components of turnover are sales and transfers out of goods both produced and not produced by the establishment, all other operating revenues (including bounties and subsidies on production, and imputed commission for work done or sales carried out on behalf of other establishments of the same enterprise), and capital work done for own use.

Total materials consumption (M)

M was defined as total purchases, transfers in and selected expenses less the change in both inventories of materials, fuels, etc. and work in progress. Purchases and transfers in encompasses purchases of materials, components and supplies, electricity and fuels, containers and other packing materials, and goods for resale. Selected expenses include payments for commission and subcontract work, repair and maintenance expenses, and outward freight and cartage expenses.

Labour input (L)

L ideally should be measured in terms of labour hours, with allowances made for part-time workers and absenteeism. In the absence of the requisite data, L was based on the average level of employment over the year. Further, following Griliches and Ringstad (1971) the labour variable was calculated to take account of the difference in relative annual compensation and productivity between production and the sum of non-production workers and working proprietors. That is, L was the sum of the number of production workers, and the number of non-production workers and working proprietors converted into production worker equivalents. This conversion involved dividing the annual wage bill of non-production workers by the average wage of production workers (so that non-production worker compensation was expressed as an equivalent number of production workers) and multiplying the number of working proprietors by the ratio of the average wage rates of non-production to production workers.

Capital input (K)

The K variable was defined as the sum of owned plus rented buildings and plant, plus the average value of total inventories.

The following procedure was used to derive capital stock estimates (of owned and leased assets) for individual establishments. In the case of single-establishment enterprises, the enterprise and establishment capital stock are synonymous, hence the book values (owned assets) could be used. For multi-establishment enterprises, where all establishments operated by an enterprise were in-scope in 1977–8, the reported enterprise book value of building and machinery stocks for 1977–8 were allocated across individual establishments on the basis of their relative energy and fuel usage. In the cases where some establishments operated by an enterprise were out-of-scope in 1977–8, the reported enterprise book value of capital stocks was allocated between the in- and out-of-scope establishments on the basis of their shares in enterprise value added. The derived estimates of in-scope capital stocks were then allocated across in-scope establishments on the basis of their relative energy and fuel usage.

The breakdown of total rent, leasing and hiring expenses by asset was unavailable for 1977–8. To derive an estimate of the value of leased building and machinery assets it was assumed that:

1. The shares in total rent, leasing and hiring expenses for each four-digit ASIC class accounted for by land and buildings and by motor vehicles, plant, machinery and equipment in 1977–8 could be proxied by the corresponding shares in 1980–1 (the first year for which suitable data were available).
2. The shares calculated for a given four-digit ASIC class were suitable proxies for the shares of each establishment within the class. The values of leased building and plant assets of an establishment were estimated assuming a 12 per cent discount rate, a 40-year building life and a 13-year machinery life.

Appendix 2

Technical inefficiency rankings by Button (1992)

Ten most efficient industries

1. Other printing, publishing, bookbinding.
2. Metal industries (n.e.s).
3. Precision chains & other mechanical engineering.
4. Dresses, lingerie, infants wear, etc.
5. Timber.
6. Furniture & upholstery.
7. Plastic products (n.e.s).
8. Other machinery.
9. Women's and girls' tailored outerwear.
10. Men's and boys' tailored outerwear.

Ten most inefficient industries

1. Cement.
2. Food – margarine.
3. Fertilisers.
4. Chemical industries – polishes.
5. Textiles industries – asbestos.
6. Chemical industries – printing ink.
7. Sugar.
8.= Tobacco.
8.= Chemicals – pesticides.
10. Electrical goods – batteries.

Note: the soft modelling technique allowed Button to include 148 industries in his analysis, as compared to our 72.

Table 1. Estimates of error term parameters and associated statistics, gross output frontier, truncated-normal/normal error structure (Australia)

ASIC Code	Class	Skewness	J.B. Statistic	σ_v	σ_U	μ	ATI	ATE
2115	Meat	0.145	273.500[c]	0.021	0.103	−0.064	(1)	0.994
2116	Poultry	0.486[b]	6.068[d]	0.058	0.093	−0.181	0.006	0.984
2117	Bacon, ham & small goods	0.107	0.211				0.016	
2121	Liquid milk & cream	0.602[a]	22.200[c]				(1)	
2122	Butter	0.094	0.084	0.030	0.117	0.150	0.150	0.861
2123	Cheese	0.503	1.548	0.015	0.115	0.173	(1)	0.841
2124	Ice-cream & frozen confections	0.606	2.866	0.024	0.138	0.019	0.173	0.973
2131	Fruit products	0.295	1.064				0.028	
2132	Vegetable products	0.402	2.429				(1)	
2140	Margarine, oils & fats nec	−0.258	0.587	0.061	0.027	0.096	0.103	0.903
2151	Flour mill products	0.216	1.064	0.005	0.047	0.097	0.097	0.907
2153	Cereal foods & baking mixes	0.911[a]	7.654[d]				(1)	
2161	Bread	0.282[a]	23.790[c]				(1)	
2162	Cakes & pastries	0.191	2.478				(1)	
2163	Biscuits	0.476	1.407				(1)	
2173	Confectionery & cocoa	0.099	0.200	0.090	0.124	0.004	0.073	0.931
2174	Processed seafoods	−0.326	16.410[c]	0.191	0.094	−0.311	0.080	0.925
2175	Prepared animal & bird foods	1.058[a]	25.570[c]				(1)	
2176	Food products nec	1.485[a]	236.600[c]				(1)	
2185	Soft drinks, cordials & syrups	0.395[b]	7.627[d]				(1)	
2186	Beer	0.113	0.173	0.029	0.087	0.101	0.101	0.904
2187	Malt	1.035[b]	4.854[d]				(1)	
2188	Wine & brandy	−0.127	48.790[c]	0.165	0.230	0.631	0.631	0.539
2344	Man-made fibre, b/w fabrics	0.565	1.674				(1)	
2345	Cotton yarns & b/w fabrics	−0.093	0.038	0.051	0.063	0.042	0.060	0.942
2347	Woollen yarns & b/w fabrics	0.059	0.206	0.018	0.076	0.070	0.070	0.933
2348	Narrow woven & elastic textiles	0.908[b]	7.849[d]				(1)	
2349	Textile finishing	0.345	4.382				(1)	
2351	Household textiles	−0.057	7.015[d]				(3)	

Table 1. *continued*

ASIC Code	Class	Skewness	J.B. Statistic	σ_V	σ_U	μ	ATI	ATE
2352	Textile floor coverings	-0.319	0.659	0.088	0.041	0.114	0.131	0.880
2354	Canvas & associated products nec	0.047	0.316	0.047	0.140	0.126	0.126	0.882
2356	Textile products nec	-0.337	1.264	0.154	0.095	0.059	0.147	0.868
2441	Hosiery	0.291	0.657				(I)	
2442	Cardigans & pullovers	0.229	1.965				(I)	
2443	Knitted goods nec	0.452[b]	3.010				(I)	
2451	Men's trousers & shorts (work)	-0.053	58.480[c]	0.131	0.203	0.066	0.132	0.880
2452	Men's suits & coats (waterproof)	-0.379	1.938	0.187	0.101	-0.111	0.115	0.895
2453	Women's outerwear nec	0.173[b]	170.200[c]				(I)	
2454	Foundation garments	0.051	1.868	0.031	0.063	-0.034	0.015	0.985
2455	Underwear & infants' clothing nec	0.019	13.080[c]	0.004	0.183	0.024	0.024	0.977
2456	Headwear & clothing nec	-0.058	10.410[c]	0.152	0.174	-0.001	0.121	0.890
2460	Footwear	-0.059	23.060[c]				(3)	
2531	Log sawmilling	-0.032	117.300[c]				(I)	
2532	Resawn & dressed timber	0.335[b]	12.790[c]				(I)	
2533	Veneers & manufactured boards	0.517[b]	8.137[c]				(I)	
2534	Wooden doors	0.194	0.244	0.035	0.076	-0.044	0.017	0.983
2535	Wooden structural fittings & joinery nec	0.105	39.870[c]				(I)	
2536	Wooden containers	-0.292	5.161[d]	0.389	0.124	-1.512	0.090	0.917
2538	Wood products nec	0.154	4.214				(I)	
2541	Furniture (excl sheet metal)	-0.024	176.200[c]				(I)	
2542	Mattresses (excl rubber)	0.061	0.252	0.095	0.105	-0.214	0.033	0.968
2632	Paper bags (incl textile bags)	0.066	0.103	0.026	0.062	0.075	0.075	0.928
2633	Solid fibreboard containers	0.074	0.089				(I)	
2634	Corrugated fibreboard containers	-0.280	0.728	0.083	0.045	0.110	0.126	0.884
2635	Paper products nec	0.916[a]	28.470[c]				(I)	

Table 1. *continued*

ASIC Code	Class	Skewness	J.B. Statistic	σ_V	σ_U	μ	ATI	ATE
2641	Publishing	-0.066	1.234	0.206	0.237	-0.213	0.107	0.902
2642	Printing & publishing	-0.035	25.040[c]	0.153	0.235	-0.009	0.119	0.892
2643	Paper stationery	0.310	8.857[c]	0.076	0.147	0.002	0.061	0.941
2644	Printing & bookbinding	0.020	127.300[c]	0.100	0.166	0.001	0.080	0.925
2645	Printing trade services nec	0.073	5.553[d]				(1)	
2751	Chemical fertilisers	-0.495	1.326	0.060	0.017	0.059	0.077	0.927
2753	Synthetic resins & rubber	0.081	0.284	0.087	0.000	0.463	0.463	0.632
2754	Organic industrial chemicals nec	0.263	0.413				(1)	
2762	Paints	0.574[a]	20.090[c]				(1)	
2763	Pharmaceutical & veterinary products	0.463[b]	9.853[c]				(1)	
2764	Pesticides	0.372	0.653				(1)	
2765	Soap & other detergents	0.937[a]	25.560[c]				(1)	
2766	Cosmetics & toilet preparations	0.131	0.842				(1)	
2767	Inks	-0.201	0.243	0.176	0.097	-0.386	0.062	0.941
2780	Petroleum & coal products nec	-0.721	1.732	0.091	0.017	0.044	0.091	0.914
2850	Glass & glass products	0.464	1.425				(1)	
2861	Clay bricks	0.091	0.159	0.014	0.196	0.105	0.105	0.901
2863	Ceramic tiles & pipes	0.145	0.175				(1)	
2864	Ceramic goods nec	-0.003	0.106	0.048	0.192	0.000	0.038	0.963
2872	Ready mixed concrete	2.982[a]	16756.000[c]	0.020	0.124	0.058	0.058	0.944
2874	Concrete products nec	0.064	4.803[d]				(1)	
2882	Stone products	0.207	0.491				(1)	
2884	Non-metallic mineral products nec	0.112	4.821[d]				(1)	
2941	Iron & steel basic products	0.924[a]	78.500[c]				(1)	
2942	Iron casting	-0.414[b]	15.170[c]	0.404	0.102	-1.636	0.090	0.917
2943	Steel casting	-0.662	3.484	0.191	0.062	-0.270	0.086	0.920
	Iron & steel forging	0.995[b]	4.584				(1)	

Table 1. *continued*

ASIC Code	Class	Skewness	J.B. Statistic	σ_V	σ_U	μ	ATI	ATE
2945	Steel pipes & tubes	-0.545	4.707[d]	0.323	0.097	-0.788	0.106	0.903
2957	Secondary recovery & alloying	1.393[a]	19.990[c]				(1)	
2961	Aluminium rolling, drawing, extruding	-0.523	0.960	0.092	0.032	0.066	0.104	0.904
2963	Non-ferrous metal casting	0.570[b]	8.486[c]				(1)	
3141	Fabricated structural steel	0.303[a]	161.900[c]				(1)	
3142	Architectural aluminium products	0.094	3.628	0.053	0.136	0.026	0.053	0.949
3143	Architectural metal products nec	-0.082	0.372	0.173	0.149	-0.317	0.068	0.936
3151	Metal containers	0.108	0.857				(1)	
3152	Sheet metal furniture	-0.135	0.876				(3)	
3153	Sheet metal products nec	0.249[a]	92.910[c]	0.039	0.178	0.022	0.041	0.960
3161	Cutlery & hand tools nec	-0.628[b]	10.620[c]	0.345	0.081	-1.090	0.094	0.914
3162	Springs & wire products	0.231	7.068[d]				(1)	
3163	Nuts, bolts, screws & rivets	0.698[a]	12.610[c]				(1)	
3164	Metal coating & finishing	0.101	7.440[d]				(1)	
3165	Non-ferrous steam, gas & water fittings	0.295	1.060	0.028	0.116	0.031	0.038	0.963
3166	Boiler & plate work	-0.138	1.039	0.176	0.036	0.427	0.431	0.659
3167	Metal blinds & awnings	0.769[a]	16.050[c]				(3)	
3168	Fabricated metal products nec	0.363[a]	22.690[c]				(1)	
3231	Motor vehicles	0.133	0.970				(1)	
3232	Motor vehicle bodies, trailers, caravans	0.522[a]	23.840[c]				(1)	
3233	Motor vehicle instruments	-0.057	0.602				(3)	
3234	Motor vehicle parts nec	0.311[a]	32.690[c]	0.062	0.160	0.050	0.073	0.931
3241	Ships	0.707[b]	14.280[c]				(1)	
3242	Boats	-0.105	86.430[c]	0.151	0.170	0.028	0.131	0.881

Table 1. *continued*

ASIC Code	Class	Skewness	J.B. Statistic	σ_V	σ_U	μ	ATI	ATE
3243	Railway rolling stock & locomotives	-0.075	0.024	0.037	0.048	0.050	0.057 (1)	0.945
3245	Transport equipment nec	0.264	0.722	0.149	0.015	0.178	0.211 (3)	0.816
3341	Photographic & optical goods	-0.497	1.014					
3342	Photographic film processing	0.037	0.147					
3343	Measuring, professional & scientific equipment nec	0.686[a]	54.500[c]	0.087	0.166	-0.001	0.069 (1)	0.934
3351	Radio & TV receivers, audio equipment	0.410	1.208				(1)	
3352	Electronic equipment nec	0.223	1.920					
3353	Refrigerators & household appliances	-0.064	1.210	0.138	0.151	-0.162	0.068 (3)	0.936
3354	Water heating systems	-0.101	0.789					
3355	Electric & telephone cable & wire	0.077	1.784	0.030	0.054	-0.068	0.010 (3)	0.990
3356	Batteries	-0.070	1.022					
3357	Electrical machinery & equipment nec	0.311[a]	86.250[c]	0.013	0.190	0.043	0.043 (1)	0.958
3361	Agricultural machinery	0.945[a]	114.900[c]	0.015	0.134	0.054	0.054	0.947
3362	Construction machinery	0.100	0.228					
3363	Materials handling equipment	0.218	5.811[d]	0.040	0.167	-0.024	0.025 (1)	0.976
3364	Wood & metal working machinery	0.313	1.585					
3365	Pumps & compressors	0.689[a]	21.550[c]					
3366	Commercial space heating & cooling	-0.089	0.206	0.117	0.107	-0.167	0.053 (1)	0.949
3367	Dies, saw blades & machine tool accessories	0.093	0.433				(1)	
3368	Food processing machinery	-0.399	1.892	0.203	0.103	-0.164	0.115 (1)	0.900
3369	Industrial machinery & equipment nec	0.449[a]	294.400[c]					
3451	Leather tanning & fur dressing	0.918[a]	18.690[c]	0.053	0.114	-0.007	0.040 (1)	0.961
3452	Leather & leather sub goods nec	0.112	0.860					

Table 1. *continued*

ASIC Code	Class	Skewness	J.B. Statistic	σ_v	σ_U	μ	ATI	ATE
3461	Rubber tyres, tubes, belts, hoses & sheets	0.579[b]	6.757[d]				(1)	
3462	Rubber products nec	0.096	16.730[c]	0.002	0.159	0.041	0.041	0.960
3471	Flexible packaging & abrasive papers	-0.226	12.140[c]	0.181	0.127	-0.142	0.103	0.905
3474	Plastic products nec	0.242[a]	52.900[c]				(1)	
3481	Ophthalmic articles	0.313	1.586				(3)	
3482	Jewellery & silverware	0.048	0.102	0.099	0.160	-0.085	0.055	0.948
3483	Brooms & brushes	0.589	2.108				(1)	
3484	Signs & advertising displays	0.032	2.012				(1)	
3485	Sporting equipment	0.403[b]	16.060[c]				(1)	
3486	Writing & marking equipment	0.543	2.003	0.079	0.127	0.002	0.064	0.939
3487	Manufacturing nec	-0.022	0.635	0.087	0.180	0.000	0.070	0.934

Skewness $\mu_3/\mu_2^{3/2}$, where μ_2 and μ_3 are, respectively, the second and third moments of the regression residuals.

J.B. statistic χ_2^2 statistic for testing deviations of the regression residuals from normality, using the second, third and fourth moments (Jarque and Bera, 1980).

σ_v Square root of variance variable of truncated-normal error component (systematic error term).

σ_U Square root of variance variable of normal error component (random error term).

μ Mode of truncated-normal error component.

ATI Average technical inefficiency.

ATE Average technical efficiency.

(1) Case (1) failure, $\sigma_v < 0$.

(3) Case (3) failure, $\mu/\sigma_v < -5$.

a Significant at the 2 per cent level (two-tail test).

b Significant at the 10 per cent level (two-tail test).

c Significant at the 2 per cent level (one-tail test).

d Significant at the 10 per cent level (one-tail test).

nec not elsewhere classified.

Table 2. Estimates of error term parameters and associated statistics, value added frontier, truncated-normal/normal error structure (Australia)

ASIC Code	Class	Skewness	J.B. Statistic	σ_V	σ_U	μ	ATI	ATE
2115	Meat	0.384[a]	35.950[c]	1.160	0.305	−5.334	(1)	0.810
2116	Poultry	−0.363	3.394	0.169	0.260	0.124	0.233	0.833
2117	Bacon, ham & small goods	−0.058	0.057				0.191	
2121	Liquid milk & cream	−0.204	0.827	0.352	0.299	0.129	0.333	0.735
2122	Butter	−0.299	1.103	1.141	0.489	−2.647	0.387	0.716
2123	Cheese	0.469	2.337	0.097	0.296	0.007	0.080	0.925
2124	Ice-cream & frozen confections	0.423	0.911				(1)	
2131	Fruit products	−0.210	0.728	0.426	0.011	0.868	0.889	0.444
2132	Vegetable products	0.293	0.775				(1)	
2140	Margarine, oils & fats nec	−0.656	2.157	0.467	0.001	0.415	0.570	0.601
2151	Flour mill products	0.235	0.921				(1)	
2153	Cereal foods & baking mixes	0.743[b]	6.622[d]				(1)	
2161	Bread	−0.297[a]	15.760[c]	0.760	0.300	−2.272	0.215	0.821
2162	Cakes & pastries	0.016	0.713				(1)	
2163	Biscuits	0.375	1.021				(1)	
2173	Confectionery & cocoa	−0.120	0.514	0.320	0.027	0.788	0.795	0.474
2174	Processed seafoods	−0.351	1.461	0.478	0.232	0.518	0.641	0.565
2175	Prepared animal & bird foods	−0.298	3.228	1.487	0.438	−6.899	0.296	0.770
2176	Food products nec	0.530[a]	20.380[c]				(1)	
2185	Soft drinks, cordials & syrups	0.401[b]	5.787[d]				(1)	
2186	Beer	−0.494	0.863	0.358	0.029	0.438	0.514	0.624
2187	Malt	−0.743	1.833	0.384	0.029	0.260	0.423	0.680
2188	Wine & brandy	−0.500[b]	14.520[c]	1.694	0.433	−6.368	0.402	0.710
2344	Man-made fibre, b/w fabrics	0.557	1.606				(1)	
2345	Cotton yarns & b/w fabrics	−0.174	0.387	0.198	0.030	0.435	0.443	0.654
2347	Woollen yarns & b/w fabrics	−0.013	0.526	0.061	0.183	0.204	0.204	0.817
2348	Narrow woven & elastic textiles	0.531	1.278				(1)	
2349	Textile finishing	0.314	1.656				(1)	
	[...] textiles	0.045	9.180[c]	0.185	0.348	−0.289	0.080	0.926

Table 2. *continued*

ASIC Code	Class	Skewness	J.B. Statistic	σ_V	σ_U	μ	ATI	ATE
2352	Textile floor coverings	−0.970[b]	7.531[d]	0.761	0.162	−0.987	0.358	0.729
2354	Canvas & associated products nec	0.062	0.240	0.032	0.334	−0.007	0.023	0.978
2356	Textile products nec	−0.438	2.699	0.617	0.273	−0.788	0.292	0.768
2441	Hosiery	0.401	1.627				(1)	
2442	Cardigans & pullovers	0.187	0.871				(1)	
2443	Knitted goods nec	0.145	1.924				(1)	
2451	Men's trousers & shorts (work)	−0.684[b]	165.300[c]	1.304	0.197	−5.616	0.276	0.782
2452	Men's suits & coats (waterproof)	−0.538[b]	4.300	0.386	0.156	−0.378	0.204	0.827
2453	Women's outerwear nec	0.047	91.150[c]				(1)	
2454	Foundation garments	−0.589	1.331	0.308	0.103	0.150	0.309	0.750
2455	Underwear & infants' clothing nec	−0.233	21.910[c]				(3)	
2456	Headwear & clothing nec	−0.255	3.007	0.624	0.282	−1.643	0.194	0.836
2460	Footwear	−0.256	8.816[c]	0.869	0.244	−4.191	0.167	0.856
2531	Log sawmilling	−0.418[a]	109.400[c]	1.431	0.310	−6.486	0.291	0.773
2532	Resawn & dressed timber	−0.704[a]	56.680[c]	1.251	0.237	−4.854	0.289	0.774
2533	Veneers & manufactured boards	0.176	0.337				(1)	
2534	Wooden doors	0.265	0.377				(1)	
2535	Wooden structural fittings & joinery nec	−0.156[b]	28.160[c]	0.764	0.279	−3.282	0.162	0.860
2536	Wooden containers	−0.654[b]	5.487[d]	0.431	0.093	0.275	0.465	0.657
2538	Wood products nec	−0.174	1.118	0.329	0.301	0.084	0.295	0.761
2541	Furniture (excl sheet metal)	−0.461[a]	118.500[c]	1.055	0.254	−4.175	0.240	0.805
2542	Mattresses (excl rubber)	−0.280	0.983	0.351	0.243	−0.020	0.273	0.777
2632	Paper bags (incl textile bags)	−0.107	0.435				(3)	
2633	Solid fibreboard containers	0.483[b]	2.614				(1)	
2634	Corrugated fibreboard containers	−0.154	1.024	0.232	0.223	−0.023	0.177	0.845
2635	Paper products nec:	0.035	0.300	0.044	0.369	0.027	0.047	0.955

Table 2. *continued*

ASIC Code	Class	Skewness	J.B. Statistic	σ_V	σ_U	μ	ATI	ATE
2641	Publishing	-0.502[b]	6.370[d]	1.183	0.324	-4.052	0.302	0.766
2642	Printing & publishing	-0.425[a]	35.690[c]	1.129	0.285	-3.913	0.286	0.776
2643	Paper stationery	-0.032	10.860[c]	0.102	0.304	0.666	0.666	0.517
2644	Printing & bookbinding	-0.382[a]	133.700[c]				(3)	
2645	Printing trade services nec	-0.263	2.375	0.339	0.243	-0.017	0.264	0.783
2751	Chemical fertilisers	0.001	1.982				(3)	
2753	Synthetic resins & rubber	0.188	1.056				(1)	
2754	Organic industrial chemicals nec	0.001	0.043				(3)	
2762	Paints	-0.105	0.582	0.554	0.353	-1.459	0.172	0.852
2763	Pharmaceutical & veterinary products	-0.328	3.926	1.212	0.335	-5.369	0.251	0.798
2764	Pesticides	0.586	1.756				(1)	
2765	Soap & other detergents	-0.008	21.310[c]				(1)	
2766	Cosmetics & toilet preparations	-0.049	0.863	0.119	0.310	0.142	0.169	0.849
2767	Inks	-0.964[b]	3.621	0.505	0.022	0.033	0.415	0.690
2780	Petroleum & coal products nec	0.519	0.915				(1)	
2850	Glass & glass products	0.073	0.072				(1)	
2861	Clay bricks	-0.093	0.661	0.474	0.339	-1.111	0.160	0.861
2863	Ceramic tiles & pipes	-0.229	0.832	0.611	0.283	-1.621	0.189	0.839
2864	Ceramic goods nec	-0.466	2.225	0.450	0.214	-0.237	0.285	0.771
2872	Ready mixed concrete	-0.134	3.409	0.939	0.534	-2.581	0.283	0.777
2874	Concrete products nec	-0.356[a]	7.214[d]	0.484	0.288	-0.065	0.364	0.720
2882	Stone products	-0.155	0.926	0.777	0.304	-3.288	0.167	0.856
2884	Non-metallic mineral products nec	-0.186	8.283[c]	0.986	0.324	-4.341	0.205	0.829
2941	Iron & steel basic products	0.910[a]	15.550[c]				(1)	
2942	Iron casting	-0.227	1.774	0.619	0.245	-2.153	0.156	0.864
2943	Steel casting	-0.502	1.189	0.259	0.001	0.314	0.370	0.706
2944	Iron & steel forging	0.585	1.740				(1)	

Table 2. *continued*

ASIC Code	Class	Skewness	J.B. Statistic	σ_V	σ_U	μ	ATI	ATE
2945	Steel pipes & tubes	−0.438	1.120	0.349	0.142	0.315	0.428	0.675
2957	Secondary recovery & alloying	0.709[b]	3.431				(1)	
2961	Aluminium rolling, drawing, extruding	−0.489	0.981	0.232	0.009	0.288	0.336	0.728
2693	Non-ferrous metal casting	−0.165	0.515	0.274	0.125	0.542	0.558	0.591
3141	Fabricated structural steel	−0.518[a]	260.100[c]	1.353	0.311	−5.107	0.320	0.755
3142	Architectural aluminium products	−0.380[a]	9.751[c]	0.990	0.277	−4.099	0.217	0.821
3143	Architectural metal products nec	−0.192	2.706	0.863	0.296	−3.831	0.178	0.848
3151	Metal containers	−0.300	1.095	0.337	0.226	0.035	0.282	0.770
3152	Sheet metal furniture	0.369	1.393				(1)	
3153	Sheet metal products nec	−0.123	9.016[c]	0.415	0.309	−0.749	0.165	0.857
3161	Cutlery & hand tools nec	−0.771[b]	7.346[d]	0.638	0.159	−1.413	0.223	0.815
3162	Springs & wire products	0.342[b]	10.690[c]				(1)	
3163	Nuts, bolts, screws & rivets	0.181	0.797				(1)	
3164	Metal coating & finishing	−0.218[b]	10.130[c]	0.909	0.287	−3.974	0.190	0.839
3165	Non-ferrous steam, gas & water fittings	−0.083	0.274	0.281	0.228	−0.579	0.103	0.906
3166	Boiler & plate work	−0.454[b]	10.200[c]	0.988	0.307	−2.614	0.307	0.762
3167	Metal blinds & awnings	0.033	0.812				(1)	
3168	Fabricated metal products nec	0.119	7.329[d]				(1)	
3231	Motor vehicles	0.042	1.014	0.165	0.476	−0.023	0.124	0.887
3232	Motor vehicle bodies, trailers, caravans	0.050	19.600[c]				(1)	
3233	Motor vehicle instruments	0.008	0.035				(3)	
3234	Motor vehicle parts nec	−0.925[a]	301.200[c]	1.124	0.167	−3.257	0.327	0.751
3241	Ships	−0.386	1.761	0.453	0.245	−0.241	0.287	0.770
3242	Boats	−0.859[a]	82.090[c]	1.216	0.249	−3.519	0.354	0.735

Table 2. continued

ASIC Code	Class	Skewness	J.B. Statistic	σ_V	σ_U	μ	ATI	ATE
3243	Railway rolling stock & locomotives	-0.437	9.323[c]	0.813	0.159	-3.822	0.160 (1)	0.861
3245	Transport equipment nec	0.504	4.593					
3341	Photographic & optical goods	-0.257	0.642	0.402	0.010	0.988	0.995	0.399
3342	Photographic film processing	-0.172	0.752	0.319	0.081	0.685	0.698 (1)	0.521
3343	Measuring, professional & scientific equipment nec	0.052	0.332					
3351	Radio & TV receivers, audio equipment	-0.042	1.296				(3)	
3352	Electronic equipment nec	-0.184	1.610	0.379	0.008	0.933	0.940	0.418
3353	Refrigerators & household appliances	-0.167	1.462	0.322	0.192	0.662	0.678 (1)	0.531
3354	Water heating systems	0.128	0.671				(1)	
3355	Electric & telephone cable & wire	0.175	0.606					
3356	Batteries	-0.117	0.285	0.223	0.322	0.555	0.559	0.585
3357	Electrical machinery & equipment nec	-0.158	34.110[c]	1.112	0.328	-5.380	0.214	0.823
3361	Agricultural machinery	-0.279	3.900	1.129	0.329	-5.278	0.223	0.817
3362	Construction machinery	0.039	0.058				(1)	
3363	Materials handling equipment	-0.124	0.473	0.336	0.287	-0.369	0.170	0.852
3364	Wood & metal working machinery	-0.156	0.795				(3)	
3365	Pumps & compressors	-0.170	0.743	0.248	0.196	0.369	0.404	0.683
3366	Commercial space heating & cooling equipment	-0.244	0.599	0.351	0.226	-0.349	0.185	0.841
3367	Dies, saw blades & machine tool accessories	-0.117	0.842	0.607	0.314	-2.233	0.146	0.872
3368	Food processing machinery	-0.369	1.701	0.321	0.005	0.499	0.539	0.606
3369	Industrial machinery & equipment nec	-0.009	61.880[c]	0.628	0.365	-2.957	0.123	0.890
3451	Leather tanning & fur dressing	-0.157	0.390	0.252	0.113	0.532	0.543	0.597
3452	Leather & leather sub goods nec	0.203	0.890				(1)	

Table 2. continued

ASIC Code	Class	Skewness	J.B. Statistic	σ_V	σ_U	μ	ATI	ATE
3461	Rubber tyres, tubes, belts, hoses & sheets	−0.495	2.525	0.352	0.146	0.205	0.370	0.712
3462	Rubber products nec	0.391	45.320[e]				(1)	
3471	Flexible packaging & abrasive papers	−0.613[a]	9.325[e]	0.810	0.285	−1.009	0.389	0.712
3474	Plastic products nec	−0.496[a]	81.890[e]	0.938	0.268	−2.537	0.287	0.774
3481	Ophthalmic articles	0.168	1.759	0.007	0.250	0.051	0.051	0.950
3482	Jewellery & silverware	−0.373[b]	3.884	0.378	0.198	0.309	0.445	0.666
3483	Brooms & brushes	0.201	0.257				(1)	
3484	Signs & advertising displays	−0.659[a]	27.990[e]	1.507	0.272	−7.435	0.285	0.777
3485	Sporting equipment	−0.710[a]	10.620[e]	0.606	0.197	−0.359	0.374	0.717
3486	Writing & marking equipment	0.008	0.526				(3)	
3487	Manufacturing nec	−0.365	2.307	0.888	0.284	−3.141	0.221	0.817

Skewness $\mu_3/\mu_2^{3/2}$, where μ_2 and μ_3 are, respectively, the second and third moments of the regression residuals.

J.B. statistic χ_2^2 statistic for testing deviations of the regression residuals from normality, using the second, third and fourth moments (Jarque and Bera, 1980).

σ_V Square root of variance variable of truncated-normal error component (systematic error term).

σ_U Square root of variance variable of normal error component (random error term).

μ Mode of truncated-normal error component.

ATI   Average technical inefficiency.

ATE   Average technical efficiency.

(1)   Case (1) failure, $\sigma_\varepsilon < 0$.

(3)   Case (3) failure, $\mu/\sigma_\varepsilon < -5$.

a   Significant at the 2 per cent level (two-tail test).

b   Significant at the 10 per cent level (two-tail test).

c   Significant at the 2 per cent level (one-tail test).

d   Significant at the 10 per cent level (one-tail test).

nec   not elsewhere classified.

Table 3. Industry level inefficiency measures (UK)

SIC Code	Industry	Number of plants	Failure case	SIGMAE	ATINON	LAMBDA	ATE	SKEWNESS
2210	Grain milling	64	(1)	0.515	0.000	0.000	0.000	0.491
2120	Bread & flour confection	341		0.380	0.300	1.668	0.733	−0.354
2130	Biscuits	37	(1)	0.353	0.000	0.000	0.000	0.581
2140	Bacon, meat & fish products	364	(1)	0.605	0.000	0.000	0.000	0.669
2150	Milk & milk products	210	(1)	0.569	0.000	0.000	0.000	0.012
2170	Chocolate & sugar products	89	(2)	0.588	0.575	0.000	0.503	−1.327
2180	Fruit & vegetable products	99	(2)	0.718	0.647	0.000	0.449	−1.311
2190	Animal & poultry feed	178		0.613	0.492	2.506	0.567	−0.577
2210	Oils & fats	50	(2)	0.873	0.694	0.000	0.413	−1.076
2292	Starch & miscellaneous foods	84		0.680	0.499	1.991	0.562	−0.451
2310	Brewing & malting	92		0.594	0.435	1.759	0.612	−0.383
2320	Soft drinks	107	(1)	0.731	0.000	0.000	0.000	0.404
2391	Spirit & distilling	61		0.608	0.330	0.951	0.698	−0.122
2400	Tobacco	21	(1)	0.729	0.000	0.000	0.000	0.562
2610	Coke ovens & fuel	25	(2)	0.813	0.687	0.000	0.419	−1.258
2620	Mineral oil & refining	22	(1)	0.547	0.000	0.000	0.000	0.382
2630	Lubricating oils & grease	44	(1)	0.545	0.000	0.000	0.000	0.418
2711	Inorganic chemicals	56		0.428	0.361	22.141	0.672	−0.491
2712	Organic chemicals	65	(2)	0.751	0.631	0.000	0.461	−1.006
2713	Other chemicals	117	(2)	0.853	0.741	0.000	0.379	−1.705
2720	Pharmaceuticals	101	(1)	0.646	0.000	0.000	0.000	0.106
2730	Toilet preparations	53		0.659	0.492	2.041	0.567	−0.465
2740	Paint	85	(1)	0.386	0.000	0.000	0.000	1.361
2750	Soap & detergents	41	(1)	0.521	0.000	0.000	0.000	0.390
2761	Synthetic resins & plastic	112		0.462	0.389	2.268	0.649	−0.523
2770	Dyes & pigments	28		0.283	0.123	0.620	0.880	−0.042
2780	Fertilisers	28		0.610	0.391	1.229	0.647	−0.230
2791	Polishes	26		0.397	0.190	0.729	0.819	−0.064
2792	Adhesives, gelatine etc.	30		0.442	0.285	1.162	0.735	−0.188
2793	Explosives & fireworks	18	(1)	0.420	0.000	0.000	0.000	0.551

Table 3. *continued*

SIC Code	Industry	Number of plants	Failure case	SIGMAE	ATINON	LAMBDA	ATE	SKEWNESS
2794	Formulated pesticides etc.	17		0.731	0.463	1.390	0.590	−0.263
2795	Printing ink	18		0.231	0.170	1.278	0.837	−0.226
2796	Surgical bandages	16	(1)	0.493	0.000	0.000	0.000	0.267
3110	Iron & steel	243		0.451	0.357	1.832	0.675	−0.405
3120	Steel tubes	86		0.413	0.269	1.162	0.750	−0.187
3130	Iron castings	273	(2)	0.343	0.392	0.000	0.646	−1.311
3210	Aluminium	137		0.434	0.405	3.481	0.636	−0.732
3220	Copper, brass etc.	110		0.365	0.201	0.872	0.809	−0.100
3230	Other base metals	73		0.489	0.288	1.022	0.733	−0.143
3310	Agricultural machinery	71	(1)	0.431	0.000	0.000	0.000	0.129
3320	Metal working tools	194	(2)	0.416	0.501	0.000	0.560	−1.997
3331	Pumps	59	(2)	0.598	0.671	0.000	0.431	−2.757
3332	Valves	73	(1)	0.440	0.000	0.000	0.000	0.400
3333	Compressors	1044		0.364	0.225	1.037	0.787	−0.148
3340	Industrial engines	29		0.367	0.342	2.792	0.688	−0.632
3350	Textile machinery	106		0.375	0.350	2.891	0.691	−0.649
3360	Earth-moving equipment	79		0.492	0.411	2.315	0.631	−0.534
3370	Mechanical handling equipment	196	(2)	0.404	0.419	0.000	0.624	−1.045
3380	Office machinery	23	(1)	0.553	0.000	0.000	0.000	0.012
3391	Mining machinery	63	(1)	0.371	0.000	0.000	0.000	0.221
3392	Printing & paper machinery	69	(1)	0.260	0.000	0.000	0.000	0.482
3393	Refrigerating machinery	186		0.398	0.353	2.428	0.679	−0.560
3395	Scales & weighing machinery	33		0.312	0.188	0.972	0.821	−0.128
3397	Food & drink processing machinery	88		0.484	0.426	2.867	0.620	−0.645
3399	Other machinery	255		0.364	0.302	1.854	0.721	−0.412
3414	Constructional steelworks	147	(1)	0.472	0.000	0.000	0.000	0.040
3451	Other iron & steel	349	(1)	0.454	0.000	0.000	0.000	0.912
3420	Ordnance & small arms	24		0.383	0.353	2.813	0.678	−0.636
3491	Ball & roller bearings	34	(1)	0.242	0.000	0.000	0.000	0.092
3492	Precision chains	574	(2)	0.361	0.436	0.000	0.611	−1.706

Table 3. *continued*

SIC Code	Industry	Number of plants	Failure case	SIGMAE	ATINON	LAMBDA	ATE	SKEWNESS
3510	Copying equipment	16	(1)	0.316	0.000	0.000	0.000	0.440
3520	Watches & clocks	14		0.274	0.231	1.738	0.783	−0.376
3530	Surgical instruments	130	(1)	0.328	0.000	0.000	0.000	0.675
3540	Scientific instruments	313	(2)	0.447	0.534	0.000	0.534	−2.142
3610	Electrical machinery	264	(1)	0.375	0.000	0.000	0.000	0.031
3620	Insulated wires & cables	37		0.272	0.235	1.841	0.779	−0.408
3630	Telephone apparatus	54		0.404	0.283	1.322	0.737	−0.241
3640	Radio components	222		0.351	0.271	1.533	0.749	−0.311
3652	Broadcast receiving equipment	31		0.769	0.606	3.792	0.490	−0.765
3660	Electronic computers	32	(2)	0.932	0.728	0.000	0.388	−1.177
3670	Electronic capital goods	146	(1)	0.445	0.000	0.000	0.000	0.435
3680	Domestic electrical goods	80		0.367	0.380	9.357	0.656	−0.950
3691	Vehicle electrical goods	31	(2)	0.386	0.417	0.000	0.627	1.164
3692	Primary batteries	20	(1)	0.365	0.000	0.000	0.000	0.258
3694	Electrical lamps	108		0.378	0.371	4.078	0.664	−0.791
3700	Shipbuilding	198		0.400	0.317	1.720	0.708	−0.371
3800	Wheeled tractors	17	(1)	0.302	0.000	0.000	0.000	0.320
3811	Motor vehicle manufacturing	382	(2)	0.326	0.359	0.000	0.674	−1.084
3812	Trailers, caravans etc.	89		0.398	0.331	1.961	0.697	−0.442
3820	Motor cycles & bicycles	25	(1)	0.227	0.000	0.000	0.000	0.100
3830	Aerospace	141	(1)	0.333	0.000	0.000	0.000	0.486
3840	Locomotives	21	(2)	0.473	0.543	0.000	0.527	−1.947
3900	Engineers' small tools	335	(1)	0.255	0.000	0.000	0.000	0.099
3910	Hand tools	64	(1)	0.369	0.000	0.000	0.000	0.489
3920	Cutlery	65	(1)	0.286	0.000	0.000	0.000	0.205
3930	Nuts & bolts	117	(1)	0.302	0.000	0.000	0.000	0.184
3940	Wire	145		0.452	0.447	10.997	0.603	−0.962
3950	Cans & metal boxes	48		0.307	0.283	2.371	0.739	−0.547
3962	Jewellery & precious metals	74		0.688	0.457	1.498	0.594	−0.299
3991	Metal furniture	78		0.434	0.321	1.513	0.705	−0.304
3995	Drop forgings	55		0.284	0.124	0.624	0.879	−0.041

Table 3. *continued*

SIC Code	Industry	Number of plants	Failure case	SIGMAE	ATINON	LAMBDA	ATE	SKEWNESS
3996	Domestic holloware	70		0.353	0.280	1.635	0.740	-0.344
3998	Needles & pins etc.	1099	(1)	0.376	0.000	0.000	0.000	0.134
4110	Manmade fibres	25		0.491	0.327	1.276	0.700	-0.225
4120	Spinning of cotton	119		0.467	0.405	2.568	0.636	-0.590
4130	Weaving	138		0.342	0.190	0.870	0.819	-0.099
4140	Woollen & worsted	308	(2)	0.502	0.659	0.000	0.440	-4.251
4150	Jute	23	(1)	0.540	0.000	0.000	0.000	0.023
4160	Rope, twine & net	27	(1)	0.508	0.295	1.010	0.727	-0.140
4171	Hosiery	336	(2)	0.391	0.440	0.000	0.608	-1.400
4172	Warp knitting	38		0.408	0.335	1.912	0.694	-0.428
4180	Lace	28	(1)	0.368	0.000	0.000	0.000	0.207
4190	Carpets	61	(2)	0.656	0.605	0.000	0.480	1.221
4210	Narrow fabrics	70		0.296	0.285	2.750	0.736	-0.624
4221	Household textiles	87		0.475	0.215	0.695	0.796	-0.057
4222	Canvas goods	61		0.352	0.259	1.392	0.758	-0.264
4230	Textile finishing	223		0.343	0.353	5.449	0.679	-0873
4291	Asbestos	19	(1)	0.282	0.000	0.000	0.000	0.344
4292	Other textiles	29		0.481	0.469	16.980	0.585	-0.981
4310	Leather tanning	118	(2)	0.717	0.754	0.000	0.368	-3.216
4320	Leather goods	94	(2)	0.620	0.654	0.000	0.443	-2.165
4330	Fur	23	(1)	0.544	0.000	0.000	0.000	0.054
4410	Weatherproof outerwear	74		0.412	0.397	4.146	0.642	-0.796
4420	Men's outerwear	170	(2)	0.407	0.472	0.000	0.582	-1.670
4430	Women's outerwear	135	(1)	0.368	0.000	0.000	0.000	0.797
4440	Overalls & men's shirts	178	(1)	0.328	0.000	0.000	0.000	0.339
4450	Dresses, infants' wear etc.	301	(1)	0.432	0.000	0.000	0.000	0.626
4460	Hats & millinery	35	(2)	0.540	0.538	0.000	0.531	-1.254
4491	Corsets & swimwear	76	(1)	0.346	0.000	0.000	0.000	0.595
4492	Gloves	33	(1)	0.420	0.000	0.000	0.000	0.317
4500	Footwear	203		0.271	0.175	1.054	0.833	-0.153

Table 3. *continued*

SIC Code	Industry	Number of plants	Failure case	SIGMAE	ATINON	LAMBDA	ATE	SKEWNESS
4611	Refractory goods	57	(1)	0.442	0.000	0.000	0.000	0.191
4612	Non-refractory goods	100		0.506	0.290	0.987	0.732	−0.133
4620	Pottery	108	(1)	0.256	0.000	0.000	0.000	0.304
4630	Glass	101		0.325	0.331	4.346	0.697	−0.811
4640	Cement	13		0.368	0.115	0.431	0.888	−0.058
4691	Abrasives	33	(1)	0.318	0.000	0.000	0.000	0.246
4692	Other building materials	355		0.590	0.130	0.303	0.873	−0.007
4710	Timber	390		0.484	0.401	2.227	0.639	−0.513
4720	Furniture & upholstery	319	(2)	0.547	0.631	0.000	0.461	−2.601
4730	Bedding	89	(2)	0.703	0.614	0.000	0.473	−1.072
4740	Shop & office fittings	133	(2)	0.580	0.689	0.000	0.417	−3.513
4750	Wooden containers	96	(2)	0.426	0.503	0.000	0.558	−1.900
4790	Miscellaneous wood & cork	124	(2)	0.409	0.486	0.000	0.572	−1.845
4810	Paper & board	136		0.416	0.415	6.865	0.638	−0.914
4821	Cardboard boxes etc.	254		0.343	0.347	4.569	0.683	−0.826
4822	Paper packaging	90	(1)	0.371	0.000	0.000	0.000	0.169
4830	Manufactured stationery	206		0.336	0.204	0.992	0.806	−0.134
4841	Wallpaper	16		0.330	0.251	1.469	0.764	−0.290
4842	Other paper & board	71		0.418	0.398	3.855	0.641	−0.771
4850	Newspaper printing	319	(2)	0.418	0.502	0.000	0.559	−2.006
4890	Other printing	899		0.423	0.426	12.355	0.630	−0.968
4910	Rubber	212		0.393	0.312	1.724	0.712	−0.372
4920	Lino & plastic flooring	25		0.440	0.351	1.840	0.680	−0.407
4930	Brushes & brooms	38	(2)	0.738	0.693	0.000	0.414	−1.753
4941	Toys & games	90		0.413	0.398	4.205	0.641	−0.801
4943	Sports equipment	58	(2)	0.497	0.487	0.000	0.571	−1.043
4950	Miscellaneous stationers' goods	43		0.569	0.436	1.948	0.611	−0.439
4960	Other plastics	587		0.389	0.356	2.742	0.676	−0.623
4991	Musical instruments	26		0.311	0.134	0.619	0.870	−0.026
4992	Other	105	(1)	0.382	0.000	0.000	0.000	0.306

(1) denotes case (1) failure, (2) denotes case (2) failure.
ATINON denotes non-normalised ATI – this allows us to directly read average technical inefficiency as percentage inefficiency.

Table 4(a).   Efficiency ranking of all industries (ranked by ATI) (**UK**)

SIC Code	Industry	ATI	Skewness
4640	Cement	0.115	−0.058
2770	Dyes & pigments	0.123	−0.042
3995	Drop forgings	0.124	−0.041
4692	Other building materials	0.130	−0.007
4991	Musical instruments	0.134	−0.026
2795	Printing ink	0.170	−0.226
4500	Footwear	0.175	−0.153
3395	Scales & weighing machinery	0.188	−0.128
2791	Polishes	0.190	−0.064
4130	Weaving	0.190	−0.099
3220	Copper, brass, etc.	0.201	−0.100
4830	Manufactured stationery	0.204	−0.134
4221	Household textiles	0.215	−0.057
3333	Compressors	0.225	−0.148
3520	Watches & clocks	0.231	−0.376
3620	Insulated wires & cables	0.235	−0.408
4841	Wallpaper	0.251	−0.290
4222	Canvas goods	0.259	−0.264
3120	Steel tubes	0.269	−0.187
3640	Radio components	0.271	−0.311
3996	Domestic holloware	0.280	−0.344
3950	Cans & metal boxes	0.283	−0.547
3630	Telephone apparatus	0.283	−0.241
2792	Adhesives, gelatine, etc.	0.285	−0.188
4210	Narrow fabrics	0.285	−0.624
3230	Other base metals	0.288	−0.143
4612	Non-refractory goods	0.290	−0.133
4160	Rope, twine & net	0.295	−0.140
2120	Bread & flour confection	0.300	−0.354
3399	Other machinery	0.302	−0.412
4910	Rubber	0.312	−0.372
3700	Shipbuilding	0.317	−0.371
3991	Metal furniture	0.321	−0.304
4110	Man-made fibres	0.327	−0.225
2391	Spirit & distilling	0.330	−0.122
4630	Glass	0.331	−0.811
3812	Trailers, caravans, etc.	0.331	−0.442
4172	Warp knitting	0.335	−0.428
3340	Industrial engines	0.342	−0.632
4821	Cardboard boxes, etc.	0.347	−0.826
3350	Textile machinery	0.350	−0.649
4920	Lino & plastic flooring	0.351	−0.407
4230	Textile finishing	0.353	−0.873
3393	Refrigerating machinery	0.353	−0.560
3420	Ordnance & small arms	0.353	−0.636
4960	Other plastics	0.356	−0.623
3110	Iron & steel	0.357	−0.405
2711	Inorganic chemicals	0.361	−0.491
3694	Electrical lamps	0.371	−0.791
3680	Domestic electrical goods	0.380	−0.950
2761	Synthetic resins & plastic	0.389	−0.523
2780	Fertilisers	0.391	−0.230

Table 4(a). *continued*

SIC Code	Industry	ATI	Skewness
4410	Weatherproof outerwear	0.397	−0.796
4842	Other paper & board	0.398	−0.771
4941	Toys & games	0.398	−0.801
4710	Timber	0.401	−0.513
4120	Spinning of cotton	0.405	−0.590
3210	Aluminium	0.405	−0.732
3360	Earth-moving equipment	0.411	−0.534
4810	Paper & board	0.415	−0.914
4890	Other printing	0.426	−0.968
3397	Food & drink processing machinery	0.426	−0.645
2310	Brewing & malting	0.435	−0.383
4950	Miscellaneous stationers' goods	0.436	−0.439
3940	Wire	0.447	−0.962
3962	Jewellery & precious metals	0.457	−0.299
2794	Formulated pesticides, etc.	0.463	−0.263
4292	Other textiles	0.469	−0.981
2190	Animal & poultry feed	0.492	−0.577
2730	Toilet preparations	0.492	−0.465
2292	Starch & miscellaneous foods	0.499	−0.451
3652	Broadcast receiving equipment	0.606	−0.765

Table 4(b). Efficiency ranking of all industries (ranked by skewness) (**UK**)

SIC Code	Industry	Skewness	ATI
4692	Other building materials	−0.007	0.130
4991	Musical instruments	−0.026	0.134
3995	Drop forgings	−0.041	0.124
2770	Dyes & pigments	−0.042	0.123
4221	Household textiles	−0.057	0.215
4640	Cement	−0.058	0.115
2791	Polishes	−0.064	0.190
4130	Weaving	−0.099	0.190
3220	Copper, brass, etc.	−0.100	0.201
2391	Spirit & distilling	−0.122	0.330
3395	Scales & weighing machinery	−0.128	0.188
4612	Non-refractory goods	−0.133	0.290
4830	Manufactured stationery	−0.134	0.204
4160	Rope, twine & net	−0.140	0.295
3230	Other base metals	−0.143	0.288
3333	Compressors	−0.148	0.225
4500	Footwear	−0.153	0.175
3120	Steel tubes	−0.187	0.269
2792	Adhesives, gelatine, etc.	−0.188	0.285
4110	Man-made fibres	−0.225	0.327
2795	Printing ink	−0.226	0.170
2780	Fertilisers	−0.230	0.391
3630	Telephone apparatus	−0.241	0.283
2794	Formulated pesticides, etc.	−0.263	0.463
4222	Canvas goods	−0.264	0.259
4841	Wallpaper	−0.290	0.251
3962	Jewellery & precious metals	−0.299	0.457
3991	Metal furniture	−0.304	0.321
3640	Radio components	−0.311	0.271
3996	Domestic holloware	−0.344	0.280
2120	Bread & flour confection	−0.354	0.300
3700	Shipbuilding	−0.371	0.317
4910	Rubber	−0.372	0.312
3520	Watches & clocks	−0.376	0.231
2310	Brewing & malting	−0.383	0.435
3110	Iron & steel	−0.405	0.357
4920	Lino & plastic flooring	−0.407	0.351
3620	Insulated wires & cables	−0.408	0.235
3399	Other machinery	−0.412	0.302
4172	Warp knitting	−0.428	0.335
4950	Miscellaneous stationers' goods	−0.439	0.436
3812	Trailers, caravans, etc.	−0.442	0.331
2292	Starch & miscellaneous foods	−0.451	0.499
2730	Toilet preparations	−0.465	0.492
2711	Inorganic chemicals	−0.491	0.361
4710	Timber	−0.513	0.401
2761	Synthetic resins & plastic	−0.523	0.389
3360	Earth-moving equipment	−0.534	0.411
3950	Cans & metal boxes	−0.547	0.283
3393	Refrigerating machinery	−0.560	0.353
2190	Animal & poultry feed	−0.577	0.492
4120	Spinning of cotton	−0.590	0.405

Table 4(b). *continued*

SIC Code	Industry	Skewness	ATI
4960	Other plastics	−0.623	0.356
4210	Narrow fabrics	−0.624	0.285
3340	Industrial engines	−0.632	0.342
3420	Ordnance & small arms	−0.636	0.353
3397	Food & drink processing machinery	−0.645	0.426
3350	Textile machinery	−0.649	0.350
3210	Aluminium	−0.732	0.405
3652	Broadcast receiving equipment	−0.765	0.606
4842	Other paper & board	−0.771	0.398
3694	Electrical lamps	−0.791	0.371
4410	Weatherproof outerwear	−0.796	0.397
4941	Toys & games	−0.801	0.398
4630	Glass	−0.811	0.331
4821	Cardboard boxes, etc.	−0.826	0.347
4230	Textile finishing	−0.873	0.353
4810	Paper & board	−0.914	0.415
3680	Domestic electrical goods	−0.950	0.380
3940	Wire	−0.962	0.447
4890	Other printing	−0.968	0.426
4292	Other textiles	−0.981	0.469

5

Determinants of inefficiency

The previous two chapters discussed how inefficiency should be measured and analysed the results of our estimation of inefficiency for a 151-industry breakdown of manufacturing in the UK and a 140-industry breakdown for Australian manufacturing. In this chapter we go on to the second phase of our research and explore what determines inefficiency, suggesting reasons why inefficiency varies by industry. Here we restrict our empirical analysis to the UK before moving on in Chapter 6 to compare the work with similar analyses, most of them stemming from Phase 2 of the six-country project.

We have already explained that variation in behaviour among firms is a natural part of the dynamic process of competition in markets, which thrive on imperfections and exhibit considerable variation in products. In the previous chapter we showed how that variation in the performance of firms could be explained by three groups of factors. The first was the characteristics of production within the industry suggesting, in the form of a production function, how inputs are transformed into output. By using a flexible functional form, augmented by variables that admit differences in the composition of inputs, we are able to account for a considerable proportion of variation among firms, caused by scale, factor proportions and, to a lesser extent, quality. Second, we have argued that the remaining variation can be split into two components, one of which represents a measure of what we have described as 'inefficiency' and the other a largely random component representing the myriad of detailed forces we have omitted from the analysis. Of course, the residuals will also reflect the extent to which the data have been mismeasured, any misspecifications in our production model and any drawbacks to our estimation methods.

Hence, in turning our focus now on to what determines the extent of inefficiency in each industry, we must bear in mind that the measures of inefficiency we are starting with are themselves imprecise and reflect aspects of variety within each industry that may not represent technical inefficiency in the strict sense of Farrell (1957).

As inefficiency can only occur for substantial periods in imperfect markets, the simplest approach to explaining it is to try to set out the causes of imperfection and measures of their extent. We are, of course, restricted in our analysis by the data available for a breakdown of industry similar to that in the Standard Industrial Classification (1968) for the *Annual Census of Production*, which we used for the measures of inefficiency.[1] Our ambition, therefore, has to be tempered by the different concerns which governed data collection by others. Fortunately we have not been limited entirely to official statistics.

Within this framework, imperfections can be characterised in six ways: competitive conditions, heterogeneity, industry dynamics, spatial disparities, managerial/organisational influences and public policy.[2] We therefore explore the first five groups as sets of hypotheses about what might explain inter-industry variations in inefficiency.

1. *Competitive conditions.*   In a highly competitive environment there is less scope for inefficiency. At one end of the spectrum we have perfect competition. We described earlier how in a perfectly competitive market a large number of homogeneous firms competing under the same market and production conditions will produce at their optimal point, where inputs are allocated and utilised in the most efficient way to produce the maximum possible output. In such a competitive environment the product price is set by the market and firms are price takers, because no individual firm is influential enough to be otherwise. In this situation it is easy to see that an inefficient firm will rapidly go out of business. In the short term a firm may be able to suffer the losses incurred from higher costs of production, but in the long term it will be unable to compete with the more efficient firms and will leave the industry. Of course, the reverse is true – a firm may earn excess profits in the short term due to super-efficient behaviour, but in the long term these gains will attract new firms into the industry and compete away the profits.

   At the other extreme is the monopoly situation, where the sole firm in the industry faces no competition due to some barrier preventing the entry of new firms, this may be high fixed costs, hostile behaviour, patented product, government regulation, etc. A monopolist can either choose how much to produce and let the market set the price or choose what price to set and let the market set the demand for the product at that price. While it too would maximise profits by operating where marginal revenue is the same as marginal cost this will be at a lower level of output, higher price and hence higher profit than for a perfectly competitive industry. A monopolist has less incentive to optimise production because there are no competitors threatening its excess profits. Thus not only may profits not be maximised in the price-setting process, but the firm may show inefficiencies of all forms – allocative, technical, scale and dynamic – because the incentives to use the most up-to-date technology, to innovate and squeeze the last drop of efficiency out of the system are lower. Input factors such as management and labour can extract some of the monopoly profits from the firm, leaving themselves better off, but leading to higher marginal costs and output prices and further reductions in output relative to the competitive or, indeed, monopoly outcome. However, most monopolies, or near-monopolies, are regulated in industrial countries to provide at least some degree of alternative pressure to act in the interests of the purchasers.

Even if there is more than one firm in the industry a position similar to a monopoly can emerge because this limited number of firms can observe each other's actions and infer their intentions, thereby coming either to implicit or explicit agreements to limit competitive behaviour, as all know they will suffer sharply reduced profits if they step out of line and trigger a competitive war. Such collusion in this oligopoly is also subject to tight regulation. In the UK this comes through both the Office of Fair Trading and the Monopolies and Mergers Commission. Although action is taken or threatened by the authorities in *prima facie* cases of anti-competitive behaviour, such cases can be difficult to prove and hence competition can be restricted for extended periods of time; Rees (1993) provides a recent discussion of the UK salt industry. Much of the reality lies between these two extremes, with many players, but in general the more competitive the industry, the more efficient it is likely to be.

2. *Heterogeneity.* In order to secure market share firms may attempt to differentiate their product from their competitors, for example through the use of brand names. In these cases, although the product may in practice be highly substitutable, like different sorts of baked beans or instant coffee or washing powder, producers are able to build up considerable brand loyalty which enables them to charge different prices and yet keep market share. This ability to reduce cross-price elasticities enables producers to increase margins, or have slacker control over costs and yet still remain competitive. Insofar as firms have variable success in achieving this, further variety in performance will be observed. One way in which inefficiency of this form may be manifested is through a high level of advertising or other promotional costs in order to maintain the brand image. The more the products of an industry are differentiated, the more efficiency can vary. However, in many industries the differentiation will not be partly an illusion

created by the brand image and imperfections in information acquired by the purchaser but actual differences caused by including a wide range of products under the same industry heading. In part this is a comment on the inappropriateness of estimating a single frontier production function for the sector. In the absence of a time- or budget-constraint it would have been desirable to test the estimated models with a range of diagnostic procedures and to refine the models to ensure that the results were statistically adequate.[3]

3. *Industry dynamics.* Efficiency is a dynamic concept and in a changing environment we would expect to see varying behaviour amongst firms. In fact, the faster the rate of change in a sector, the greater the spread of (in)efficiency within an industry, as at any one time different firms will be at different stages of adjustment. This applies whether the industry is contracting, expanding, or innovating, although we cannot expect to see the same spread of behaviour in each case.

4. *Spatial disparities.* In the same way that increased variation in performance is possible as variation in the product increases, so the more geographically diverse the market, and the more variety there is in production; the more performance can vary. If production is spread out across the country this may give an opportunity for differences in efficiency because of differences in productive conditions and reduced competitive pressures due to the natural protection afforded by transport costs.

5. *Managerial and organisational influence.* In many respects organisation and management of the firm is the archetypal source of residual or X-inefficiency. Once we have taken account of all the identifiable factors relating to the quality of inputs and other items set out in hypotheses 1 to 4, the only option left lies in how the firm is run. However, as it is very difficult to quantify accurately we used a different treatment and tried to identify explicit organisational differences, for example, the greater the number of plants in a firm, the greater the chance of heterogeneity and weaker control, hence greater inefficiency.

In the rest of this chapter we explore each group of hypotheses in turn. Although we shall be looking at each hypothesis separately it must be remembered that the relationships are not independent and the model used is a multivariate one taking into account all of these factors simultaneously.

5.1 The full model

In Chapter 4 we considered how behaviour varied within each industry and derived a set of estimates for inefficiency. In this chapter we are seeking to explain the variations across industries, so our starting point is the inefficiency estimates for the 151 industries. However, as we could not decompose the residuals satisfactorily for some industries, fewer than 151 industries have been included in the analysis of those measures that require decomposition, and our coverage of manufacturing is no longer complete. Hence, our new model is of the form:

$$\Pi_j = h(X_{jk}) \qquad j = 1, \ldots, n; \, k = 1, \ldots, m \qquad (5.1)$$

where Π_j is an estimate of average inefficiency in industry j and the X_k are the m variables used to explain how inefficiency varies across industries. We are, of course, measuring relative inefficiency, i.e. how an industry's actual performance compares with the potential for that industry, assessed relative to the best performing plants with various input mixes and output scales. We have estimated (5.1) in the form of a linear model:

$$\Pi_j = \sum_{k=1}^{m} h_k X_{jk} + w \qquad (5.2)$$

where w is residual with the usual assumption of a $N(0, \sigma_w^2)$ distribution.

Throughout the study our main concern lay with the full model, which is multivariate and considers all the factors affecting inefficiency (X_k) together. Using each of the five measures of inefficiency – skewness, ATI, ATE, sigmae and lambda – as the dependent variable, the model enabled us to observe the estimated ability of our chosen variables to explain inefficiency and thus test our five hypotheses. The full model is given in the Appendix to this chapter and is discussed in detail later. First, however, we consider variables in the model one at a time, looking at their ability to explain inefficiency. To ease exposition we shall refer to all the measures in terms of *in*efficiency, which involves reversing the signs for ATE and skewness so that a higher value implies higher inefficiency.

5.2 Competitive conditions

Competitive conditions are the obvious starting point for our analysis. By definition, if there is perfect competition then inefficiency is precluded. Perfect competition entails a large number of identical firms (same size, using the same technology, etc.) producing a homogeneous product. Both purchasers and suppliers have full information about market conditions. Producers' objectives are assumed to be to maximise profits, therefore, under perfect competition, all firms will produce at the most efficient point on their identical production functions.

Almost all real-world markets differ from this paradigm in every respect: within an industry products are not identical, a Ford car is not the same as a Vauxhall; different firms will sell their goods for different prices; firms will differ in productivity, inputs used, etc. and there is disagreement over the extent to which profits are the appropriate maximand, as some companies may put a greater emphasis on market share. Here we need to identify the extent to which competition is revealed to be imperfect. All sorts of measures exist for this. We can look at market structure. For example, we can observe the degree to which monopoly power has been built up. Even though competition policy seeks to reduce monopoly power, cartels and oligopoly, through restricting horizontal mergers and acquisitions, and seeks to limit the exploitation of that power through the outlawing of restrictive practices, just examining the extent of monopoly in an industry would give a *prima facie* indication of the opportunity for monopoly to exist. Although not all firms' monopoly power is inefficient, its presence can permit inefficiency. Clearly the less concentrated an industry the more closely it mirrors one of the characteristics of perfect competition.

In our particular case we will not observe complete monopoly as our industries have to be large enough to avoid the statistics from any one establishment being inferred and large enough to permit the satisfactory estimation of a model with at least half a dozen parameters. However, monopoly power is exercised by firms, not individual establishments, so an industry may be more concentrated than the total number of establishments suggests.

A second way of deciding whether an industry exhibits free or open competition is to look at the spread of prices for particular products within it. Unless the market can be segmented consumers can shop around seeking the lowest prices. This normally forces even independent producers to exhibit a fairly low spread of prices. A lack of information and high shopping around costs will permit substantial discrepancies to appear. Products that are difficult to transport or need to be consumed near the point of production or sale automatically increase the opportunity to segment. This approach of examining price dispersion is used by the European Commission in its assessment of the opportunity for change in the European Single Market (Buigues and Ilzkowitz, 1988).

Following the Buigues and Ilzkowitz methodology a little further, one would attempt direct measurement of the height of the barriers between segments of the market. They consider only geographical segmentation, but barriers can be introduced between products as well, say through broad patents or exclusive dealing requirements. Buigues and Ilzkowitz use a questionnaire to help establish the extent of segmentation (Nerb, 1987) where industrialists are invited to identify barriers and their importance is indicated largely by a count of the replies.

This rather subjective and weakly graded measure is therefore supplemented by other measures of the openness of the market such as import penetration and price dispersion. Even though a market may have considerable domestic monopoly, if at the same time there are substantial imports the monopolists are unlikely to have a major opportunity to exploit their power and hence be subject to considerable inefficiency.

In the same way we can judge the effectiveness of barriers in an industry by looking at the ease of entry of new producers. Thus, even if a monopoly exists, if new entrants can challenge it, then competition is likely to be strong. So the number of new entrants might indicate a strongly competitive market. However, strong competition results in deaths as well as births, new entrants squeeze out existing players, they do not merely gain market share and expand the whole market. Hence exit as well as entry is a measure of competitive pressure. High sunk costs in a business may make exit difficult and hence enable existing producers to restrict entry.

These measures relate to revealed behaviour. One of the advances of recent years (Baumol *et al.*, 1988) is to articulate the idea of 'contestability'. What creates competitive pressure is not just that a market is contested, as we have just described, for example, by new entrants and importers, but that it is *contestable*, i.e. the entry of new producers is possible and likely if existing firms behave inefficiently. In this case the incumbent firms will conduct a wholehearted drive for efficiency to make sure that entry never takes place. Hence, we need measures of openness to competition, which do not necessarily require actual entry for their estimation. This is a tall order and, in our choice of measures of competitiveness to use in this analysis, we have to be directed by the availability of the information. Perfect contestability, like perfect competition, relies on the absence of the imperfections that characterise most real-world situations, in this case that there are no sunk costs (Bollard *et al.*, 1993). Dixit (1992) allows for such sunk costs, uncertainty and imperfect information. His analysis suggests, for example, that there can be deviations from Marshallian theory (which suggests that prices are capped by entry at long-term average costs and have a floor due to exit at variable costs) for long periods (ten years or more) that are perfectly consistent with dynamic competition under uncertainty. It is thus possible to admit rather more complexity than some of the foregoing arguments might seem to imply.

In order to estimate the effect of competitive conditions on inefficiency we were able to use three measures of competitiveness: firm concentration; openness of the market to imports, in terms of actual market share; and extent to which the industry in contested, i.e. levels of entry and exit of firms into and out of the industry.

5.2.1 *Firm concentration*

Firm concentration is a widely used measure of competitive conditions. In an industry where the number of firms is small or where production is concentrated in the hands of a few large producers, the large companies can exercise market power by restricting the ability of smaller companies to compete. Cartels are a prime example of such a situation; together members of the cartel can effectively act as a monopoly and prevent the entry of potential competitors. Although cartels are usually illegal, in industries where the market is concentrated in the hands of a few firms these firms can act together without any explicit collusion, through pricing policies, to restrict competition. Thus we can hypothesise that in an industry where firm concentration is high these firms will tend to be more inefficient. However, this is not a hard and fast rule – one may observe an industry composed of small specialised producers who face little competition in their segments, and another composed of a small number of volume producers competing with a range of more standardised products. In such a situation the concentrated industry could be efficient and the non-concentrated industry, comprising smaller firms, inefficient because it is segmented.

There is therefore no reason to expect to find a consistent positive linear relationship between concentration and inefficiency. It may be the case that up to a particular level of concentration firms are actually more efficient, or that once concentration reaches very low levels firms find niches in the market in which to specialise, thus limiting the competition that encourages efficient behaviour. Empirical evidence has suggested a curvilinear relation between concentration and inefficiency. The US study (Caves and Barton, 1990b) found that efficiency rises with concentration up to a four-firm concentration ratio of 40 per cent and thereafter it falls away. These results were replicated in the Japanese study (Uekusa and Torii, 1985).

There is considerable argument about how concentration should be measured. Should it include merely the largest firms, such as concentration ratios, or should it include all firms, as in the case of Herfindahl index? Should the chosen variable, according to which concentration is measured, be value added or sales?

Concentration ratios are a popular method in empirical work and measure either the proportion of output attributable to the top n firms in the industry, or alternatively the number of firms that comprise x per cent of the industry's output. They can be thought of as relating to points on a concentration curve (Figure 5.1). Consider industry A, if we look at the top three firms our concentration ratio is 75 per cent, because they account for 75 per cent of the total industry output. On the other hand, using the second method, if we look at the number of firms that produce 75 per cent of industry A's output, our concentration ratio is three. Theoretically both these methods provide a good measure of concentration,[4] however the former method is the most commonly used because the data required are more easily accessible, often given by industrial census. Figure 5.1

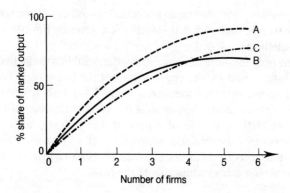

Figure 5.1 Industry concentration ratios (*source*: Hay and Morris, 1981).

does, however, illustrate a potential problem when comparing concentration in different industries. Consider industries B and C. Using a three-firm concentration ratio, B is the more concentrated, however using a five-firm ratio the reverse is true.

Unlike the concentration ratio, which only considers the dominant firms in an industry, the Herfindahl index takes into account all firms and their relative sizes, it is given by:

$$H = \sum_i s_i^2 \qquad (5.3)[5]$$

where s_i is the market share of the *i*th firm. It is, however, debatable whether the inclusion of all firms is beneficial, as it can be argued that the entry and exit of firms at a small-scale have little effect on concentration (Hart, 1971).

The Herfindahl index can additionally be used as a numbers-equivalent index, i.e. it can be translated into the number of equal-sized firms that would give the same value of the index. Once again, theoretically the Herfindahl index is a good measure of concentration and empirically it is possible to calculate without information on all firms (Adelman, 1969), however it does require access to individual firm data which we were unable to obtain.

In the discussion up till now we have considered measures of concentration using sales or gross output. In manufacturing industries the production of a finished good usually involves a number of different stages. The use of sales/gross output presents a problem because it also includes interfirm sales, which do not enter the final markets. One way around this problem is to use value added and to treat each separate stage of production as the 'final market' for the semi-processed product. However, the problems of obtaining such detailed information severely limit the practicality of this method.

In practice the only measure of concentration available was the five-firm concentration ratio based on the gross output of the five largest firms in the industry. The use of other measures might have lead to markedly different results. This concentration ratio is recorded in the *Annual Census of Production* (ACOP) as a ratio of output in the industry as a whole (Table 5.1). However, this measure introduces an extra concept as, in practice, market competition occurs between firms (enterprises) whereas the basis of our analysis is establishments (plants).

Table 5.1 Concentration in UK manufacturing industry, 1977

Five-firm concentration ratio (%)	Industries	
	Number	Per cent
0–24	25	17
25–49	59	39
50–74	39	26
75–100	28	19
Total	151	100

nb: columns may not sum due to rounding.

One important point to note is that using our data it was not always possible to identify effective concentration. As our industries are defined by statistical categories and not in homogeneous economic terms, the industry could be characterised by two somewhat separate markets. We have already mentioned the brewing and malting industry, where brewing is concentrated in six large firms and malting consists of a large number of very small firms. Thus not all firms in the same industry may be facing the same competitive conditions. Second, if an industry has strikingly different firm sizes, those firms rather different factor prices. In the case of capital (and material and service inputs), these prices are likely to be lower for large firms who tend to buy in large quantities and are in a better position to secure purchasing deals, but in the case of labour the position is not so clear. Stronger trade union activity in larger firms may drive up wage costs but, on the other hand, a large firm may be able to pay lower wages by offering other benefits, for example greater job security (Prais, 1981a). Finally, firms of different sizes may differ in their ability to innovate and thus in their productivity. The effect of size on innovation is strongly debated. Schumpeter (1951) suggested that large firms would have the resources to be more innovative (this argument is discussed in greater detail in Section 5.4). However, entrepreneurs in small firms will be less held back by bureaucracy and hierarchical structures and hence could be more innovative.

The five-firm concentration ratio, referred to as CONC1 (the variables and the definitions are listed in the Appendix to this chapter), can be misleading because it treats the market as if only domestic output matters. This approach is mistaken in two respects; first, because the concentration of domestic suppliers becomes irrelevant if the UK market is dominated by importers; second, because the domestic market could be fragmented and the large firms mainly export-oriented. There are two ways to deal with the problem. The first is to expand the definition of the market to include imports; we did this by including the variable,

$$ \text{CONC2} = \text{CONC1} \left(\frac{\text{sales}}{\text{sales} + \text{imports}} \right) $$

The second is to measure the openness of the industry to foreign trade as a separate issue from concentration. We consider this in Section 5.2.2.

Concentration is the first of our variables to be examined. Table 5.2 shows the relationship between the five inefficiency measures and concentration, using CONC1 and CONC2. It should be noted that while the skewness and standard error measures relate to the combined residual and can therefore be estimated for all the industries (151), the remaining measures relate only to those 72 industries where the residuals could be satisfactorily decomposed. Table 5.2 shows that there is a significant (at the 5 per cent level) positive correlation between skewness and both concentration measures. The correlations between the concentration measures and the other efficiency measures are considerably weaker, with only that between ATI and the trade-adjusted concentration measure reaching the 10 per cent significance level.

Table 5.2 Correlation between inefficiency and concentration

Inefficiency measure	CONC1	CONC2	Number of industries
skewness	0.06**	0.06**	151
σ_e	0.00	0.00	151
ATI	0.03	0.04*	72
ATE	0.03	0.03	72
λ	0.01	0.01	72

** indicates significance at the 5 per cent level; * indicates significance at the 10 per cent level.

In the full model the concentration measures are significant at the 10 per cent level at least for all measures of inefficiency (in the full model in the Appendix table, skewness, σ_e and λ are referred to as SKEW, SIGMAE and LAMBDA). Concentration is not rejected from the final form in any case although the individual co-efficients are only marginally significant in some specifications. In general the greater the concentration the greater the inefficiency (or the less the efficiency in the case of the ATE measure). However the sign is sometimes the opposite, which suggests the existence of multi-collinearity in the model or the possibility of misspecification in the industry regressions that yield the measures of inefficiency – and by consequence the cross-industry regressions.

There is no specific reason to believe that the relation between concentration and efficiency is linear as opposed to curvilinear. A curvilinear relation can be modelled by including the square of concentration in the regression, i.e. CONSQ1 and CONSQ2 corresponding to CONC1 and CONC2. However, this relation was less clearly borne out, with significant co-efficients only in the case of ATI and ATE (our preferred specifications). In addition we cannot reject it in the case of λ. All have the same inverted U form with increasing concentration first increasing and then decreasing inefficiency (see Appendix table).

In a purely numerical sense, the smaller the industry, the more likely it is to be concentrated. However, conversely, the more firms in the industry, the greater the chance that some of them will exhibit divergence from the industry 'norm'. In other words, inefficiency could be positively related to the number of firms in the industry. This has not only been observed empirically in the US (although not in Japan) but has been justified by Caves and Barton (1990b) in theoretical terms in a deterministic model. Therefore, we looked simply at the hypothesis that inefficiency is related to the number of plants (CASES in our list of variables). This was only borne out for the skewness and σ_e measures, although it is also weakly significant for the λ measure. However, in the case of σ_e inefficiency was *negatively* correlated with the number of cases, this contradicts both the theory and the American data, and we should therefore question its validity.

In order to explore the bilateral relation between concentration and *efficiency* we have drawn up a grid of the two measures – Table 5.3. We see here the two effects, first, the relation between concentration and inefficiency, and second, the way in which the concentration measures are concentrated in 25–49 per cent, and to a lesser extent 50–74 per cent ranges (Table 5.1).

Therefore the main conclusion drawn from these results is that inefficiency rises with increasing concentration, at least up to concentration in the 50–74 per cent range (values of ATI are on average higher). Beyond that interval the values appear a little lower so, in common with examples from other countries, particularly the US, the relationship may actually

Table 5.3 Concentration and efficiency in UK industry

Concentration (%)	Efficiency (% of total in group)			
	Case (1) failures	ATI below mean	ATI above mean	Case (2) failures
0–24	19	26	12	10
25–49	38	48	30	41
50–74	23	13	36	33
75–100	21	13	21	18
Total	100	100	100	100
Number of cases	48	31	33	39

peak rather than rise monotonically with concentration. This is also broadly consistent with the results from the multiple regression analysis discussed below.

5.2.2 Actual market share

The extent of competition may also be measured by the openness of the market to imports. This is measured not in potential terms, but in terms of actual market share – imports/sales (IMPORTS in our list of explanatory variables). In theory, the more the market is open to foreign competition the smaller the opportunity for inefficiency, inefficient firms will be unable to compete and quickly go out of business. However, a high import ratio could actually indicate that the industry *is* inefficient relative to firms abroad, not that foreign competition drives out inefficient domestic firms, i.e. the fact that there is excess market share which the foreign firms are able to fill could point to absolute inefficiency of the domestic firms. Therefore one should perhaps also look at the industry's ability to export – exports/sales (EXPORTS in our list). The greater the ability of an industry to export, the greater its international competiveness and hence the lower the absolute inefficiency. Once again we must be aware that our measures of inefficiency do not show absolute levels but variation in domestic performance within industries. It is important not to confuse measured technical efficiency with comparative advantage. A highly technically efficient industry might have difficulty competing with imports or exporting if foreign relative prices are very different, say because of very low material or labour costs.

Looking at import/sales or exports/sales within an industry ignores the existence of intra-industry trade, which is increasingly tending to characterise trading patterns. Under these circumstances it is possible to specialise within market segments, hence we could see both higher imports and exports with continuing measured technical inefficiency simply because the market is highly segmented. We therefore included in our specification two further explanatory variables which are widely used to measure the extent of intra-industry trade, NETTRADE and GROSSTRADE. These are defined as:

$$\text{NETTRADE} = \left(\frac{\text{imports} - \text{exports}}{\text{sales}} \right)$$

$$\text{GROSSTRADE} = \left(\frac{\text{exports} + \text{imports}}{\text{sales}} \right)$$

If our theory holds we would expect these to be positively correlated with inefficiency insofar as they show the existence of intra-industry trade.

However, rather to our surprise these variables were rather poorly correlated with inefficiency and it was only the lambda, λ, measure that showed much in the way of a significant relationship. In the final specification of the full model IMPORTS and EXPORTS were included in the ATI and ATE equations (see Appendix table). In the ATI equation IMPORTS has a negative co-efficient while that for EXPORTS is positive; the opposite is true for the ATE equation as ATE is a measure of *efficiency*. EXPORTS alone was included in the λ equation (see Appendix table); its sign was positive.

To conclude, our results show that higher imports do appear to be associated with higher levels of efficiency. These results indicate that foreign competitors do appear to drive out some of the inefficient domestic firms, but not all. However, higher exports also coincide with higher inefficiency (the same sign is observed in the skewness equation but an insignificant co-efficient of the reverse sign is obtained for the σ_e equation), this appears to contradict our hypothesis. It may, however, be that this result is caused by the fact that exports are concentrated in a relatively small proportion of establishments. These plants may be very efficient but the industry may also contain a large number of very inefficient firms. Hence our measures would indicate an inefficient industry. These results are replicated by those from the US study (Caves and Barton, 1990b).

Part of this confusion over the relationship between import/exports and inefficiency is that trade is a static or 'snapshot' measure of a changing environment. If high imports drive out inefficient domestic producers, we need to know the history of imports to know whether that process of driving out has only just begun or is long established. Caves and Barton found that productivity growth increases with the growth rate of import penetration. An alternative means of examining this phenomenon is to measure it directly by looking at the number of firms leaving and entering an industry, which we do shortly. To explore this process of 'driving out' firms we would require data on the firms which exit and on their market share, which unfortunately we do not have at present.[6]

5.2.3   *Entries and exits*

Highly competitive industries tend to be highly contested, i.e. show high levels of entries of new firms and exits of existing firms. These industries should exhibit lower levels of inefficiency because new firms entering the industry will push out inefficient ones. As Baldwin and Gorecki (1989) have shown, in the case of Canada it tends to be the less productive plants which exit, thus promoting an industry's efficiency. However, highly competitive industries might exhibit higher rather than lower levels of measured technical inefficiency as the new, more efficient, entrants raise the frontier relative to the incumbents. Only when the incumbents react or go out of business will the range of efficiency contract. Dixit (1992) suggests that there can be significant persistence of observed 'inefficient' firms if they believe that the economic conditions for them will improve in the future. There is thus considerable scope for extending this analysis if it is possible to work directly on the data relating to individual plants over time.

Further empirical evidence on foundries (Baden-Fuller, 1989) suggests that although the less efficient exit, many of the least efficient continue if they have no alternative plants or products to which they can switch their product line. Thus one may find that subsidiaries of larger companies exit before single plant firms. Alternatively, it may be that small firms are more prone to exit as a result of normal market fluctuations, because they have no alternative activities or sources of funds to use to offset these difficulties. These firms may not necessarily be the most inefficient. Capital intensive industries, where individual firms have high sunk and fixed costs, will tend to suffer most from market fluctuations. Sunk costs are investment costs which cannot be recouped whereas fixed costs are sunk only in the short term. For some firms a decrease in industry demand will involve a cut in profits, but others will be making losses. The ability of firms to take these losses will depend not only on alternative sources of funds but also on how they financed the original investment. In the case of large firms, finance may well be from retentions – they will suffer no financial difficulties. However, small firms tend to borrow either from banks or on debentures at a fixed interest rate, in this case there is the danger that gross profit during a downturn will be insufficient to meet the interest repayments.

Industries that lack competition are often characterised by barriers to entry, hence restricting entry; or high costs of exit, making existing firms reluctant to leave. These will cut down the changes in the number of firms, thus encouraging inefficiency. Many of the barriers arise largely from sunk costs and the use of assets that are specific to the particular production process. A new entrant needs to incur these costs, much of which are likely to be financed by borrowing against the future income stream, while existing incumbents have already incurred the expenditure. If there is no alternative use for the assets and no good second-hand market it is worth their while continuing in production as long as they cover their current costs, as they will in any case have to write off the assets if they go out of business. Even if they are currently covering full costs it is worth their while, if the size of the market is limited, to make a credible threat to prospective entrants that they will cut prices to the level of current costs, if necessary, to deter entry. Such credibility can usually be obtained from actions in the face of previous entry attempts or aggressive pricing among the existing incumbents. Using data on entries and exits[7] we were able to create four variables.

$$\text{ENTI} = \frac{\text{average number of entrants} - }{\text{average number of exits, 1973–6}}$$
$$\text{ENTI} = \frac{\text{average number of exits, 1973–6}}{\text{number of establishments}}$$

$$\text{ENT2} = \frac{\text{average sales of entrants} - }{\text{average sales of exits, 1973–6}}$$
$$\text{ENT2} = \frac{\text{average sales of exits, 1973–6}}{\text{average industry sales, 1973–6}}$$

$$\text{PENTS} = \frac{\text{average sales of entrants, 1973–6}}{\text{average industry sales, 1973–6}}$$

$$\text{PEXITS} = \frac{\text{average sales of exits, 1973–6}}{\text{average industry sales, 1973–6}}$$

This enabled us to see not just how many firms are changing, but what their importance is to the industry as a whole. However, unfortunately we had no explanatory success with any of these variables, except some limited correlation between ENT2 and σ_e.

The data used also covered the average annual change in the number of enterprises over the years 1973–6[8], denoted as ENTRY in the regression model. This variable had a clear negative relation with σ_e and a weaker one with ATI, i.e. greater change in the number of firms decreases inefficiency. We therefore conclude that there is some evidence of a relation between this aspect of competition and efficiency.

These measures are, of course, indicators of the extent to which the industry is contested, rather than contestable (Baumol *et al.*, 1982). This again provides a problem of interpretation as actual entry could be low. First, if there are effective barriers to entry, in which case there is an incentive for the incumbents to be inefficient; second, where the incumbents are so efficient that potential entrants see little gain from entry. To distinguish between those industries in the first category and those in the second we would need an independent measure of barriers to entry.

Therefore in our study the use of a single measure may confuse the two influences. Finally, entry and exit will tend to reflect the position in the product life-cycle of the various establishments. As the market for a new product expands, potential new firms will see an opportunity to profit by entering the industry, entry will therefore be rapid. However, towards the end of a product's life, demand will be diminishing and hence firms will exit the industry, possibly to move into an expanding one. In many industries the product range is too great to distinguish this effect.

The dynamic forces of competition are also modelled explicity by including variables measuring the relation between rate of change and efficiency. This is discussed in the next section of this chapter. The problems observed here with the use of variables related to entry and exit may be offset to some extent by these direct measures of the change in the industries.

5.3 Product differentiation and heterogeneity

Heterogeneity of the product is the second major potential characteristic that can lead to the existence of technical inefficiency as we have measured it. This can take two forms: product differentiation and heterogeneity, i.e. one group heading covering a wide range of products.

5.3.1 *Product differentiation*

Product differentiation is one of the most widely used forms of 'non-price' competition. The use of brand names enables firms to differentiate their product from those of competitors and establish consumer loyalty. The technique most commonly used to promote a product is advertising, although other methods (promotional offers, trial samples, demonstrators, lobbyists) are all used to varying extents. Advertising expenditure is probably the best method of detecting and the most important source of product differentiation (Bain, 1956) and it can take many forms, including newspapers and magazines, billboards, television and radio, and direct mail. Advertising is likely to affect the efficiency of an industry, although there are opposing views as to the direction. On the one hand some see advertising as an information provider (Telser, 1964) . Adverts provide the consumer with useful information on price, product quality, retail location, etc. They reduce the cost and help the consumer make a rational choice between brands. Thus it could be claimed that advertising actually encourages competition because it reduces product differentiation associated with customer ignorance. In addition, the industry at large will tend to be *more* efficient as efficient new firms can capture the demand of already existing firms. This will generally discourage inefficient behaviour of those in the industry. Thus, even though this characteristic of the industry may have little implication for any loss of welfare, it is essential to include it in the regression as an explanation of variation in efficiency in order to avoid any misspecification of the relationship with factors, such as competition or public policy, which can lead to a loss of welfare.

On the other hand, advertising creates effective barriers to entry because it takes many years to establish new brands, and existing incumbents always have the option to try to match the new entrant's expenditure and hence make the task of entry harder. Therefore with barriers to entry in existence, the industry will tend to be more inefficient. However, where the new entrant is already established in a different part of the market, and hence already has a brand image, advertising will be a less effective barrier. Under these circumstances advertising can provide stability for an existing informal cartel (Comanor and Wilson, 1967). One problem with the use of advertising and branding is that it tends to be firm-specific rather than plant-specific, hence one cannot be certain that it will be clearly related to plant efficiency, nor that it will be correctly allocated to the appropriate industry, when a firm covers several different industries.

We used the variable ADSALES = advertising expenditure/sales (for 1977) in our regression analysis. However, the data[9] did not cover all industries and did not match our existing classification exactly. Therefore the variable could only be incorporated in a regression with some of the observations excluded. This subset of data was not random, relating mainly to industries where advertising is important. Unfortunately we obtained no results to suggest that advertising was an important variable affecting efficiency.

5.3.2 *Heterogeneity*

We have mentioned before that industry classifications may not define a single industry but one comprising a number of 'subindustries' producing a range of products. Therefore, to some extent, it may be inappropriate to fit a single production function to the data. By heterogeneity we do not necessarily mean some wildly differentiated group, such as mainframe computers and portable electric typewriters, coming under the same heading of Office Equipment, but even examples such as machine tools, where it is possible to define several major different types and over 200 types of installed capacity (*Metalworking Production*, five-yearly surveys). In the latter case, not only does the value range from just a few pounds for minor components to several millions for major systems for the motor car industry, but the precision required and the degree of automation possible in its production vary enormously. Hence there will be considerable variation in the way producers would combine labour and capital inputs, even if they were equally efficient in their own product segments. When fitting our single production function to the data we must take these factors into account. It may be that these departures from common behaviour are random and hence picked up in the random components of the residual. However, on the other hand they may have systematic tendencies and will therefore be picked up in the skewed residual and treated as technical inefficiency. Thus we have to appreciate that technical inefficiency may have a rather wider meaning in these circumstances.

Heterogeneity can be measured for all industries, albeit crudely, simply by adding up the number of five-digit categories (activity headings) in each three-digit industry (division class group). This is a very arbitrary measure but at least it gives some indication of the variability of the product structure. A second and more helpful ratio is that of total sales of principal products by the industry to total sales of goods produced and work done (SPECIAL in our regression).[10] The greater the proportion of output that is produced in the principle product industry, the lower is the level of heterogeneity and hence the more efficient the industry as a whole is likely to appear according to our data.

Table 5.4 Specialisation of industries

Specialisation (%)	Number	%
90–100	87	62
80–89	39	27
70–79	11	8
60–69	5	4
Total	142	100

nb: columns may not sum due to rounding.

The vast majority of industries have plants that are heavily focused on their products, with ratios between 90 per cent and 100 per cent, and, as Table 5.4 shows, specialisation tails off rapidly towards a minimum of 60 per cent.

Table 5.5 Spread of inefficiency and specialisation

Specialisation (%)	Case (1) failure	Below mean ATI	Above mean ATI	Case (2) failure
90–100	25 (57)	18 (56)	26 (66)	18 (68)
80–89	15 (34)	11 (34)	7 (18)	7 (25)
70–79	4 (9)	1 (3)	2 (5)	1 (4)

nb: lower specialisation levels excluded.

It is apparent from Table 5.5 that there is a tendency for greater specialisation to be associated with greater measured inefficiency. On a bivariate basis we found the correlations to be weak but once the variable was used in the full model the estimates were significant in all cases except skewness (see Appendix table). Had this variable referred to the individual plant and not the industry then this relation would have been explicable. As it is, it appears counterintuitive.

5.4 Industry dynamics

Earlier on in this chapter we talked briefly about the importance of dynamic factors upon an industry's efficiency. A simple example is rapid growth of demand. If an industry is growing rapidly then capacity will tend to be insufficient to meet demand, hence there will be enough room for all firms, both efficient and inefficient, in the market. The spread of efficiency may also widen as firms invest and expand capacity. Those with new plants will be at high levels of absolute efficiency compared with those with older plants, particularly where they are using marginal capacity to meet the higher levels of demand. This would tend to be the case even if technology was largely similar in the new and old plants. However, the chances are that there will be considerable embodied technical progress, and the new plants will be capable of higher efficiency than their older counterparts. These new plants will therefore push the stochastic production frontier outwards. Closure of some of the gap in efficiency between the old and new plants will therefore not be possible by the older plants. Indeed, compared with their potential, old plants may be considerably more relatively efficient, even if their absolute efficiency is lower. However, this is not a one-sided relationship, as it takes time to get up to full speed with new equipment. Indeed, in some industries it is unusual for the learning curve to have levelled off with one set of products or technology before the next is implemented. Therefore it is not only the technology but the position on the learning curve that generates the competitive advantage.

There are several possible indicators of the rate of change. In theory we could look at how fast the production frontier for the industry changes over time or we could directly measure technical change; for Phase 2 of our research this option was not open to us but future research should enable us to consider it. Work that is currently being undertaken on Phase 3 will extend this measurement of inefficiency over the period 1979–89. This should allow us to determine the extent to which the rapid increase in productivity in the UK manufacturing industry over the 1980s was due to improvements in the efficiency of continuing business relative to the prevailing best practice. However, for Phase 2 we could measure effort going into achieving such change by looking at R&D expenditures or alternatively by looking at proxy measures of output of innovation, for example, registration of patents or the number of 'significant' innovations. There are problems with both approaches. First, measuring R&D expenditure is a notoriously inaccurate indicator of innovation. Not only may the research be unsuccessful but even if research successfully generates new products or processes these in turn may not be successful in the market. In other words, R&D is a very hit-and-miss affair in the early stages, and hence the amount of effort put into innovation may not be a good measure of the amount of technical change in the industry. In addition, the technical change can spill over into other industries, with one industry's R&D leading to change elsewhere through a form of 'technological externality'. Nevertheless Griliches (1987) finds a significant contribution of R&D to productivity growth in the largest US manufacturing corporations, particulary for company- (as distinct from government-) financed R&D and for basic R&D.

R&D expenditure will vary over different industries, particularly between science-based and the more traditional industries. Some industries have much higher research expenditure than others (Buxton *et al.*, 1990), although this does not necessarily make them more innovative. In the case of pharmaceuticals, it merely reflects the fact that research in this industry is an extremely expensive process, given the need for extensive clinical trials. Nor, indeed, does it make them more competitive, as competitiveness is a relative concept. The firm or country that does best is one that discovers a new and successful product and hence, if R&D is equally effective, the one that spends more than its competitors in the *same* industry. The scale of operation is another factor affecting R&D expenditure. Schumpeter (1951) suggested that large firms will be more innovative than small firms. Large firms are able to bear the costs of R&D better than small firms, due to economies of scale. They can pool the risk involved in R&D investment by undertaking innovations in different projects, thus they are more able to bear failures. Finally, large firms with a large element of market control will be in a better position to reap the rewards of innovation.[11]

There is also considerable argument about the 'winners' curse'. The innovator is the firm that first meets the difficulties and teething problems and has to put them right. The companies that follow can learn from the innovator's mistakes, without the same expense. In some cases the main gainers may be the followers, not the innovators. However, if this expectation were true then one might ask why anyone would bother to innovate (Ray, 1984). One response is that firms have different access to information and hence differing abilities both to innovate or to follow in any one instance.

Firms may use patents to protect their innovations from competitors, hence the registration of patents can be used as a proxy measure of the output of innovations. Griliches (1990) surveys a number of studies that use patent statistics as economic indicators and concludes that in the cross-sectional dimension patent data are good indicators of inventive input and output. There are several drawbacks to using patent statistics at the individual firm level and for inter-industry comparisons. These mainly lie in the fact that not all firms obtain patents. Evidence from the US indicates that since 1940 there has been a decline in the propensity to patent innovations largely due to the legal factors involved, e.g. anti-trust legislation and the expense and difficulties of registering a patent (Comanor and Scherer, 1969). Second, patents are more commonly of products than of processes. Patenting a product is more effective because it is easier to police whether a product is being copied. In addition, products can easily be bought and copied,[12] whereas processes can be effectively protected from competitors through secrecy and security within the firm. Third, as with R&D expenditure, the propensity to patent varies between industries and also within an industry between firms of different sizes. Large firms have a lower tendency to patent as their market dominance and techno-logical superiority are often sufficient to protect their innovation, on the other hand small firms are more open to exploitation by competitors, both large and small, and will want to protect themselves by patenting. Finally, patent statistics do not reflect the 'quality' of the innovations. For example, a firm may obtain patents for various applications connected with a useful innovation. This is particularly the case in the pharmaceutical industry where the production of one drug involves a number of processes, each of which may be patented. One could look at the number of 'significant' innovations as an alternative proxy measure, but here we must question whether it is really possible to distinguish between the useful and useless.

The variable we tried in our regression analysis, on the input to R&D activity, was RSALES = R&D expenditure/sales.[13] Unfortunately, once again we were hampered from using the full data set because the classifications did not match well with the SIC. Little useful explanatory power appeared.

A similar story unfolded when we tried an 'output' measure of innovation, namely the average number of patents per industry over the years 1973–6.[14] This covered only 115 industries and was defined as:

$$\text{INNSIZE} = \frac{\text{average number of patents 1973–6}}{\text{number of establishments}[15]}$$

This worked little better than RSALES but we could not justify, on empirical grounds, the inclusion of either of these two variables in the final specification. However, patenting is more commonly used to protect innovations in some industries than others, making use of the measure difficult (Ray, 1984).

We were therefore forced to use more indirect measures of industry dynamics. The simplest was to look at the change in employment in the industry, EMP = rate of change in employment 1973–7; or change in productivity, PROD = rate of change in net output per head 1973–7. Our initial belief was that the latter would be the preferred indicator because of the strong cyclical movements that occur in productivity which are directly related to efficiency, as productivity rises in upturns and falls in the early stages of downturns. This absolute improvement and worsening could be associated with movement of plants towards or away from the frontier respectively. However, the relation, certainly at the bivariate level, was closer for EMP, with skewness, ATI and ATE all showing significant bivariate relations at the 5 per cent level. This pattern was repeated in our final preferred equations (see Appendix table). However, the relationship was positive in each case – the faster the change in employment the greater the level of inefficiency.

It is easy to provide an argument in favour of these results. Where an industry is in trouble it not only has inefficiency but a falling workforce. Therefore in this case the perceived correlation is the result of common cause (difficult conditions) rather than causation from employment change to efficiency which is the implicit structure of the model. In the LAMBDA equation, both EMP and PROD are included as it is possible to distinguish their effects. The measured industry inefficiency is only observed when some firms react much more successfully than others to the difficult conditions. Employment growth is likely to be concentrated on the more efficient in firms, which could result in an increase in the spread of measured efficiency in the industry. Inefficient behaviour by all firms in an industry, by comparison with other countries, would not be picked up by our measures.

In completing this part of the study we felt that capital would also have a role to play. Where capital/labour ratios are high there are considerable sunk costs which will inhibit change. Thus, *prima facie*, the greater the capital/labour ratio the more we might expect inefficiency to appear. We unfortunately had no clear measures of capital stock and so had to be content with investment/labour ratios:

$$\text{KINTENSE} = \frac{\text{capital expenditure} + \text{hiring and leasing of plant}}{\text{and machinery} + \text{acquisitions} - \text{disposals}}{\text{total wage bill}}$$

In four cases out of five KINTENSE did indeed have positive coefficients, but in the remaining case (σ_e) not only was the relationship much more significant, and sufficiently so to be included in the final specification on statistical grounds, but it was also of the opposite sign, i.e. a greater capital/labour ratio implies *lower* inefficiency. However, this may reflect our initial argument about the influence of technology. An industry that is increasing its efficiency rapidly will be investing more heavily or at any rate cutting surplus labour, hence increasing the capital/labour ratio. However, here again it is not clear that absolute efficiency and the spread relative to the frontier will necessarily move in this related manner.

5.5   Spatial disparities

There are two main ways in which spatial factors can have an influence on efficiency in industries. The first occurs where inputs, particularly of materials, are locally based and vary across the country. We have already discussed this in relation to agriculture and horticulture, where the quality of produce may vary considerably. This will certainly have repercussions on food manufacturing industries. Skills in different labour markets will also vary across the country. This applies not just to the direct labour input but also to bought-in services. For example, the general quality of business services may be higher in the main business centres. Thus the sheer distribution of production across the country may give an opportunity for differences in efficiency because of differences in productive conditions.

The second effect of geographical dispersion occurs through demand. If demand is very localised, or if market size is limited because of the need for freshness or closeness to the producer, as is the case for many food products and business and consumer services, then it is possible for there to be considerable variation in competitive conditions. Near-monopolies may exist in rural areas, while there may be considerable competition in the larger cities. Second, country-wide measures of competition may be misleading because they are calculated on the basis that the appropriate market definition is the whole country. The more fragmented the market the less the competitive pressures for any given national measure.

We were only able to get suitable data on the first of these two phenomena, namely the dispersion of production. The measure available from ACOP was:

GEOG = percentage of industry output concentrated in the
largest geographical production area

This variable performed moderately well in three cases, σ_e, ATI and ATE, which all exhibited the expected sign, namely the greater the geographical spread of production, the greater the level of inefficiency (the lower the efficiency). The same relation was observed for skewness but more weakly.

5.6 Managerial and organisational influences

Once we have taken into account all the other factors affecting heterogeneity of inputs, technology and products, and the competitive pressures
in the market, the main source of variation lies in how the plant is organised
and managed. Some problems of management relate to competence, which
is difficult to measure in aggregate, but others occur for structural reasons.
A simple one is that the more diverse the activities of the firm, the more
difficult it is to manage all of them very successfully; those in peripheral
industries may suffer.

This organisational problem can be replicated within an industry. If a
firm has many plants it may find it more difficult to run all of them
efficiently compared to the firm that only has one or a few plants. ACOP
provides data on enterprises as well as establishments so we were able to
incorporate the establishment/enterprise ratio (ESTENT) into the analysis.
Only in the case of σ_e was the result at all significant. As we would expect,
the sign was positive, indicating that rises in the ratio, which could also
imply increasing concentration, are correlated with rising levels of inefficiency.

5.7 The characteristics of inefficiency

Although up until now we have discussed each of the five hypotheses
separately, the model is a multivariate one and hence these factors should
be considered together. Indeed, our analysis was conducted on the full
model throughout. The discussion has been divided into the five groups
in this chapter simply to make it easier to follow. We followed the normal
procedure of starting with the most general specification and testing down
to a better specified and more parsimonious model, primarily through
zero restrictions on the co-efficients. The testing-down procedure is shown
in the Appendix table for the five inefficiency measures in turn: SIGMAE,
SKEW, ATI, LAMBDA and ATE. The form of the final preferred
equations is summarised in Table 5.6. Taking the five inefficiency measures
as a whole, factors from each of the five groups we have discussed generally
have an influence in the way we suggested. However, there are some
potentially perverse results and considerable differences between the five
inefficiency measures.

Although adjustments had to be made before estimation to account for
missing values in some of the explanatory variables and to eliminate
outliers, the resulting simple correlations together with the eventual sample
size can be seen from Table 5.7. The regressions were also corrected for

heteroscedasticity of the residuals because of the different sizes of the various industries,[16] and the results are shown in the Appendix table.

Table 5.6 Summary of multiple regression results on relation between industry characteristics and inefficiency

Exogenous variable	Endogenous variable				
	SIGMAE(σ_e)	SKEW*	ATI	ATE*	LAMBDA(λ)
CONC1	– – –	–	+	+	+
CONSQ1		– – –		–	–
SPECIAL	+ + +		+		+ + +
ENTRY	– – –	(–)			
ESTENT		(+)			
IMPORTS			– – –		–
EXPORTS		+	+ + +	+ + +	+ + +
WORKRAT	+ +	+	+	+	
GEOG	– – –	–	–	–	
KINTENSE	– – –	+ +	+		+
EMP		+	+ + +	+ + +	+
PROD	+	+			+ + +
CASES	– –	+			+

Number of pluses and minuses indicate: 1, co-efficient > standard error; 2, 10 per cent significance level; 3, 5 per cent significance level.
Parentheses indicate variable excluded from preferred regression.
* Signs are reversed for comparability.

Table 5.7 Correlation of inefficiency measures and explanatory variables

Explanatory Variables	Inefficiency Measures					
	SKEW	NEWSKEW	SIGMAE	ATI	ATE	LAMBDA
BIGNO	0.257	0.304	−0.015	−0.202	0.199	−0.137
KINTENSE	−0.083	−0.201	−0.269	−0.144	−0.150	0.051
SPECIAL	0.001	−0.055	0.100	0.133	−0.129	0.216
EMP	0.013	−0.117	0.085	0.324	−0.318	0.048
PROD	0.100	0.009	0.086	0.135	−0.144	0.185
GEOG	0.055	0.033	−0.164	−0.144	0.163	−0.079
CHANGEK	−0.075	0.029	0.021	0.075	0.077	0.036
ENTRY	0.039	0.014	−0.182	0.148	−0.141	0.030
ESTENT	−0.100	−0.052	0.126	−0.043	0.050	−0.091
IMPORTS	0.032	−0.082	−0.038	−0.144	0.146	−0.150
EXPORTS	−0.043	−0.085	−0.039	0.022	−0.017	−0.263
TRADE	0.044	0.084	0.039	−0.045	0.040	−0.272
CASES	−0.240	−0.259	−0.081	0.140	−0.122	0.141
WORKRAT	0.010	−0.017	0.169	0.155	−0.064	−0.114
n	125	125	128	63	63	60

Skewness is clearly the most difficult measure of inefficiency to explain. The closest explanation accounts for only 15 per cent of the total variation.

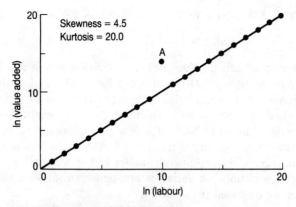

Figure 5.2 Hypothetical production relationship between value added and labour, one efficient plant (the estimated OLS relationship is: ln (value added) = 0.232 + 0.997 ln (labour)) (*source*: BIE, 1988).

Although the preferred equation includes concentration, capital intensity, change in employment, number of firms and exports, significant levels for the individual co-efficients are weak. Overall there is little source of systematic variation other than concentration, which alone explains 9 per cent of the total. The level of explanation for the remaining four measures was also low, at around 27–30 per cent. Although this is a much weaker level of explanation than in the US case (Caves and Barton, 1990b), where about half the variance was explained, in the context of cross-section analysis this is still a reasonable result. The major disappointment is that it was not possible to include measures of all the facets of the explanatory factors we identified, hence we cannot tell if those parts of the hypotheses would have been rejected.

One of the problems of the decomposed residual method of estimating inefficiency is that it requires the inefficiency to be the unusual behaviour. If, on the other hand, there are just a few efficient establishments and the bulk of the industry is inefficient, then it is this bulk of establishments that will have the major effect on the position of the production frontier and the resulting residuals will be positively skewed. This industry would then be omitted from consideration under the skewness and other decomposition measures. This is illustrated in Figure 5.2 where only case A is more efficient than the general run of firms.

In an effort to examine the information content of the set of positive skewness values, we reversed their sign and augmented the vector of original, negative skewness values.[17] Thus the measure NEWSKEW referred to in Table 5.7 is defined as:

$$\text{NEWSKEW} = \text{SKEW} \qquad \text{where } \text{SKEW} \leqslant 0$$

$$= \text{SKEW}(-1) \qquad \text{where } \text{SKEW} > 0$$

This turns skewness into another measure of inefficiency which can be estimated for all industries.[18] However, from Table 5.7 it is clear that this transformation was not particularly successful in terms of correlation with the hypothesised characteristics of inefficiency. The results from the multiple regression model of NEWSKEW are therefore not reported.[19]

The only remaining measure that covers all of the industries is σ_e. Here we were more successful (see Appendix table). In the preferred regression, imposing zero restrictions on variables not significant at least at the 10 per cent level, we obtained the equation:[20]

$\sigma_e = 0.5000$ $-$ $0.2100\ \text{KINTENSE} -$ $0.0100\ \text{ENTRY}$ $+0.0022\ \text{SPECIAL}$

$\quad(4.21)$ $\quad(-5.63)$ $\quad(-3.70)$ $\quad(1.75)$

$\quad -0.0015\ \text{CONCI}$ $\quad -0.0005\ \text{CASES} +$ $\quad 0.0024\ \text{ESTENT}$

$\quad(-2.87)$ $\quad(-1.78)$ $\quad(3.22)$

$R^2 = 0.286 \qquad n = 131$

These results show, as expected, that greater competition in the form of entry into the industry increases efficiency. The rest of the findings are more contentious. The more specialised, the less capital intensive and concentrated the industry, the smaller the number of establishments and the larger the number of establishments per enterprise, the greater the inefficiency.

The difference in the structure of the other three equations makes comparison difficult. The ATI model did not show significant relationship with KINTENSE, ENTRY, CASES or ESTENT. However, it did add EXPORTS, IMPORTS, EMP and, to a marginal extent, GEOG to the list of explanatory variables.[21] We see in this case the expected relation with respect to concentration, i.e. increasing concentration being associated with increasing inefficiency, but only up to a point. Beyond this, inefficiency falls with further increases in concentration. Additionally, this equation gave a trade relationship which appeared to be counterintuitive, with higher export ratios being associated with lower inefficiency. We argued in Section 5.2.2 that this could be related to intra-industry specialisation. However, the finding that higher import competition was associated with increased efficiency is as expected. The ATE equations (see Appendix table) were similar but with the signs reversed as the dependent variable relates to efficiency. The lambda equations confirmed the trade picture, with higher export and lower import ratios being associated with higher inefficiency. They also confirmed the association of faster growth with greater measured inefficiency, which we expected to emerge from the increased opportunity for variety in behaviour.

5.8 Summary

Taken together, the results from our final specification were promising but not without problems. We were able to explain up to 30 per cent of the variation in inefficiency by variables related to competition, product differentiation, the rate of change, spatial variation and the organisational structure of firms. Our clearest result concerned the effect of import competition leading us to conclude that greater import competition does seem to be related to lower measured technical inefficiency. In common with US and Japanese experience there does appear (from the ATI, ATE and LAMBDA results) to be a maximum to the adverse impact of concentration, after which further concentration actually decreases inefficiency. Although the spatial factor was weak in its influence it was consistent with our hypothesis, that increasing geographical spread of production is positively related to inefficiency. Unfortunately the other three main categories of influence showed some confusion in their results. However, the more rapidly changing industries do appear to be measured as more efficient.

Ironically, while having the benefit of covering the whole of the manufacturing industry, and hence being generalisable, this analysis also suffered from being comprehensive. There were more problems with data quality and compatibility than there would be with a specialised study of individual industries. Unfortunately, the Statistics of Trade Act prevented us from having information on individual firms and hence this option was not open to us. However, while our results do not come up to the quality of Førsund and Hjalmarsson (1979) in looking at individual industries they provide a first attempt to cover the whole of UK manufacturing and provide a rich source of information for further study. Comparisons between the UK and Australia (Green *et al.*, 1989) and between the US and Japan (Torii and Caves, 1992) showed that there are common elements to their experiences. In the next chapter we shall examine whether the spread of inefficiency by industry is the same across a selection of different countries.

Notes

1. The least efficient firms are likely to go out of business altogether but they will not have been caught in our sample, which normally relates to a full trading year only.
2. Public policy variables were not available for the UK study and are not discussed in this section.
3. Relevant test procedures would include tests for incorrect functional form and omitted variables (Ramsey, 1969; Anscombe, 1961), heteroscedasticity (Breusch and Pagan, 1979) and parameter stability (Chow, 1960). Some work

along these lines has been done with respect to establishment size in the US and Japanese studies discussed in Chapter 6.

4. Hannah and Kay (1977) suggested four general criteria that measures of concentration should meet:

   1. If one concentration curve lies *entirely* above another it represents a higher level of concentration.
   2. If sales are transferred from a small firm to a large firm, concentration has increased (the sales transfer principle).
   3. If firms merge concentration increases.
   4. The entry of a new firm increases the number of firms in the industry and hence decreases concentration.

5. In its general form this is a symmetric strictly concave function, given by:

$$R = \sum_i s_i^\alpha$$

where s_i is the market share of the ith firm, and α is an elasticity parameter, the value of which determines the weight given to large firms relative to small ones.

6. We are pursuing this approach in our current work which considers the behaviour of plants in the UK throughout the 1980s.

7. These data, collected by S. Toker at the London Business School, related to 116 industries over the years 1973–6.

8. This was obtained from the 1977 ACOP database.

9. These data were obtained from a major survey of advertising expenditure in 1977 by the Mirror Group.

10. These data were obtained from ACOP but unfortunately they were only available for 142 out of the 151 industries.

11. Others argue that the small firms are a major source of innovation. Our concern is merely that innovation may vary by firm size.

12. The purchase is the easy part, the reverse engineering can turn out to be impossible or even lead to a better product, a finding frequently attributed to Japanese companies.

13. Ideally one might have used some measure which 'capitalised' past R&D effort as the results of R&D take a long time to come through to the market – more than a decade in the case of pharmaceuticals (Griliches, 1987).

14. These data were supplied by Toker at the London Business School using original data collected by the Science Policy Research Unit at the University of Sussex.

15. We tried a number of other means of scaling the number of patents for the size of the industry.

16. Size was measured in terms of number of establishments not employment or value added. If the form of heteroscedasticity is different from that implied by this adjustment for size then this 'correction' may not in fact lead to an improvement in the estimates.

17. A more sophisticated approach would have been to employ the techniques for a stochastic cost frontier, in which the correct skewness of the regression residuals is positive, to derive an estimate (in per cent) for an ATE construct. The ATE construct would then have been subtracted from its maximum value (100 per cent) to derive NEWATE, an estimate for ATE in cases similar to that for the industry shown in Figure 5.2.

18. Zvi Griliches has suggested an innovative way of circumventing this problem by running the regression through an upper quantile instead of through the

mean as is conventional. This would ensure something much more akin to a genuine frontier.

19. We also explored whether the two facets of NEWSKEW had equal co-efficients by including them in a 'stacked' regression.

20. Exclusion of some of the variables with missing observations enabled us to increase the number of industries by three.

21. We also added a variable WORKRAT (the ratio of operatives to total employment in the industry) in these specifications. This acted as a measure of differences in the structure of employment not captured by the original production function.

Appendix

Explanatory variables for inefficiency measures

ADSALES	advertising expenditure/sales, 1977 (Mirror Group Publication).
BIGEMP	percentage of employment accounted for in an industry by the five largest producers, 1977.
CASES	number of establishments in the industry, 1977.
CHANGEK	rate of change in capital equipment expenditure, 1973–7.
CONC1	percentage of net output produced by the five largest producers in the industry, 1977.
CONC2	CONC1 × (1 − Imports/(Imports + Sales)), 1977.
COSIZE	CONC1 × SALES, 1977.
COVERAGE	IMPORTS/EXPORTS.
EMP	rate of change in employment, 1973–7.
ENTRANTS	average number of entrants to the industry, 1973–6 (LBS).
ENTRY	change in the number of establishments, 1973–6 (LBS).
ENTSIZE	ENTRANTS/CASES
ENT1	(ENTRANTS − EXITS)/CASES.
ENT2	(SALESENT − SALESEX)/average industry sales, 1973–6
ESTENT	ratio of establishments to enterprises, 1973–7 (LBS).
EXITS	number of exits from the industry, 1976 (LBS).
EXPORTS	value of exports/total sales, 1977 (*World Trade Statistics*).
EXSIZE	EXITS/CASES.
GEOG	percentage of output concentrated in largest geographical production area, 1977.
GROSSTRADE	(Exports + Imports)/(Sales + Imports), 1977.
IMPORTS	value of imports/total sales, 1977.
INNOV	average number of innovations (patents), 1973–6 (LBS).
INNSIZE	INNOV/CASES.
KINTENSE	capital expenditure/labour cost, 1977.
NEWTRADE	IMPORTS + EXPORTS.
NETTRADE	(Imports − Exports)/Sales, 1977.
OPWAGPH	wages of operatives per head, 1977.
OTHWAGPH	wages of non-operatives per head, 1977.
PENTS	SALESENT/average industry sales, 1973–6 (LBS).
PEXITS	SALESEX/average industry sales, 1973–6 (LBS).
PROD	rate of change in Net Output per Head (NOPH), 1973–7.
RSALES	(expenditure on research and development)/sales, 1979 (CSO *Research & Development Expenditure* Occasional Publication, RDEOP).

SALESENT	sales of entrants to the industry, 1976 (LBS).	
SALESEX	sales of exiters from the industry, 1976 (LBS).	
SIZEENT	SALESENT/ENTRANTS (LBS).	
SIZEEX	SALESEX/EXITS (LBS).	
SPECIAL	total sales of principal products/total sales of goods produced and work done.	
TRADE	IMPORTS − EXPORTS.	

Variables are from 1977 *Annual Census of Production* unless stated otherwise.

LBS indicates data supplied by S. Toker at the London Business School, from their industrial database.

Table (a) Explanations of inefficiency using SIGMAE as the dependent variable

CASES	−0.0002	−0.0002	−0.0002	−0.0002	−0.0002
	(−1.91)	(−2.03)	(−1.83)	(−1.78)	(−1.74)
CHANGEK	−0.0002				
	(−0.55)				
CONC1	−0.0039	−0.0041	−0.0019	−0.0017	−0.0017
	(−1.59)	(−1.67)	(−2.92)	(−2.73)	(−2.69)
CONCSQ	−0.0001	0.0000			
	(−0.85)	(−0.92)			
EMP	0.0753				
	(0.22)				
ENTRY	−0.0093	−0.0097	−0.0092	−0.0091	−0.0078
	(−2.53)	(−2.77)	(−2.64)	(−2.62)	(−2.30)
ESTENT	0.0012	0.0012	0.0013	0.0013	
	(1.29)	(1.36)	(1.49)	(1.46)	
EXPORTS	−0.0012	−0.0005			
	(−0.76)	(−0.78)			
GEOG	−0.0018	−0.0017	−0.0019	−0.0018	−0.0016
	(−2.14)	(−2.11)	(−2.28)	(−2.23)	(−2.00)
IMPORTS	0.0060				
	(0.52)				
KINTENSE	−0.1800	−0.1740	−0.1658	−0.1711	0.1803
	(−3.60)	(−3.65)	(3.53)	(−3.65)	(−3.86)
PROD	0.2276	0.2384	0.2351		
	(1.08)	(1.16)	(1.23)		
SPECIAL	0.0041	0.0041	0.0036	0.0035	0.0040
	(2.42)	(2.43)	(2.22)	(2.14)	(2.52)
WORKRAT	0.1344	0.1298	0.1197	0.1122	0.1267
	(1.86)	(1.89)	(1.76)	(1.65)	(1.88)
Constant	0.3322	0.3279	0.3130	0.3779	0.3186
	(1.77)	(1.80)	(1.73)	(2.18)	(1.88)
R^2	0.2867	0.2833	0.2736	0.2643	0.2512
ADJR^2	0.2054	0.2154	0.2183	0.2148	0.2075
DF	113	116	118	119	120

t-values shown in parentheses.
  Multiple regression estimates include adjustment for heteroscedasticity.
  DF indicates degrees of freedom.
  ADJR^2 indicates adjusted R^2.

Table (b) Explanations of inefficiency using SKEW as the dependent variable

CASES	−0.0001	−0.0006	−0.0006	−0.0005	−0.0006	−0.0006
	(−1.36)	(−1.52)	(−1.53)	(−1.45)	(−1.67)	(−1.59)
CHANGEK	−0.0008	−0.0008				
	(−0.59)	(−0.61)				
CONC1	0.0083	0.0042	0.0045	0.0043	0.0034	0.0041
	(0.81)	(1.62)	(1.77)	(1.72)	(1.42)	(1.70)
CONCSQ	−0.0004					
	(−0.41)					
EMP	−1.8105	−1.8582	−1.8169	−1.6771	−2.0801	
	(−1.34)	(−1.39)	(−1.38)	(−1.29)	(−1.65)	
ENTRY	0.0165	0.0157	0.0135			
	(1.15)	(1.12)	(0.99)			
ESTENT	−0.0032	−0.0032	−0.0035	−0.0025		
	(−0.90)	(−0.90)	(−1.03)	(−0.77)		
EXPORTS	−0.0029	−0.0031	−0.0032	−0.0032	−0.0031	
	(−0.47)	(−1.22)	(−1.26)	(−1.27)	(−1.24)	
GEOG	0.0040	0.0041	0.0042	0.0038		
	(1.17)	(1.25)	(1.30)	(1.19)		
IMPORTS	−0.0027					
	(−0.06)					
KINTENSE	−0.0277	−0.0291	−0.0268	−0.0258	−0.0202	−0.0161
	(−1.94)	(−2.12)	(−2.04)	(−1.98)	(−1.63)	(−1.32)
PROD	−0.6250	−0.6411	−0.5486			
	(−0.76)	(−0.79)	(−0.69)			
SPECIAL	−0.0034	−0.0028				
	(−0.51)	(−0.43)				
WORKRAT	−0.3202	−0.3058	−0.2858	−0.2698		
	(−1.14)	(−1.12)	(−1.09)	(−1.03)		
Constant	−0.1095	−0.0718	−0.4109	−0.5137	−0.5304	−0.6111
	(−0.15)	(−1.00)	(−1.26)	(−1.77)	(−2.57)	(−3.06)
R^2	0.1818	0.1805	0.1766	0.1659	0.1454	0.1202
ADJR^2	0.0777	0.0927	0.1043	0.1083	0.1095	0.0984
DF	110	112	114	116	119	121

t-values shown in parentheses.
  Multiple regression estimates include adjustment for heteroscedasticity.
  DF indicates degrees of freedom.
  ADJR^2 indicates adjusted R^2.

Table (c) Explanations of inefficiency using ATI as the dependent variable

CASES	0.0001	0.0001	0.0001			
	(0.73)	(0.79)	(0.72)			
CHANGEK	0.0001					
	(0.00)					
CONC1	0.0046	0.0047	0.0042	0.0029		
	(1.46)	(1.56)	(1.44)	(1.21)		
CONCSQ	−0.0004	−0.0005	−0.0004	−0.0003	−0.0001	−0.0001
	(−1.76)	(−1.84)	(−1.75)	(−1.60)	(−1.60)	(−2.04)
EMP	1.0009	1.0063	1.0528	0.9363	0.9897	1.0030
	(2.68)	(2.75)	(2.96)	(2.79)	(2.95)	(3.07)
ENTRY	0.0021	0.0022				
	(0.58)	(0.63)				
ESTENT	−0.0005	−0.0006				
	(−0.72)	(−0.73)				
EXPORTS	0.0037	0.0038	0.0040	0.0035	0.0039	0.0040
	(2.29)	(2.43)	(2.61)	(2.47)	(2.83)	(2.89)
GEOG	−0.0011	−0.0012	−0.0013	−0.0012		
	(−1.13)	(−1.25)	(−1.42)	(−1.35)		
IMPORTS	−0.0289	−0.0298	−0.0309	−0.0278	−0.0297	−0.0297
	(−2.25)	(−2.46)	(−2.60)	(−2.51)	(−2.73)	(−2.73)
KINTENSE	0.0045	0.0047	0.0050			
	(0.90)	(1.02)	(1.08)			
PROD	0.0852					
	(0.31)					
SPECIAL	0.0026	0.0026	0.0024	0.0024	0.0025	
	(1.45)	(1.45)	(1.56)	(1.52)	(1.55)	
WORKRAT	0.1451	0.1504	0.1432	0.0966	0.0746	
	(1.57)	(1.69)	(1.70)	(1.30)	(1.02)	
Constant	−0.0820	−0.0671	−0.0366	0.0779	0.1045	0.3711
	(−0.35)	(−0.31)	(−0.18)	(0.45)	(0.62)	(18.18)
R^2	0.3600	0.3586	0.3492	0.3299	0.2965	0.2641
ADJR^2	0.1773	0.2047	0.2240	0.2306	0.2211	0.2134
DF	48	50	52	54	56	58

t-values shown in parentheses.
  Multiple regression estimates include adjustment for heteroscedasticity.
  DF indicates degrees of freedom.
  ADJR^2 indicates adjusted R^2.

152 Inefficiency in industry

Table (d) Explanations of inefficiency using LAMBDA as the dependent variable

CASES	0.0028	0.0028	0.0028	0.0023			
	(1.03)	(1.13)	(1.12)	(0.96)			
CHANGEK	0.0063	0.0060	0.0059				
	(0.96)	(0.96)	(0.97)				
CONC1	0.0717	0.0751	0.0705	0.0664	0.0454		
	(1.38)	(1.52)	(1.46)	(1.39)	(1.07)		
CONCSQ	-0.0006	-0.0007	-0.0006	-0.0006	-0.0005	-0.0001	
	(-1.45)	(-1.61)	(-1.58)	(-1.53)	(-1.48)	(-1.26)	
EMP	7.6210	7.5042	7.9716	8.4512	5.9108	5.9212	
	(1.19)	(1.20)	(1.32)	(1.40)	(1.07)	(1.07)	
ENTRY	0.0139	0.0129					
	(0.23)	(0.21)					
ESTENT	-0.0100	-0.0101					
	(-0.74)	(-0.81)					
EXPORTS	0.0528	0.0521	0.0564	0.0542	0.0471	0.0313	0.0269
	(1.95)	(1.99)	(2.23)	(2.15)	(2.03)	(2.45)	(2.18)
GEOG	0.0037						
	(0.21)						
IMPORTS	-0.2045	-0.2029	-0.2263	-0.2020	-0.1609		
	(-0.96)	(-0.97)	(-1.11)	(-1.00)	(-0.86)		
KINTENSE	0.0795	0.0863	0.0938	0.0664			
	(0.93)	(1.14)	(1.27)	(0.97)			
PROD	8.5104	8.2000	8.0181	7.2249	7.7942	8.8829	8.5545
	(1.83)	(1.85)	(1.85)	(1.70)	(1.85)	(2.18)	(2.11)
SPECIAL	0.0342	0.0364	0.0322	0.0330	0.0395	0.0416	0.0475
	(1.11)	(1.35)	(1.29)	(1.32)	(1.62)	(1.72)	(2.04)
WORKRAT	-0.3295						
	(-0.21)						
Constant	-5.3618	-5.6717	-5.1552	-4.5093	-3.8502	-3.2241	-4.0621
	(-1.31)	(-1.61)	(-1.87)	(-1.68)	(-1.48)	(-1.30)	(-1.70)
R^2	0.2908	0.2896	0.2797	0.2658	0.2406	0.2155	0.1738
ADJR^2	0.0702	0.1082	0.1326	0.1337	0.1384	0.1429	0.1295
DF	45	47	49	51	52	54	56

t-values shown in parentheses.
  Multiple regression estimates include adjustment for heteroscedasticity.
  DF indicates degrees of freedom.
  ADJR^2 indicates adjusted R^2.

Table (e) Explanations of inefficiency using ATE as the dependent variable

CASES	−0.0001	−0.0001				
	(−0.58)	(−0.64)				
CHANGEK	0.0000					
	(0.008)					
CONC1	−0.0039	−0.0041	−0.0029	−0.0027		
	(−1.47)	(−1.58)	(−1.44)	(−1.36)		
CONCSQ	0.0004	0.0004	0.0003	0.0003	0.0001	0.0001
	(1.80)	(1.90)	(1.77)	(1.76)	(1.58)	(2.03)
EMP	−0.8170	−0.8223	−0.8537	−0.7673	−0.8838	−0.8361
	(−2.57)	(−2.64)	(−2.82)	(−2.69)	(−3.14)	(−2.99)
ENTRY	−0.0017	−0.0017				
	(−0.55)	(−0.59)				
ESTENT	0.0005	0.0005	0.0003			
	(0.75)	(0.76)	(0.58)			
EXPORTS	−0.0030	−0.0031	−0.0032	−0.0029	−0.0034	−0.0033
	(−2.17)	(−2.31)	(−2.42)	(−2.36)	(−2.88)	(−2.83)
GEOG	0.0011	0.0012	0.0012	0.0012		
	(1.32)	(1.46)	(1.53)	(1.58)		
IMPORTS	0.0238	0.0248	0.0259	0.0231	0.0259	0.0251
	(2.18)	(2.40)	(2.57)	(2.45)	(2.78)	(2.69)
KINTENSE	−0.0035	−0.0037	−0.0036			
	(−0.82)	(−0.94)	(−0.94)			
PROD	−0.0861					
	(−0.37)					
SPECIAL	−0.0026	−0.0022	−0.0024	−0.0020	−0.0015	
	(−1.46)	(−1.46)	(−1.69)	(−1.50)	(−1.19)	
WORKRAT	−0.1263	−0.1317	−0.1286	−0.0884		
	(−1.60)	(−1.74)	(1.76)	(1.40)		
Constant	1.0457	1.0310	1.0072	0.9160	0.7994	0.6650
	(5.28)	(5.49)	(5.84)	(6.17)	(7.01)	(38.05)
R^2	0.3604	0.3850	0.3492	0.3337	0.2752	0.2571
ADJR^2	0.1739	0.2045	0.2240	0.2350	0.2116	0.2059
DF	48	50	52	54	57	58

t-values shown in parentheses.
  Multiple regression estimates include adjustment for heteroscedasticity.
  DF indicates degrees of freedom.
  ADJR^2 indicates adjusted R^2.

6

International comparisons

So far we have only compared results for inefficiency in manufacturing industry in the UK and Australia. We now address two further questions. Is the pattern of relative efficiency repeated in other countries? Are other aspects of efficiency in the UK and Australia revealed by foreign experiences?

6.1 Absolute comparisons

In Chapter 1 we showed that overall labour productivity in Australia was 17 per cent higher than in the UK in 1977. In manufacturing the difference was larger, 31 per cent.[1] Table 6.1 presents this same comparison for a wider range of countries, this highlights the poor performance of UK manufacturing in the second half of the 1970s.

Table 6.1 Manufacturing productivity comparisons with the UK, 1977

Source	Country	Productivity measure	UK = 100
Haig (1987)	Australia	Output per person hour	132
van Ark (1990b)	France	Output per person hour	142
O'Mahony (1992)	Germany	Output per person hour	146
van Ark (1990a)	Netherlands	Output per person hour	169
van Ark (1992)	US	Value added per hour worked	172

Comparison with the US and Germany is for 1977; comparison with France and Netherlands is for 1979; comparison with Australia is for 1974.

Disaggregating further, these studies were able to compare individual industry classes (at the two-digit level in the Standard Industrial Classification). With the exception of only the French chemicals industry and the Australian food, drink and tobacco industry, British industries'

154

productivity were below that of their corresponding foreign counterparts. In particular the figures for paper products show a surprisingly large difference.

Table 6.2 Productivity comparisons between some major groups of manufacturing products in the 1980s (UK = 100)

	Australia	France	Germany	Netherlands	US
Food, drink and tobacco	99	127	107	156	226
Textiles and clothing	102	121	116[g]	164[a]	174[a]
Leather and footwear	–	122	96[h]		
Paper products	–	208	185	325	–
Printing and publishing	–	112	–	134	–
Basic metals	158[b]	132[b]	111	204	187[b]
Metal products		131	144		
Machinery	–	157[d]	135	139	140[c]
Transport equipment	–	141	115	–	
Electrical engineering	–	102	130	–	
Chemicals, rubber and plastic products	160[f]	113	95[f] 120[i]	170	138[e]

Data years vary between studies – US (1982), Australia (1983), France and Netherlands (1984) and Germany (1987).
[a] Textiles, clothing, footwear and leather.
[b] Basic metals and metal products.
[c] Machinery, electrical engineering and transport equipment.
[d] Mechanical engineering and transport equipment.
[e] Chemicals, petroleum, rubber and plastic products.
[f] Chemicals.
[g] Clothing, footwear and leather.
[h] Textiles.
[i] Rubber, plastics and other manufacturing.

Although, the figures in the tables relate to productivity not 'efficiency', it is possible to use these productivity figures as a measure of the actual levels of efficiency achieved, in the sense that they show the output that has been achieved per unit of labour input. In the two tables productivity tends to be defined as net output or value added per head (or per worker hour). This represents an attempt to define a standard unit of input but it neglects the capital input altogether and there is substantial argument in favour of measures of total factor productivity (O'Mahony and Oulton, 1989).

Making these comparisons across the countries is subject to a raft of well-known drawbacks. First of all, because published sources give data on nominal value added, for comparison between countries these need to be converted into a common currency. This sort of productivity comparison is both controversial and difficult because it involves information on the relative prices of products. A number of alternative methods have been used by researchers to construct relative prices, which when used on

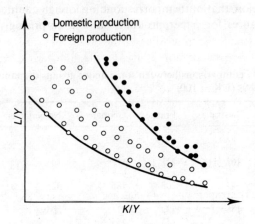

Figure 6.1 Comparing inefficiency across countries

identical data give differing results. The first uses information on quantities and sales of a range of manufactured products to estimate their unit values in both countries, examples of this method include O'Mahony (1992) and van Ark (1990a, 1990b). These 'unit value ratios' are then weighted to reflect the importance of products in matched sales at the industry level and the importance of each industry in total manufacturing. These 'matched product' price ratios are then assumed to be representative of 'non-matched product' price ratios within each industry. This method gives price ratios closely reflecting producer prices. The second alternative is to use purchasing power parity prices (PPP) (Summers and Heston, 1988). PPPs are measures of relative retail prices, thus they differ from producer prices in that they exclude prices of semi-finished products and exports but include the prices of imported goods. A third possibility is to use the official exchange rate, however this is the most unreliable method as it is affected by short-term capital movements.

Although the studies in Tables 6.1 and 6.2 use a benchmark and are measuring the productivity of one country relative to another, they are, to some extent, a measure of absolute efficiency because they compare productivity levels between industries rather than within them. However, this begs a whole range of further questions about comparability as these data do not stem from matched samples of firms but from industry averages.

Illustrating this diagrammatically (Figure 6.1) the industry in the home country may appear to have low inefficiency because there is little divergence of production away from its production frontier (in this case the combined residual, of random variation and inefficiency, will have a small tail). However, compared to a competitor abroad it can be inefficient if the competitor's production frontier is well 'above' that of the home industry. Figure 6.1 shows the frontier as an isoquant so that the focus is not on the impact of scale. Frontiers nearer the origin require fewer inputs per unit of output and are hence more efficient in absolute terms. Moreover, Figure 6.1 indicates that a study measuring efficiency in the foreign country alone would show this industry to be highly *in*efficient as production within the industry is spread away from its frontier (in this case the combined residual will have a long tail).

6.2 Matched industry studies

Table 6.3 Productivity comparisons from matched industry studies (UK = 100)

Source	Country	Industry	Average productivity
Daly *et al.* (1985)	Germany	Metal-working	163
Steedman and Wagner (1987)	Germany	Kitchen furniture	230
Steedman and Wagner (1989)	Germany	Clothing	140
Mason *et al.* (1993)[a]	Netherlands	Biscuits	125
	Germany		140
	France		120

Matched plant studies were conducted in: 1983–4 (Daly *et al.*, 1985), 1986–7 (Steedman and Wagner, 1987), 1986 (Steedman and Wagner, 1989) and 1989–91 (Mason *et al.*, 1993).
[a] Measures of productivity are 'quality adjusted' output per employee hour.

Table 6.3 shows the matched industry comparative studies for selected manufacturing industries. In all cases the British plants sampled were less productive than their counterparts abroad. This is consistent with the aggregate studies although on the whole the results from the matched studies suggest a greater differential in labour productivity. For example, the matched plant study of the clothing industry found German productivity to be 40 per cent greater than in the UK (Steedman and Wagner, 1989), whereas using aggregate data the differential was only 16 per cent (O'Mahony, 1992). To a large extent this is caused by the limited number of plants selected to represent the industry and therefore not too much weight can be placed in these measures. However, the advantage of these matched plant studies is that they enable the researcher to look further into the causes of productivity differences. To a large extent these studies have attributed this to inadequate training in British manufacturing industries.

The Bureau of Industry Economics in Canberra has conducted even more closely matched research by considering plants in different countries within the same firm (BIE, 1990, 1991a). These covered South Australian Brewing Holdings Ltd (SABH) water heaters and Kodak paper finishing. In the case of paper finishing (Figure 6.2) the difference between the UK

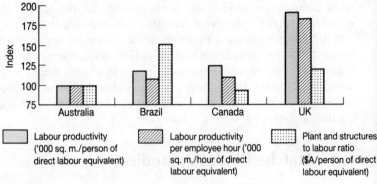

Figure 6.2 Labour productivity (*source*: BIE, 1990).

and Australia in labour productivity is striking. Indeed, Australia comes off worst of all four countries studied. However, the advantage is exaggerated, as the British plant was able to operate at a more efficient scale and not have to reset machines for different batches so frequently. Even after allowing for the difference in wage rates, the labour cost per unit of output was clearly lower in the UK than Australia (Figure 6.3). A number of factors leading to this are cited (BIE, 1990) including demarcation between production and maintenance workers, more limited skills and training, inhibition of change by trade unions and ineffective use of machines. A range of changes including teamwork might improve both productivity and motivation. In the case of water heaters there was a noticeable difference between the two Australian plants, with that in Sydney experiencing a much wider range of problems than its smaller Melbourne counterpart (BIE, 1991a). Industrial relations at the Sydney plant were characterised by suspicion and conflict. 'Unproductive hours'

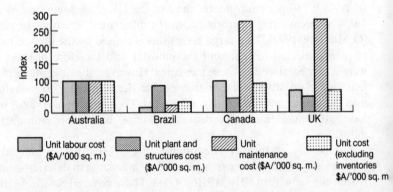

Figure 6.3 Unit cost indices for labour, capital, maintenance and total (*source*: BIE, 1990).

alone account for 25 per cent of the shortfall in productivity compared with the US.

All these suggestions would have been made for the UK plant as well in the 1970s, and one of the interesting features of the conclusion in BIE (1990) is that it cites the ability of the British plant to have made the changes as an indicator of what could be achieved in Australia.

6.3 Relative measurements

It is often argued, not least by the firms themselves, that the best British companies are world class and able to compete on an equal basis with other companies around the world. Such companies include ICI, parts of British Aerospace, Glaxo, leading financial institutions, conglomerates like Hanson, the food and drink majors, BP, etc. (Porter, 1990). There are two possible reasons why average labour productivity in the UK is so low. First, we have slightly lower labour costs, so competitiveness is achievable with greater use of labour. Second, there is a much longer tail of inefficient firms. Although largely supported by the detailed matched plant studies, other international studies have found that, on average, inefficiency within British manufacturing industries differs little to that in other countries (Table 6.4).

Table 6.4 Estimates of technical efficiency

Source	Country	Year	Technical efficiency (%)	Level of disaggregation[d]
Harris	Australia	1977	76(VA), 91(GO)	4
Lee and Tyler	Brazil	1971	63	
Corbo and de Melo[a]	Chile	1967	72–81	
Tyler and Lee[b]	Colombia	1974	55–99	
Meeusen and van den Broeck[c]	France	1962	71–94	2
Uekusa and Torii	Japan	1977	70(VA/L)	4
Yoo	Korea	1977	67(VA/L) 78(GO/N)	4
Green and Mayes	UK	1977	65(VA)	4
Caves and Barton	US	1977	63(VA/L) 88(GO/N)	4

[a] Efficiency estimated in 43 manufacturing industries.
[b] Efficiency measures for a sample of five industries: food products, apparel, footwear, furniture and metal products.
[c] Efficiency measures for ten French manufacturing industries: glass products, milk products, textiles, machine construction and mechanical tools, electrical machinery, vehicles and cycles, industrial chemicals, paper, footwear, sugar works, distillery and beverages.
[d] Equivalent disaggregation to digit level of Australian Industrial Classification.
(.): Dependent variable.
Lee and Tyler (1978), Tyler and Lee (1979) and Meeusen and van den Broeck (1977) use a stochastic Cobb–Douglas production frontier.

Measurement of relative efficiency aims to tackle the latter point by looking at the performance of the actual establishments that make up manufacturing industry. Thus we can understand more about the structure of countries' and industries and how this contributes to their performance relative to foreign competitors.

Studies like our own have been carried out in several countries, for example France (Meeusen and van den Broeck, 1977), Brazil (Lee and Tyler, 1978) and Chile (Corbo and de Melo, 1983). Many have used differing assumptions for the structure of the production function, the distribution of the inefficiency component of the residual, etc. Our studies were part of an international project involving researchers in the US, Japan, Korea and Canada (Caves, 1992b). The one main advantage of such a project was that a single general strategy could be adopted by the researchers. First, a common year for analysis was chosen by all the researchers (1977 or 1978). Second, with one exception, namely Canada, all the researchers used the stochastic frontier production function model, opting for the translog production function. In choosing an assumption for the distribution of the inefficiency component of the residuals the researchers opted for a half-normal distribution.

Table 6.4 shows estimates of technical efficiency for a number of countries. With one clear exception the estimates of average technical efficiency lie in the range 60–90 per cent of the 'maximum' attainable in the various countries for each industry.[3] The UK results are fairly typical, but those for Australia are rather better than average, implying a smaller tail of inefficiency. However, as these studies use both Cobb–Douglas and translog production functions, care has to be taken in making comparisons. Furthermore, the measures from France and Colombia are based on a sample of industries rather than on the whole of manufacturing industry. The degree of disaggregation also varies. The broader the classification, the more variable behaviour is likely to be in the 'industry' as it increases the chance that using a single production function is inappropriate, thus confusing product heterogeneity with inefficiency.

It is interesting to compare these results on inefficiency with those on differences in labour productivity based on more aggregate data. In comparison with French productivity levels British industry lagged by 30 per cent in the late 1970s (van Ark, 1990a, 1990b). However, the measures shown in Table 6.4 indicate that within industry the extent of technical efficiency in the UK was not that much lower than in France. Similarly Anglo-American productivity comparisons showed that value added per hour worked in British manufacturing industry was only 58 per cent of the corresponding American level in 1977. Furthermore, only a small percentage of this difference could be attributed to the lower capital intensity in the UK (van Ark, 1992). On the other hand, the results on inefficiency from establishment data (Caves and Barton, 1990b) showed no difference between the extent of technical efficiency in British and American industry on the basis of one of the two measures, while with value added per unit of labour input as the dependent variable American efficiency was estimated at only 28 per cent, less than half that of the UK using value added.

Table 6.5 Technical efficiency estimates for individual industries

Country	Year	Industry	Efficiency (%)
Colombia	1974	Apparel	55
		Footwear	56
		Food	64
		Furniture	98
		Metal products	99
France	1962	Glass products	94
		Milk products	93
		Textiles	91
		Machine construction & mechanical tools	90
		Electrical machinery	86
		Vehicles & cycles	82
		Industrial chemicals	79
		Paper	79
		Footwear	· 76
		Sugar works, distillery & beverages	71
Ghana	1972	Logging	71(LP), 92(OLS)
		Sawn-timber	71(LP), 90(OLS)
		Furniture	74(LP), 94(OLS)
USSR	1974	Cotton refining	93
Sweden	1973	Dairy	65

(LP) using linear programming production function; (OLS) using the residuals of OLS estimates.

Note also that the interpretation of the results varies with the width of coverage as explained for Table 6.4.

Due to the enormous task of handling datasets covering the whole of a country's manufacturing sector other estimates of technical efficiency using establishment data have concentrated on specific industries, for example, the Swedish dairy industry (Førsund and Hjalmarsson, 1979), the Ghanaian logging, sawn timber and furniture industries (Page, 1980), USSR cotton refining (Danilin et al., 1985), ten French industries (Meeusen and van den Broeck, 1977) and five Colombian industries (Tyler and Lee, 1979), the results from these studies are given in Table 6.5.[4] The choice of specific industries has allowed researchers to minimise the effects of heterogeneity by estimating efficiency for those industries where establishments show little differences in output type, product mix and quality. Moreover, the use of a limited dataset has enabled estimates of efficiency to be extended over a period of time to examine the change in industries' productivity. Over the period 1964 to 1973 Førsund and Hjalmarsson found that the gap between best-practice and average performance of

Swedish dairy producers showed an increasing trend, which could be partly explained by rapid technical progress.

6.4 Lessons to be learnt from the international project

6.4.1 Japan, Korea and the US

Throughout this book we have talked about the international project of which the UK and Australia were participants, we now look at what can be learnt from the results obtained by the other researchers. All countries apart from Canada attempted to match each other's methods as far as possible although, as Table 6.6 indicates, there were some differences in the success rates, in particular that of the US and, to a lesser extent Australia, who were able to cleanse their data thoroughly. In comparison to the other countries, the UK's experience was not abnormal.

Table 6.6 Numbers of industries and rates of success in estimating stochastic frontier production functions

| Country | Industries analysed | Estimation failures | | Successes |
		Case (1)	Case (2)	
Australia	140	49	0	91
	100%	35%	0%	65%
Japan	351	86	121	144
	100%	25%	34%	41%
Korea*	242	85	29	128
	100%	35%	12%	53%
United Kingdom	151	48	31	72
	100%	32%	20%	48%
United States	434	87	0	347
	100%	20%	0%	80%

Source: Caves (1992a, b).
Some studies report alternative estimations; the one chosen here involves the deletion of outliers, inclusion of control variables, and use of corrected ordinary least squares estimation. * indicates based on gross output per employee. Other countries based on value added per unit of labour input (denominator varies).

The major difference in the results was in the extent of case (2) failures. Through data cleansing, the US and Australia were able to eliminate it, however, amongst the other countries the proportions of case (2) failures were similar. It is not known exactly how varying proportions of case (2) failures affect measures of efficiency. Truncation resulting from this failure may bias the measures as the excluded cases could have a more extreme distribution of inefficiency.

The extent of case (1) failure varied to a lesser extent between the studies. However, these too can cause biases in overall estimators and obviously prevent full use of the dataset. Torii (1992b) suggests that as long as the speed of replacement investment is finite, some positive level of technical inefficiency is inevitable, and therefore one should not observe such high, if any, levels of case (1) failures. He employs a method that uses maximum likelihood estimators to obtain efficiency indexes and avoids case (1) failures. However, it is well known that maximum likelihood estimators show a local maximum when the inefficiency component is set at zero for a distribution of residuals for the wrong skew (Olson *et al.*, 1980). This procedure is therefore similar to reporting zero inefficiency rather than a case (1) failure.

The most important question from many points of view is 'Does British and Australian industry exhibit different levels of efficiency compared with their competitors?' As is clear from Table 6.7, which shows mean levels of four efficiency measures – ATE, ATI, skewness and lambda – substantial inefficiency was present in all the countries and it appeared that the average extent of inefficiency did not vary to any great extent between them. As not all countries estimated measures using both value added and gross output as the dependent variable, for the purpose of comparison we focus on the former. First, average technical efficiency derived from the value added frontiers is highest in Australia, well in front of the UK and US for example. As the absolute measures of efficiency imply highest efficiency in the US, followed by Australia and the UK (Table 6.1), this suggests that there is no simple relationship between a country's absolute efficiency and technical efficiency on average within a given industry sector. Second, excluding Australia, there is a remarkable similarity between average technical efficiencies derived from the value added frontiers in the other countries, which range from 63 per cent for the US to 70 per cent for Japan. Third, the estimates for average technical efficiency derived from the gross output frontiers are higher on average than those derived from the value added frontiers. However, the ranking by country for countries with data for both measures is different for each measure, with the US and Korea swapping places behind Australia. Fourth, the UK does not stand out in any way. Thus it is difficult to sustain the argument of the longer tail of UK inefficiency as opposed to simply that of absolute efficiency. Fifth, the measures tell a similar, but not identical, story.

Although the various measures of inefficiency are clearly related (Table 6.8), nevertheless there is considerable variation across them for each country. Some points can be made from this correlation comparison. As implied by the algebra,[5] there was strong correlation between ATE and ATI in all countries, except Korea, using value added as the dependent variable.[6] There was also strong correlation between lambda and skewness in most countries, the exception being Japan. However, correlation

Table 6.7 Means and standard deviations of the measures of technical efficiency

	US	Japan	Korea	UK	Australia[1]
ATE(VA)	0.632	0.699	0.672	0.646	0.756
	(0.133)	(0.095)	(0.089)	(0.125)	(0.120)
ATE(GO)	0.881	–	0.783	–	0.912
	(0.053)		(0.075)		(0.076)
ATI(VA)	0.190	0.210	0.680	0.390	0.336
	(0.078)		(0.189)	(0.141)	(0.188)
ATI(GO)	0.013	–	0.032	–	0.126
	(0.006)		(0.014)		(0.114)
LAMBDA(VA)	0.808	3.48	2.552	2.880	13.409
	(0.321)	(8.280)	(6.233)	(3.578)	(55.862)
LAMBDA(GO)	0.599	–	1.849	–	1.292
	(0.308)		(1.310)		(1.658)
SKEW(VA)	−0.717	−0.723	−0.280	−0.424	−0.120
	(0.922)	(1.107)	(0.646)	(0.879)	(0.371)
SKEW(GO)	0.113	–	−0.265	–	0.212
	(0.689)		(0.785)		(0.462)

[1] Assuming the inefficiency component is truncated-normally distributed.

(VA) Dependent variable is based on value added; (GO) Dependent variable is based on gross output; standard deviations in parentheses.

Table 6.8 Correlation matrix

	ATE,ATI	ATE,λ	ATE,SKEW	ATI,λ	ATI,SKEW	λ,SKEW
US	−0.959	−0.681	0.848	0.728	−0.864	−0.866
	(−0.996)	(−0.301)	(0.512)	(0.364)	(−0.555)	(−0.888)
Japan	−0.991	−0.475	0.740	0.285	−0.726	−0.416
Korea	−0.351	−0.853	0.853	0.332	−0.332	−1.000
	(−0.989)	(−0.758)	(0.758)	(0.748)	(−0.748)	(−1.000)
UK	−0.990	−0.470	0.770	0.480	−0.770	−0.780

Figures in parentheses indicate the correlation between measures when the dependent variable is based on gross output, all others based on value added.

Correlations refer only to industries where both measures can be estimated.

between other pairs of measures was variable and on the whole poor. It is thus difficult to draw comparisons across different measures and we restrict our remarks to those measures which are common to the studies.

Despite attempts to make the studies as comparable as possible, differences remained between them. It is interesting to look into these as lessons can be learnt from the different methods used.

The first main difference was in the definition of the dependent variable. All five country studies used a dependent variable based on value added (VA or VA/L), however in addition the US, Korea and Australia used a gross output based variable (GO or GO/N). Results with the latter variable appeared to be more variable and measures of skewness in Australia and the US were, on average, of the 'wrong' sign using a gross output based dependent variable. In BIE (1988) the Australians argue in favour of the value added approach, as gross output and material inputs are both likely to be determined within the year in question and the resulting simultaneity could lead to inconsistent OLS estimates. Therefore the decision made in the UK to deal with value added alone is unlikely to be particularly misleading. However, the lack of relationship between the ATE(VA) and ATE(GO) measures for Australia with a truncated normal/normal error structure is surprisingly comprehensive, although there is a linear relation between ATI(VA) and ATI(GO) (and the ATE equivalents), with a half normal/normal error structure (Harris, 1992).

The second difference was in the extent to which researchers were able to 'cleanse' the data. The American researchers, like the Australians, successfully eliminated case (2) failures by cleansing the data thoroughly. They were able to estimate technical (in)efficiency for up to 347 four-digit American manufacturing industries with value added per unit of labour input as the dependent variable, but for only 191 industries using gross output per employee. However, the elimination of case (2) failures was not the main reason for cleansing in the Australian study. It was largely a fortuitous result. The principal motivation was the elimination of doubtful capital stock estimates and values imputed by the Australian Bureau of Statistics for missing observations. In Japan researchers were unable to cleanse the data to the extent of the US and Australia. Their success rate was the lowest of all countries – only 41 per cent, with 25 per cent and 34 per cent, respectively, of case (1) and case (2) failures. Despite such a high failure rate they were still able to decompose the residuals for up to 144 industries, although this larger number reflects the finer disaggregation of industries used by the Japanese team. In Korea the residuals could be successfully decomposed for 128 industries (53 per cent). Cleansing the data appeared to have a major effect on the results. In the UK our weaker success does imply that our cleansing methods, although careful, would have possibly benefited from a relaxation of the time and resource constraints to which we were subject. However, some of the problem may have been due to the considerable approximation used in the estimation of the stock of capital.

Comparing the correlation between the other measures there was a fair degree of variation between the countries. The correlation between the lambda and skewness measures is around 0.8 or higher; low correlation will occur when case (2) failures are incorporated into the analysis with a zero value, as for Japan where the case (2) failure rate was as high as 34 per cent.

6.4.2 *Canada*

The Canadian study was unable to compute the stochastic frontier production function due to a lack of data on plant-level capital stocks. Instead Baldwin used a simpler measurement technique (Timmer, 1971). This method used establishment level data on output per person. Baldwin assumed that the frontier of efficient behaviour could be derived from the most productive establishments in an industry; this approach is different to estimating a frontier from a production function. He thus defined the efficient level of output per person as the sum of output divided by the sum of all employment in the most productive establishments accounting for a specific percentage of total output (10 to 40 per cent). Efficiency was then measured as the ratio of actual output to potential output, where potential output was calculated as the efficient level of output per person multiplied by the level of employment in each establishment, summed over all producing establishments.

The advantage of this technique is that it includes scale inefficiency (inefficiency due to suboptimal-sized plants) and inefficiency due to non-optimal factor proportions, whereas estimates of technical inefficiency do not include these influences, as in using a production function.

By concentrating on output per person Baldwin's method implicitly assumes that this is what firms aim to maximise and that the best in the industry will set the standard which other firms should follow. On the other hand, it could be argued that different factor proportions within an industry are optimal because of differences in factor prices, for example. We have explicitly excluded this form of *allocative* inefficiency primarily because we do not have the appropriate price and cost data to estimate it. Unfortunately there are no other suitable studies against which to compare these Canadian measures, although we are beginning some similar work for the UK.

The Canadians considered the efficiency distribution of industries in the years 1970 and 1979. In 1970 the industries in the tenth percentile, i.e. the most efficient 10 per cent, had an efficiency ratio of 77 per cent, whereas those in the ninetieth percentile, i.e. the least efficient, had a ratio of 53 per cent. These results are very similar to the range of inefficiency measures calculated from the stochastic frontier approach for the other countries. It will be interesting to see the results from the current British study when both methods are used on the same data.

6.5   Change in efficiency over time

As the Canadian study measured efficiency over a period of time they were able to show that interindustry differences in efficiency change, as indicated by the correlation between measures of efficiency in the two years.

Table 6.9 shows the correlation between efficiency estimates for 1970 and 1979. The measure EFF1 uses the top 10 per cent to estimate the efficient base line against which to measure the efficiency ratio. Correlation between EFF1(1970) and EFF1(1979) is 0.61. Similarly, EFF2, EFF3 and EFF4 correspond to the top 20, 30 and 40 per cent, respectively.

Table 6.9 Correlation between efficiency measures for 1970 and 1979

EFF1	0.61
EFF2	0.51
EFF3	0.55
EFF4	0.52

All correlations are significantly different from zero.
Source: Special tabulations, Business and Labour Market Analysis Group, *Statistics Canada*.

Changes in industry efficiency over time occur as firms' market shares change, reflecting factors such as changes in the pattern of demand or supply. The latter component is influenced in turn by changing factor prices, technology and technical, scale and price efficiencies. Consider first changes in productivity level. The efficiency measure will change with a change in productivity that is not spread evenly throughout all the firms in the industry, i.e. one that increases dispersion asymmetrically amongst firms. For example, assuming that growth does not change efficiency, if an industry's productivity grows over a period of time, inefficiency will increase if the gainers were the most efficient firms initially but will decrease if the growth is concentrated in the least efficient firms at the beginning of the period, thus narrowing the gap. Torii (1993) has looked at the role of the rate of capacity utilisation of plants and its effect on technical efficiency. He observed that, when industry demand is rising, average efficiency is high because of a high rate of capacity utilisation. However, in times of recession the relationship is less clear and depends on the rationing rule employed by the industry in response to inadequate demand. However, Albach (1980) found that during boom periods, when investment is high, average inefficiency increased in the German chemical industry, thus providing an opposing argument. Our own analysis of the relation between rates of change and inefficiency across industries in Chapter 5 indicates that faster growth tends to be correlated with a wider spread of efficiency.

In Korea, Yoo (1992b) went a step further to look into changes in technical efficiency of Korean manufacturing industries over time (1979–88). The question he was addressing was 'how stable is technical efficiency over time among and within industries?' He was thus covering two issues, the first relating simply to changes and the second to the dynamic nature of efficiency, i.e. whether the measures of technical efficiency used throughout these studies give reliable estimates across years. Over the 11-year period mean estimates of ATE showed little variation, ranging from a low of 0.699 in 1986 to a high of 0.731 in 1978. However, the rank correlation between any two consecutive years was low and in some instances revealed no correlation.

We would expect some variation as a result of the cyclical factors discussed by Albach and Torii above. Indeed Caves and Barton (1990b) take a very sanguine view of this lack of correlation suggesting that the very considerable turnover in firms from one year to the next, revealed particularly in the Canadian studies mentioned above, could change the pattern of efficiency markedly in the short term. Nevertheless, some worry remains that there may be a deficiency in the measure of technical efficiency, as it seems unlikely that an industry's ranking of efficiency should change so dramatically each year, even if it represents variation round a more stable trend. The correlations between values of ATI for consecutive years were consistently above those of ATE, which offers some hope but they were nevertheless still low. The lack of relation across years does, however, offer one important reassurance for our work on a single year as it implies that the omission of feedbacks across years will not be a significant concern (Caves and Barton, 1990b).

Further evidence is given by Bailey (1992) who analysed the variation of intraindustry productivity dispersion over the period 1963 to 1979 of British manufacturing establishments. Strictly speaking, this does not observe technical efficiency over time, however, because of the close relation between the second and third moments found in our study, one can in this case glean some insights into efficiency from the productivity dispersion. Her results gave little evidence of systematic trends in industry-wide productivity dispersions consistent with Yoo's (1992b) results.

From their longitudinal database this Canadian study and a series of others provided a most interesting and rich source of information on the effects of firm turnover, as measured by market share changes, on productivity (Baldwin and Gorecki, 1989, 1991; Baldwin, 1990). These Canadian studies have estimated efficiency for Canadian manufacturing plants that gained market share and those that lost market share over the period 1970–9. Those plants that exit the industry have been found to be less productive than average and entrants more productive than average. Furthermore, the increase in productivity from plants gaining market share outweighed the loss from those losing market share. They concluded from this that the turnover of market share contributes substantially to efficiency gains and that, without this process, declines in efficiency throughout this period would have been greater.

Baldwin and Gorecki's results have also indicated that turnover was determined by many of the same factors that determined the level of technical efficiency. Concentration, which adversely affects efficiency, was found to be negatively related to turnover. Large plants dominating market share will be able to restrict entry into an industry, and conversely they will be in a good position to ride out bad times and thus prevent exit, with a negative effect on ATE. Second, multiplant activity, which is associated with heterogeneity and thus negatively related to efficiency, also had a negative effect on turnover. However, neither multiplant activity nor heterogeneity necessarily have an adverse effect on consumers' or overall welfare. Other related factors, which all had a positive effect on turnover were union activity, diversification and suboptimal plant scale. Again the effect on welfare is unclear.

6.6 Determinants of inefficiency – external evidence on our hypotheses

The next stage of our international comparison in this chapter is to look at the determinants of (in)efficiency. In Chapter 5 we discussed in detail five hypotheses to explain inefficiency. These concerned the relationship between inefficiency and competition, product differentiation and industry heterogeneity, industry dynamics, spatial disparities, and organisational and managerial influences. We looked at the various ways in which the British study attempted to test these hypotheses and discussed our results. Here we discuss and summarise the results obtained by the researchers of the other countries in this investigation (Australia, the US, Japan, Korea and Canada) in order to compare their experience with our results. We also include a sixth hypothesis concerning public policy, which was tested by some researchers but not by ourselves through lack of data. This is helpfully summarised in Caves (1992b) so we repeat it here (Table 6.10).

6.6.1 *Competitive conditions*

Concentration had a clear impact on (in)efficiency in all countries. However, the impact was normally bounded, with concentration having its minimum promoting effect on average technical efficiency at five firm concentration ratios in the range 45 per cent to 55 per cent in most studies. As these studies are measuring relative and not absolute efficiency, this supports the suggestion that up to a point oligopoly tends to lead to greater similarity of behaviour among the main firms. Like our own experience (with SIGMAE and SKEW), the Canadian data showed a degree of linearity in the relationship.

Table 6.10 Summary of results of interindustry analysis of the determinants of technical inefficiency, by country and hypothesis

Exogenous variable	Australia	UK	Japan	US	Korea	Canada
Competition						
1. Concentration: internal minimum inefficiency	YES	NO	YES	YES	YES	NO
2. Concentration: linear effect	0	− −	0	0	0	+ +
3. Import competition	0	− −	+	−	0	+[a]
4. Exports–shipment ratios	..	+ +	0	+ +	0	−[b]
5. Change in enterprises	..	− −	..	..	..	..
Heterogeneity						
Diversity in products						
1. Intraplant diversity in industry's products	..	0	+ +	0	..	+ +
2. Product differentiation (advertising–sales ratio)	..	0	+	+ +	0	+ +
3. Product differentiation (attribute complexity)	..	..	..	0	..	..
4. Specialisation of industry	..	+ +	..	..	..	..
Diversity of inputs						
5. Interplant dispersion of materials–labour ratio	..	..	..	..	..	+ +
6. Non-production workers proportion	0	−	+ +	+ +[c]	..	+ +
7. Fuel intensity	..	..	− −	0	0	..
Differences in capital						
8. Interplant dispersion of capital intensity	..	..	..	+ +	+ +	..
9. Capital intensity (vintage)	..	+ −	+ +[d]	+ +[e]	0[f]	..
Differences in scale						
10. Intraindustry diversity of plant scale	..	..	+ +	..	..	0
Industry dynamics						
1. Research & development expenditure/sales	..	0	− −	+ +	0	0
2. Technology imports payments	..	..	− −	..	..	−
3. Technology exports receipts	..	..	− −	..	..	..
4. Rate of productivity growth	−	+	+	0	..	..
5. Rate of output growth	0	+ +	+ +	0	..	0
6. Variability of output growth rate	..	..	+ +	..	..	0
7. Patents per plant	..	0	..	..	..	..
8. Change in employment	..	+ +	..	..	..	..
9. Investment labour ratios	..	+	..	..	..	..
Spatial disparities						
1. Regional dispersion	+ +	− −	..	+	..	0
Organisation						
1. Scale of typical plant	−	..	+	− −[g]	− −[g]	−[g]
2. Inbound diversification	0	..	− −	+ +[h]	0	+ +[h]

Table 6.10 *continued*

Exogenous variable	Australia	UK	Japan	US	Korea	Canada
3. Outbound diversification	+	−	+	+ +[i]	+ +	..
4. Multiplant operation	..	0	+ +	+	+	+ +
5. Extent of subcontracting	..	..	−	..	+	..
6. Prevalence of foreign investment	+	..	..	0	..	+
7. Union members as % of employees	..	..	0	+	..	+
8. Use of part-time employees	..	..	−	− −	..	−
Public policy						
1. Tariff protection	+ +[j]	..	+ +[k]	0	0	..
2. Regulation of entry	..	..	+ +	..	..	..

The symbol + + (− −) indicates a significant and robust positive (negative) influence on inefficiency; + (−) indicates a positive (negative) influence that is marginally significant or imperfectly robust; 0 indicates no significant effect; .. indicates that no test was made.
a. In homogeneous product industries that undertake advertising.
b. Associated with resource intensive production of undifferentiated products.
c. The co-efficient of variation of plants' ratios of non-production workers to employees.
d. Measure of indivisibility of plants' capital.
e. Dispersion of vintages of industry's capital.
f. Measure of newness of capital.
g. Relative to market size (otherwise, absolute size measure).
h. Based on enterprise data (otherwise, based on establishment data).
i. Based on enterprise data; 0 when based on establishment data (like other observations in this line).
j. Includes natural protection from transport costs.
k. Includes rate of direct subsidy to industry.

It is interesting that, of all the studies, our own for the UK showed the clearest relation of foreign competition to efficiency. This may be because most of the other countries were relatively closed in the sense that either trade forms a relatively small percentage of their market or their output (the US), or because their external trade barriers are relatively high (Japan and Australia). This pressure applies both to import-competing industries and to those which are substantial exporters, although the effect might be expected to be greater in the case of imports as exporters may still be able to benefit from a protected domestic market. In the case of Canada it was the export industries that were relatively efficient and the import-competing industries that were less so – the latter result was also found for Japan. In the Canadian case this may reflect the pressures from the need to compete in the US, particularly resource-intensive production of undifferentiated products (see footnote b to Table 6.10). The US is a large and important market for Canadian firms but the reverse is not the case – Canada is a relatively small market for US exporters compared with the US domestic market. In the Japanese case, a large measure of their economic success has come from export growth. It is therefore not particularly surprising that export-oriented industries should appear relatively efficient.

6.6.2   *Product differentiation and heterogeneity*

The other studies generally had more success in showing the influence of diversity than did the UK. They were able to look at this from four points of view:

1. Diversity in products.
2. Diversity in inputs.
3. Differences in capital structure.
4. Differences in scale.

There are, effectively, two separate issues associated with product diversity, one is simply heterogeneity – the more a product varies within an industry heading the more we would expect there to be variations in measured technical performance, even if there were no 'inefficiency' as such. The other is that firms can have varying success in segmenting markets and hence in reducing competitive pressures. One means of doing this is by establishing effective brand loyalty. This permits a firm to charge a margin over a rival even where there may be little to choose between the products in practice, a clear example of this is given in Grinyer *et al.* (1988) for Bells whisky, although there the company made use of the margin to improve efficiency. The additional price premium was created by an innovative marketing strategy, which offered incentives to publicans.

The need to have advertising is itself an entry barrier, thus encouraging inefficiency through restricted competition. Not all countries found a clear correlation between product diversification and inefficiency, although where there was a relation industries with greater product diversity were found to be less efficient. In the UK the lack of success with these measures was partly due to poor advertising data. However, the interaction of product heterogeneity within an industry classification is also likely to have influenced both our results and those of other countries.

Diversity in inputs implies heterogeneity amongst firms within industries and therefore one would expect a positive relation with measured inefficiency. The most commonly used variables were the proportion of non-production workers and fuel intensity. High levels of non-production workers may imply a strong role for value added services, which could enable firms to differentiate. Similarly, high energy intensity implies higher cost pressures and the need to become more efficient. The latter measure was significant only for Japan where there was negative correlation with inefficiency. The 1974 oil shock would have placed considerable pressure on these industries, shaking out the inefficient. Torii (1992a) argues that these industries are characterised by fixed co-efficient technologies, which limit their ability to operate flexibly. Using the non-production workers measure, other countries had more success in finding a significant relation. As one would expect, this was positive as high proportions of non-production workers would be associated with high levels of staff in areas such as sales promotion or R&D, which would be consistent with industry heterogeneity and thus measured technical inefficiency. Here again, not all of these sources of diversity represent 'inefficiency' in a sense that would imply a loss of potential welfare. These influences need to be included in the regressions to avoid misspecification of the influences of factors such as competitive structure which are thought to affect technical efficiency as we have defined it.

Difference in capital structure is yet another measure of heterogeneity. The role of fixed costs in replacement capital increases inefficiency when the number of firms is large (Torii, 1992a). When capital intensity is high the cost of upgrading technology or achieving greater efficiency may also be high. On the one hand this may encourage firms to continue as long as possible before incurring this expense. On the other hand it acts as a barrier to entry permitting inefficiency to continue – small establishments will be more reluctant or unable to invest in replacement capital to achieve optimal production, whereas large firms are often in a better position to afford to take this risk because they are likely to have access to other sources of finance. The country studies showed considerable differences in their approaches to this problem, as is clear from the variety of measures employed in Table 6.10. There is thus only limited comparability across countries. The UK, Japan, the US and Korea achieved some success in finding a significant positive relation between capital intensity, its inter-plant dispersion and inefficiency. However, a more plausible interpretation for the US and Korea is that use of 'interplant dispersion in capital intensity' is picking up the existence of different technologies in use within industries, probably including different work practices, such as number of shifts per day.

Finally, differences in scale were used by Japan and Canada to measure heterogeneity. This partly reflects the differences in firms' ability to replace capital assets. Thus a high diversity of plant scale is expected to depress technical efficiency and did so for Japan.

6.6.3 *Industry dynamics*

The other countries in this project used a variety of differing measures to test for the dynamic nature of efficiency. One might expect that the more dynamic economies would show a greater influence, but again this can reflect the problem of comparing relative rather than absolute inefficiency. A country like the US, with a strong traditional manufacturing sector, has declining as well as growing sectors, therefore one might expect these facets to emerge. However, apart from Japan and the UK the measures used were of limited success. The most common measures used in the studies were R&D expenditure and the rate of output growth. On the one hand, a high rate of output growth can increase measured inefficiency within an industry because a changing environment exacerbates the differences between firms within an industry, some firms will be able to adapt quickly whereas others will lag behind. However, on the other hand R&D operates to expand the frontier, in which case the relation with technical efficiency might be positive. In the UK, Korea and Canada there was no significant relationship between R&D expenditure and inefficiency, however the Japanese and American results showed that a higher proportion of R&D expenditure makes Japanese industry more efficient and the US less efficient. This may tell us something about the rates of diffusion of new ideas in the different countries, although when data are available on a time series basis, as for Korea, a rather fuller analysis could be contemplated. The difference between the US and Japan may also reflect institutional differences, with co-operative as opposed to competitive R&D being more common in Japan than the US. This would tend to reduce the spread of efficiency in Japan by widening the common technological base for co-operating firms in an industry.

High productivity growth makes older plants obsolete and hence increases differences between the new and dynamic, and the old and static plants. The positive effect of the rate of output growth on inefficiency, found in the UK, was replicated in the Japanese results, although there was no significant effect found in Australia, the US and Canada. In Japan several alternative measures were used to test the effects of rate of change on technical efficiency. First, a significant negative effect was found for both technology imports payments and export receipts, a negative effect was also found for the former measure in Canada, although this was only marginally significant. Although one would expect innovative industries to be more efficient it is not clear what the expected co-efficients should be in this case, as we know nothing about the distribution of the technology payments within the industry. If they were concentrated on the already efficient they would tend to increase the spread of inefficiency, while they would narrow it if they reflected the inefficient plants' attempts to catch up. The second measure, the rate of productivity growth, had only a marginally significant positive effect in the Japanese case, although no significant effect was found for this variable in the US. The final additional measure, variability of output growth rate, had a significant positive relationship with inefficiency in Japan but was not significant for Canada.

6.6.4 Spatial disparities

One would expect the effects of geographical diversity on technical inefficiency to show up much more clearly in the economies with the larger land areas, such as Australia, Canada and the US. In fact a significantly positive relation was found in Australia, the UK and the US (marginally significant only), however, in Canada there was no significant correlation. In addition to the influence of regional dispersion, these results are likely to reflect strategic behaviour and public policy as well as natural conditions. In Australia and the UK, government policies have aimed at encouraging industries towards declining or peripheral regions through subsidies and infrastructure improvements, often resulting in inefficient location patterns. The past competition for investment between the States of Australia, for example, tended to lead to a multiplicity of plants of suboptimal scale, with scope for technical inefficiency assisted by inefficient transport services that decreased competitive pressures.

6.6.5 Organisational and managerial influences

Other countries had better access to data and hence were able to use a far wider range of measures than in the UK to test for organisational and managerial influences.

Diversification

In the US there is particular evidence that diversification was overextended in the 1960s and 1970s and that activities became unrelated. This led to an extensive retrenchment of firms' activities around their primary business throughout the 1980s (Caves, 1992b). If establishments in an industry are controlled by enterprises whose primary business is in another industry this will tend to affect efficiency adversely because of factors such as lack of familiarity and lack of co-operation. This was supported by the results of the US, Korea, Japan and Australia. Inbound diversification, defined as the ratio of sales by establishments belonging to enterprises classified to other industries to sales by all establishments to this industry, was also used in the other countries. Surprisingly, using this variable, a significant negative correlation with inefficiency was found for Japan.

Multiplant operations

The second measure used in the UK was the extent of multiplant operations, although no significant relation was found. Under multiplant operations a number of plants in the same industry are controlled by one enterprise. Information can be passed more rapidly around the managers of individual plants if they are consolidated together than if they are independent, as not only will they be in constant contact with each other but there will be no incentive to hide trade secrets or operational practices. One would therefore expect the responses of plants to changes in their environment to be similar and more rapid than those of other plants, which could increase average industry inefficiency when measured for a given year.[7] In other words, multiplant operations stabilise intertemporal productivity dispersion and slow down plants' rates of adjustment to disturbances. In a changing world this increases inefficiency when measured across a single year. Possibly working in the other direction, evidence indicates that the extent of multiplant operations tends to increase with both establishment and enterprise size. A positive relation was found between multiplant operations and inefficiency from the other countries that tested this variable (significant for Japan and Canada).

Scale of establishments

Scale economies are an important source of differences in performance. To some extent this should be captured by the translog production function but some of the effect is likely to remain. The scale of a typical plant was tested in most countries in the project. Small and large plants are generally different, the former are not solely a miniature version of the latter. First, they often possess different characteristics. Large firms tend to have complex organisational hierarchies which can slow down the firm's speed of adjustment and limit the effectiveness of entrepreneurs. For example, Yotopoulos and Lau (1973) found that in India small farms were more technically efficient than large ones, although there appeared to be no difference in allocative efficiency. However, there are overheads to any operation and greater scale gives the opportunity to spread them over a larger output. Evidence also indicates that capital intensity increases with plant size (Davis, 1956; Shen, 1965; Caves and Pugel, 1980).

Second, large and small firms face different competitive environments. Large firms are better able to benefit from economies of scale thus increasing absolute and perhaps technical efficiency. In French manufacturing Meeusen and van den Broeck (1977) observed that larger firms were more efficient. Furthermore, large firms can often prevent the entry of small firms, or large initial sunk costs may act as a barrier to entry hence restricting competition and promoting inefficiency. Ideally one should disaggregate industries according to size and estimate separate efficiency frontiers for each. Meller (1976) disaggregated twenty-one Chilean industries into five classes, depending on size. He found that, on the whole, the frontiers of the smaller plants lay above those of larger ones, implying greater absolute efficiency. However, the extent of technical inefficiency within the small plant classes was greater than for the larger plants, thus the relative technical inefficiency of small firms was larger. In all countries except Japan (where a weak positive relation was found) this variable had a negative influence on inefficiency implying that the benefits for technical efficiencies of greater plant size largely outweigh the diseconomies of a complex hierarchy.

Labour relations

Trade unions are often thought to be detrimental to industrial efficiency through industrial action and the enforcement of work rules and craft demarcations. British studies using data from the Workplace and Industrial Relations Survey (WIRS) have largely shown a significant negative relation between unionisation and profitability (Blanchflower and Oswald, 1988; Machin and Stewart, 1990). On the other hand, there is some evidence that unions can improve efficiency by providing a listening ear that can act on the behalf of workers and hence reduce costly labour turnover (Freeman and Medoff, 1984). Metcalf (1990) also argues that the reduced quit rate and use of bargaining[8] by trade unions can enhance productivity, thereby offsetting some of the adverse effects from their monopoly position. In his view the empirical studies of the UK suggest that, in around 1980, highly unionised organisations had a lower level of labour productivity than corresponding less unionised ones. However, during the first half of the 1980s unionised workplaces had superior productivity growth to their less unionised counterparts, as previous inefficiencies that were imposed in the 1960s and 1970s were reduced. In the US and Canada industries with higher proportions of union members were found to be more inefficient, although these variables were only marginally significant. In Japan there was no significant relation. An analysis of the Australian Workplace Industrial Relations Survey undertaken by Crockett *et al.* (1991) suggests that, by comparison with the UK, trade unions in Australia appear still to be associated with lower relative productivity. Adverse effects of union power were particularly evident for the Sydney plant relative to the Melbourne plant considered in BIE (1991a).

The effect of part-time workers on efficiency is also controversial. Employing part-time workers involves greater fixed costs of searching, training and those of generally setting up an employee in the workplace. These in turn may give rise to inefficiencies as, during this period, employees will not have reached their full potential productivity. However, one can argue that part-time workers offer the firm greater flexibility when facing a largely unpredictable and changing environment. In the UK part-time working has become increasingly important. All countries (Japan, the USA and Canada) that tested the effects of part-time workers found a negative relation with inefficiency.

6.6.6   *Public policy*

An additional set of hypotheses was tested by some of the other countries – this was to determine the effects of public policy on efficiency. Government interventionist policies can have many rationales including the correction of market failure, the desire to redistribute income towards or maintain employment for workers in favoured industries (protection from 'unfair' foreign competition), and to develop a diversified, industrialised economy.[9] Either way they tend to distort competition and diminish incentives to improve efficiency. Thus we would expect to find a positive relation between such aspects of public policy and the extent of inefficiency. Regulation and tariff protection are alternative public policies.

Regulation

In the case of a monopoly – most commonly natural monopolies – industry regulation is used in an attempt by government to correct for market failures. Such monopolies in the US are generally heavily regulated. On the other hand, in the 1970s, British and Australian natural monopoly industries tended to be publicly owned rather than regulated, and hence subject to direct control, although this has rapidly changed in Britain with the privatisation programme of the 1980s. In Britain most of these industries lie outside manufacturing, but those such as steel and aerospace, for example, lie within the ambit of this research.

In the present context the main empirical work on regulatory effects has been limited to regulation of entry, but there are several other variables that can be targeted for regulation, for example, price, product quality, inputs such as labour, capital expenditure and R&D expenditure. One of the main sources of inefficiency in regulated industries is that control of one variable can lead to adverse affects on another; price controls, say, can affect capital expenditure decisions (Averch and Johnson, 1962). A second source of inefficiency is an imperfect flow of information between the firm and the regulator. In the case of a monopoly, the regulator's main source of information is the firm itself which is therefore in a strong manipulative position. These pressures tend to limit competition and the incentives to improve efficiency.

Just one variable was used to test for the effects of regulation, regulation of entry. Again this acts to restrict competition facing domestic producers from foreign and other competitors based in the home country. This was found to have a positive effect on inefficiency in Japan.

Tariff protection

Differing local rules on tariff protection restrict international trade and distort competition. The establishment of the free trade agreements, such as the EC, EFTA and NAFTA, removes internal tariff protection. However, externally, protection restricts the free flow of import and export goods. For example, in Australia and Japan tariff protection is higher than in many other countries, thereby limiting imports and restricting competition facing domestic producers. This in turn would encourage technical inefficiency. According to Industries Assistance Commission (1980) the average effective rate of protection in Australia was 26 per cent in 1977, although a standard deviation of 34 per cent reflects the fact that some rates were considerably higher. A tariff protection variable was used as a measure in four countries in this study. Not surprisingly a significant positive relation with inefficiency was found in Australia and Japan.

6.7 Determinants of efficiency over time

Throughout this book we have talked about efficiency as a dynamic concept. Yoo (1992b) examined measures of technical efficiency (ATE) and inefficiency (ATI) over the period 1978–88. Estimates were found to vary considerably over time, with very low rank correlation of industries' estimated efficiency levels between pairs of adjacent years. However, Yoo did find that the annual values of an industry's estimated efficiency were strongly correlated with their mean over the period as a whole, thus implying that, over time, estimated efficiency may vary randomly about a stable mean. Bailey (1992), using data on intraindustry productivity dispersion of British manufacturing establishments over a period of time, was able to investigate inter- temporal variability and its determinants. Her results indicate that industry dispersions are unlikely to display either systematic trends or auto- correlation.

Examining interindustry determinants of the intertemporal behaviour of productivity dispersion, Bailey's results complemented those of the static investigations. Changes in competitive conditions of an industry were found to have a significant effect on the stability of productivity dispersion. In particular, the greater the change in concentration the greater the intertemporal variation in the dispersion of productivity. This suggests that changing competitive conditions will affect individual firms differently and hence they will adjust to these disturbances at different rates. International competition was also found to have a destabilising effect on productivity dispersion. Of the organisational factors, only multiplant operations had a significant impact. Over the long term, having multi-plant operations had a stabilising effect, as such plants can be less vulnerable to changes in the economic environment by offsetting shocks or switching production lines. This may reduce the variance in the rates of adjustment across plants although rationalisation could result in closure of plants that would remain in business if they constituted the whole firm.

This result contrasts with the negative effect on static efficiency (Table 6.10). The number of days lost due to work stoppages was the only element of innovative activity and change that was found to have a significant impact, destabilising the productivity dispersion over time. Thus differences in management–labour relations affect the likelihood of disturbances and the rates of adjustment of individual plants, consistent with the static effects found for Canada and the US (Table 6.10). Finally, high levels of sunk capital were found to increase instability.

6.8 Conclusions and summary

Phase 1 of the study attempted to measure the extent of technical efficiency. The first and possibly most interesting observation was that there was little contradiction between the different countries' results and to a considerable extent they supported the findings in the UK and Australia. In most cases, all the countries showed similar average levels of technical efficiency using the measure ATE. Second, 'cleansing' the data appeared to make a substantial improvement to the results for Australia and the US.

Phase 2 examined the determinants of technical efficiency. Once again there was considerable support of our findings from the other countries. Furthermore, these countries provided a great deal of additional information on the determinants of efficiency. First and foremost was public policy which was found to have a positive effect on inefficiency in Australia and Japan, where protection is high. Second, labour market variables were used in some of the other countries. Trade unions appeared to have a positive effect on inefficiency whereas part-time workers had a negative influence. This has beneficial implications for the UK, which, since the late 1970s, has become less unionised and has seen an increasing proportion of part-time labour. Third, larger plants were found to be more efficient in all countries with the exception of Japan where a weak effect in the reverse direction was found.

Notes

1. These are based on average per capita labour productivity.
2. As employees in US manufacturing work more hours than their British colleagues, van Ark defines productivity as value added per hour worked rather than value added per employee to avoid bias, use of the latter measure makes the UK appear relatively less efficient.
3. To some extent these averages are misleading as they only include the industries for which average technical efficiency could be computed. It would not be appropriate to assume that the industries for which it could not be computed had the same average nor indeed that they were 100 per cent efficient.

4. There is an element of biased selection in this set of industries in Table 6.5, as they include only those for which measures of average technical efficiency can be calculated.
5. See Chapter 3, pp. 51–3.
6. There must be a question mark over the Korean results as ATE (VA) + ATI (VA) comes out closer to unity for the other countries (see Table 6.8 for the correlation of the two measures).
7. However, research does imply that managerial economies are small for multiplant operations (Scherer *et al.*, 1975).
8. This reflects the distinction common in the public choice literature between acting by using one's voice or vote to change conditions or moving to a location (in this case, firm) where the conditions are different. Both impose 'costs', the first in the form of more expensive employment conditions and the second in hiring and training costs for a larger turnover of employees.
9. In the case of Australia the level of protection was often 'tailor-made' to cover the difference between Australian costs and those of the most effective competitors (Industries Assistance Commission, 1980). Anderson and Garnaut (1987) conclude that three factors explain why the labour intensive and already highly protected textiles, clothing and footwear industries were singled out (along with motor vehicles and parts) for large increases in protection from the mid to late 1970s in Australia. First was the speed and magnitude of the changes in import competition. Second was the fact that other industrialised countries were also protecting heavily their textiles, clothing and footwear industries. The third was the adoption by the Liberal-Country Party Federal opposition, in a 1975 by-election in an electorate heavily dependent on the production of textiles and clothing, of a policy that protection would be maintained for these industries. It won the by-election and used the Labor government's liberalisation of import policies as a major point of dispute in the general election held later that year.

7

Conclusions

Australian and British manufacturing industries are clearly characterised by a very considerable variety of performance. Much of this variation is explained by the difference in size of the individual plants within each industry and by their choice of inputs. Although there are noticeable economies of scale, very considerable diversity remains in addition to these sources of variation. Some plants just seem able to gain more output than others from the same inputs. In other words, they are more efficient.

In a highly competitive world, with widespread availability of information about techniques of production, the nature of inputs and markets, it might seem unlikely that seriously inefficient plants could remain in business. Yet, in the industries for which estimates could be made, average efficiency seemed to be around two-thirds to three-quarters of that of the best plants. This is not because the best are exceptionally good. Our methodology of estimating stochastic frontier production functions ensures that the definition of 'best' allows for a considerable amount of random variation due to the myriad of minor factors, such as product variation, variation in quality of inputs and differing costs of different locations, even in efficient firms.

Our procedures are very conservative in a number of respects. Not only are extreme observations discounted but the optimum attainable is represented by the average of best observed performance within the country. We know that both Australia and the UK have an average performance in manufacturing industries towards the bottom of the range of OECD countries, so that best is likely to be well below that attained elsewhere. As, in part, this difference may be due to the use of less efficient technologies, this discrepancy may be larger than what can be achieved with the given technology. Indeed, we can draw considerable comfort from the fact that manufacturing industries in countries like the US, Japan and

Canada, which have a better overall performance, are also characterised by similar spreads in performance compared with the best within each industry.

However, by the same token the measures we have used for inefficiency may include within them other sources of variation. Any factors that lead to asymmetric variation below the frontier of best performance will be classified by our procedures as representing inefficiency. In addition, any mistaken upward shift of the frontier will cause a matching increase in estimated average inefficiency. Although our methodology is widely used and we have gone to considerable trouble to ensure that the chance of having errors in the data is minimised and that the specification and estimation methods used are as up to date as possible, the results will only be as good as the methodology permits.

Our reason for emphasising these points before drawing any further conclusions is simply that our experience in undertaking this work and our careful consideration of the results of others lead us to place some clear question marks over the estimates. It is not always possible to estimate production functions with well-determined parameters. A substantial number of industries do not exhibit the tail of inefficient behaviour we expect but show either random variation round the estimated production function or even a 'perverse' experience where the tail is upward. 'Perverse' is in inverted commas because it is by no means out of the question for efficient operation to be unusual and for there to be a common level of inefficiency leading to this apparently perverse result.

A further question mark arises, not from our own estimates, which relate to a single year, but from the work of Yoo (1992b) for Korea and Torii (1993) on the clothing and textile industries in Japan, which suggests that the estimates are decidedly unstable over time. Nevertheless, there is good reason to expect this instability, as cyclical variations in the economy will tend to lead to underutilised capacity whatever careful and dynamic approach firms use to plan their production capability. This is reflected in our own results, as industries experiencing more rapid growth are also characterised by greater inefficiency. In the case of rapid growth not only is there room in the market for the inefficient but the surge of new investment will itself tend to incorporate new technologies (and new products) which are themselves more efficient, thereby pushing the frontier outwards.

Having started with the negative we now turn to the positive as it is possible to explain up to around 30 per cent of the variation in efficiency across industries by a simple series of well-known facts. This proportion is necessarily small as we are restricted in general to employing explanatory variables which are obtainable for the same industry breakdown as that used in the *Census of Production*. There is therefore much one would like to ask about individual plants but cannot as we have to use the data which have already been collected by the Census authorities and only a very limited number of other sources.

7.1 Implications for policy

Our results confirm the strong links between the structure of industries and their performance, in particular, that industries exposed to greater competition, whether from domestic or foreign sources, seem to show a smaller variation in performance. Our results only compare performance across industries within manufacturing in both the UK and Australia. Wider evidence presented in Caves (1992b) suggests that the same arguments can be applied in general across countries.

Hence, if inefficiency is to be reduced this could be achieved by improving competition within industries at least at intermediate levels of concentration.[1] We have to recall that our data are not up-to-date, so the changes in the British and Australian economies during the 1980s and early 1990s will have already contributed to improving performance from this cause.

External barriers have been reduced markedly in Australia, and will continue to be (Figure 7.1), while barriers within the EC are being removed as part of the single market programme. These changes and the increase in competition faced by domestic producers could be expected to lead to an increase in average technical efficiency, given the positive relationship between protection and inefficiency in Australia, and the limited evidence for a negative relationship between import competition and inefficiency in the UK. Moreover, the somewhat decreased emphasis since the 1970s by the States in Australia on encouraging dispersed production for their local markets could be expected to lead to an increase in average technical efficiency, given the positive relationship between regional dispersion and

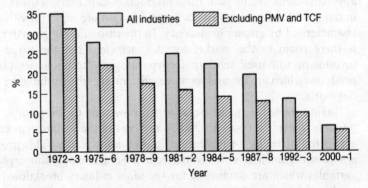

Figure 7.1 Australian manufacturing sector: average rate of effective protection, 1972–2000 (*source*: Mayes, 1993).

inefficiency, and the weak negative relation between the scale of typical plants and inefficiency in Australia.

Evidence on the importance of the 'tail' of inefficiency in manufacturing industry is more difficult to interpret. It is an obvious truth that if there were less variation and more of industry-approximated best practice then this would improve average inefficiency. However, merely looking at the length of the tail is insufficient, as it is affected by so many factors. In particular, rapidly growing industries tend to show a longer tail simply because, under these conditions, there is room for all players, even the inefficient. Thus, for such industries the problem may easily be on the way to solution, the frontier may be moving outwards, which leads to a reduction in absolute inefficiency, temporarily causing high intra-industry inefficiency. The slower and less efficient firms will also change technology in time or go out of business, thereby returning the distribution of inefficiency to more normal proportions.

This experience gives some strength to the argument that emphasis should be given to acquiring and encouraging the adoption of best practice. If it is the case that the tail of inefficiency is not especially far inside the frontier, then there is no particular reason for focusing on reducing the spread of performance within industries when there is such a large gap between best practice in the UK and Australia and that in their competitors. This reflects the thrust of current Australian industrial policy (Stanford, 1992), where the prime objective is attaining international competitiveness, complemented by what are described as 'positive adjust-ment measures' – support for R&D, encouragement of the venture capital industry, export market assistance and encouragement of specific industries such as aerospace, pharmaceuticals and information-related activities through trade-related investment measures.

In this case, the emphasis in policy has been to try to encourage the location of higher value added activities in Australia. This in itself is not so much a reaction to the distribution of efficiency within industries as a wish to switch to high productivity industries, which could themselves have a broad range of efficiency internally. Overall performance can be improved in principle by activity shifting to higher productivity industries, just as much as it can be increased by reducing the spread of efficiency below the frontier within each industry or by advancing the frontier itself.[2]

What the current study has been able to demonstrate is that a substantial proportion of the variation in efficiency within industries is due to factors related to the inherent structure of the industries and does not reflect aspects which can readily be improved by the actions of the firms themselves or which should necessarily be targeted by governments. By symmetry, of course, there is a substantial residual, which is X-inefficiency in the sense that we cannot attribute a specific cause to it. We can merely list the specific factors that have already been taken into account in its calculation.

7.2 Implications for further research

The implications for further work from these findings are straightforward. The simplest is that within the current framework it is necessary to include a time dimension. In an ideal world one would be able to trace through changes in the measured efficiency of each plant. The larger plants are observed each year through the *Annual Census of Production*. It would therefore be possible to build up a database of how each plant moves relative to the industry as a whole as has been done in Canada (Baldwin, 1990). From those results it has been possible to see, for example, the role of exit and entry in both raising average efficiency and altering its distribution. Both exits and entrants tend to have below average efficiency.[3] However, new entrants rapidly improve their position, being 4 per cent more productive than the average of all continuing firms after nine years.

Second, the time series approach would enable the identification of industries where the frontier was advancing rapidly and where average efficiency was rising (falling). It would also, as we have noted, provide a test of the stability of the frontier production function method. The analysis would not rely for its usefulness on the particular measure of inefficiency and could easily use Baldwin's methodology, for example.

A second area where it could be helpful to conduct further work is on a more suitable method for estimating capital. A time series would permit the computation of elementary perpetual inventory (PIM) estimates (Mayes and Young, 1993) but a much more satisfactory approach would be through direct estimation from asset registers. Although that might seem an expensive exercise, concern over the accuracy of capital stock estimates is such in the UK that the CSO is actively considering introducing such an approach, following successful experience with it in the Netherlands.

It is to be hoped that not only will the CSO follow this example from the Netherlands but that it and the Australian Bureau of Statistics will also follow the example of, *inter alia*, the US, Canada and Norway in putting together a longitudinal database of plant level data which can be accessed for research purposes provided no information that could be identified with an individual plant or enterprise is revealed.

A further feature of the existing analysis, which typifies industrial studies is that the information available forces a focus on manufacturing. It is not possible currently to provide a similarly comprehensive assessment of service industries. Clearly methodology would have to be changed in this instance as production functions have less meaning in this context but Baldwin's approach or that of Thiry and Tulkens (1985) is relevant. Our analysis thus far provides just one piece in the jigsaw of explaining differences in performance. Aggregate analysis, individual industry and plant studies have their part to play. We are now embarked on a time series study of UK manufacturing to try to provide a further piece, which should explain far more of the dynamics of efficiency. However, there is a long distance to go before diminishing returns set in. We hope this particular contribution of the establishment level study of inefficiency across manufacturing industry in these two countries provides a significant step forward.

Notes

1. Evidence for some countries, including Australia, the US and Japan, suggests that minimum average technical inefficiency occurs at an intermediate level of concentration (a fairly low one for Australia and the US, a higher one for Japan) whereas high concentration is associated with increased average technical inefficiency (Table 6.10 and Caves, 1992b).
2. Of course, the extent to which a programme in such areas might increase national welfare depends on a range of factors including: the magnitude of direct operational and indirect resource allocation costs; the extent of retaliation by other governments, given that the agreements reached in the recent Uruguay round of GATT negotiations effectively prohibit incentives classed as Trade-related Investment Measures; and the level of benefits obtained, given that some information relevant to the development of efficient programmes will be commercially sensitive and difficult for policy-makers to obtain. In any case there is considerable uncertainty about the significance of any economic externality benefits and about the precise activities which might lead to such externalities (Martin, 1994).
3. Efficiency is measured differently in that study, see Chapter 6, p. 165.

Bibliography

Adelman, M.A. (1969) 'Comment on the "H" concentration measure as a numbers–equivalent', *Regional Economic Statistics*, 99–101.

Afriat, S.N. (1972) 'Efficiency estimation of production functions', *International Economic Review*, **13**, 568–98.

Aigner, D.J., Lovell, C.A.K. and Schmidt, P. (1977) 'Formulation and estimation of stochastic frontier production function models', *Journal of Econometrics*, **6**, 21–37.

Aigner, S.N. and Chu, S.F. (1968) 'On estimating the industry production function', *American Economic Review*, **58**, 826–39.

Albach, H. (1980) 'Average and best-practice production functions in German industry', *Journal of Industrial Economics*, **29**, 55–70.

Anderson, K. and Garnaut, R. (1987) *Australian Protectionism: Extent, Causes and Effects*, Allen and Unwin, Sydney.

Anscombe, F.J. (1961) *Examination of Residuals*, Proceedings of the Fourth Berkley Symposium on Mathematical Statistics and Probability, vol. 2, pp. 433–6.

Australian Manufacturing Council (1990) *The Global Challenge: Australian Manufacturing in the 1990s*, Melbourne.

Averch, H. and Johnson, L.L. (1962) 'Behaviour of the firm under regulatory constraint', *American Economic Review*, **52**, 1052–69.

Baden-Fuller, C.W.F. (1989) 'Exit from declining industries and the case of steel casings', *Economic Journal*, **99**, 398.

Bailey, S.D. (1992) 'The intraindustry dispersion of plant productivity in the British Bmanufacturing sector, 1963–79', in R.E. Caves (ed.), *Industrial Efficiency in Six Nations*, MIT Press, Cambridge, MA.

Bain, J.S. (1956) *Barriers to New Competition*, Harvard University Press, Cambridge, MA.

Baldwin, J.R. (1990) 'Industrial efficiency and plant turnover in Canadian manufacturing industries', *Statistics Canada*, Business and Labour Market Analysis Working Paper.

Baldwin, J.R. (1992) 'Industrial efficiency and plant turnover in the Canadian manufacturing sector', in R.E. Caves (ed.), *Industrial Efficiency in Six Nations*, MIT Press, Cambridge, MA.

Baldwin, J.R. and Gorecki, P.K. (1989) 'Measuring the dynamics of market structure', *Annales d'économie et de statistique*, **15/16**, 316–32.

Baldwin, J.R. and Gorecki, P.K. (1990a) 'Firm entry and exit in the Canadian manufacturing sector', *Statistics Canada*, Business and Labour Market Analysis Research Paper Series, No. 23A.

Baldwin, J.R. and Gorecki, P.K. (1990b) 'Intra-industry mobility in the Canadian manufacturing sector', *Statistics Canada*, Business and Labour Market Analysis Research Paper Series, No. 23B.

Baldwin, J.R. and Gorecki, P.K. (1990c) 'Measuring entry and exit in Canadian manufacturing: Methodology', *Statistics Canada*, Business and Labour Market Analysis Research Paper Series, No. 23C.

Baldwin, J.R. and Gorecki, P.K. (1990d) 'The contribution of the competitive process to productivity growth: The role of firm and plant turnover', *Statistics Canada*, Business and Labour Market Analysis Research Paper Series, No. 23D.

Baldwin, J.R. and Gorecki, P.K. (1990e) 'Mergers and the competitive process', *Statistics Canada*, Business and Labour Market Analysis Research Paper Series, No. 23E.

Baldwin, J.R. and Gorecki, P.K. (1990f) 'Concentration statistics as predictors of the intensity of competition', *Statistics Canada*, Business and Labour Market Analysis Research Paper Series, No. 23G.

Baldwin, J.R. and Gorecki, P.K. (1990g) 'The relationship between mobility and concentration for the Canadian manufacturing sector', *Statistics Canada*, Business and Labour Market Analysis Research Paper Series, No. 23H.

Baldwin, J.R. and Gorecki, P.K. (1991) 'Firm entry and exit in the Canadian manufacturing sector, 1970–1982', *Canadian Journal of Economics*, **24**, 300–23.

Baldwin, J.R. and Gorecki, P.K. (1993) 'Profile of growing small and medium sized enterprises in Canada', *Statistics Canada*, Business and Labour Market Analysis.

Barla, P. and Perelman, S. (1989) 'Technical efficiency in airlines under regulated and deregulated environments', *Annals of Public and Co-operative Economics*, **60**, 103.

Battese, G.E. and Coelli, T.J. (1988) 'Prediction of firm-level technical efficiencies with a generalised frontier production and panel data', *Journal of Econometrics*, **38**, 387.

Baumol, W.J., Panzar, J.C. and Willig, R.D. (1982) *Contestable Markets and the Theory of Industry Structure*, Academic Press, San Diego, CA.

Belsley, D.A., Kuh, E. and Welsch, R.E. (1980) *Regression Diagnostics*, Wiley, New York.

Blanchflower, D. and Oswald, A. (1988) 'Profit-related pay: Prose discovered', *Economic Journal*, **98**, 720–30.

Bollard, A. and Mayes, D.G. (1992) 'Regionalism and the Pacific Rim', *Journal of Common Market Studies*, **30**(2), 195–209.

Bollard, A., Harper, D. and Mayes, D.G. (1993) '*Product Market Flexibility: Concepts and indicators*', report to Her Majesty's Treasury, National Institute of Economic and Social Research.

Bowen, H.P. (1991) 'Electronic components and semi-conductors', in D.G. Mayes (ed.), *The European Challenge: Industry's response to the 1992 programme*, Harvester Wheatsheaf, Hemel Hempstead.

Bravo-Ureta, B.E. and Rieger, L. (1990) 'Alternative production frontier methodologies and dairy farm efficiency', *Journal of Agricultural Economics*, **41**, 215.

Breusch, T.S. and Pagan, A.R. (1979) 'A simple test for heteroscedasticity and random coefficient variation', *Econometrica*, **47**, 1287–94.

Buigues, P. and Ilzkowitz, F. (1988) 'The sectoral impact of the internal market',

EC Brussels II/2335/88–EN.

Bureau of Industry Economics (1988) *Technical Efficiency in Australian Manufacturing Industries*, Occasional Paper 4, Bureau of Industry Economics, Canberra.

Bureau of Industry Economics (1989) *Trade Liberalisation in Australian Manufacturing Industry*, Research Report 29, AGPS, Canberra.

Bureau of Industry Economics (1990) *International Productivity Differences in Manufacturing: Photographic paper*, Research Report 34, AGPS, Canberra.

Bureau of Industry Economics (1991a) *International Comparisons of Plant Productivity: Domestic water heaters*, Research Report 38, AGPS, Canberra.

Bureau of Industry Economics (1991b) *The Pharmaceutical Industry: Impediments and opportunities*, Program Evaluation Report 11, AGPS, Canberra.

Bureau of Industry Economics (1992a) *International Performance Indicators: Rail freight*, Research Report 41, AGPS, Canberra.

Bureau of Industry Economics (1992b) *International Performance Indicators: Road freight*, Research Report 46, AGPS, Canberra.

Bureau of Industry Economics (1992c) *International Performance Indicators: Electricity*, Research Report 40, AGPS, Canberra.

Bureau of Industry Economics (1992d) *International Performance Indicators: Telecommunications*, Research Report 48, AGPS, Canberra.

Bureau of Industry Economics (1993) *International Performance Indicators: Waterfront*, Research Report 47, AGPS, Canberra.

Business Monitor (1977) *Report on the Census of Production (1977), Summary Tables*, Department of Industry, Business Statistics Office, HMSO, London.

Button, K.J. (1985) 'Potential differences in the degree of X-inefficiency between industrial sectors in the United Kingdom', *Quarterly Review of Economics and Business*, **25**, 85–95.

Button, K.J. (1992) *Technical Inefficiency in Manufacturing Industries Revisited*, mimeo, Loughborough University, Loughborough.

Button, K.J. and Weyman-Jones, T.G. (1992a) 'Ownership structure, institutional organisation and measured X-efficiency', *American Economic Review, papers and proceedings*, **82**, 439–45.

Button, K.J. and Weyman-Jones, T.G. (1992b) *X-efficiency and Technical Efficiency*, Economic Research Paper 92/1, Loughborough University, Loughborough.

Buxton, A., Mayes, D.G. and Murfin, A. (1990) 'R&D, innovation and trade performance', in B. Dankbaar, J. Groenewegen and H. Schenk (eds.), *Perspectives in Industrial Organisation*, Kluwer, Dordrecht.

Caves, R.E. (1982) 'Interindustry determinants of technical inefficiency', *Working Memorandum*, Harvard University, mimeo.

Caves, R.E. (1984) 'Scale, openness and productivity in Australian manufacturing industries', in R.E. Caves and L.B. Krause (eds.), *The Australian Economy: A view from the North*, Brookings Institution, Washington.

Caves, R.E. (1985) 'Interindustry differences in productivity growth and technical efficiency', Harvard Institute of Economic Research, Discussion Paper No. 1130.

Caves, R.E. (1988) *The Measurement of Technical Inefficiency for U.S. Manufacturing Industry*, Harvard University.

Caves, R.E. (1992a) 'Determinants of technical efficiency in Australia', in R.E. Caves (ed.), *Industrial Efficiency in Six Nations*, MIT Press, Cambridge, MA.

Caves, R.E. (1992b) *Industrial Efficiency in Six Nations*, MIT Press, Cambridge, MA.

Caves, R.E. and Barton, D.R. (1990a) *Corrections to Efficiency in US Manufacturing Industries*, mimeo.

Caves, R.E. and Barton, D.R. (1990b) *Efficiency in U.S. Manufacturing Industries*,

MIT Press, Cambridge, MA.

Caves, R.E. and Pugel, T.A. (1980) 'Intra-industry differences in conduct and performance, viable strategies in US manufacturing industries', Monograph Series in *Finance and Economics*, No. 1980-2, New York, Graduate School of Business Administration, New York University.

Census of Production (1977) *Summary Tables, Statistics of Production Concentration*, HMSO, London.

Chow, G.C. (1960) 'Tests for equality between sets of coefficients in two linear regressions', *Econometrica*, **28**, 591-605.

Christensen, L.R., Jorgenson, D.W. and Lau, L.J. (1971) 'Conjugate duality and the transcendental logarithmic function', *Econometrica*, **39**, 255-6.

Cohen, D. (1992) 'Growth, productivity and access to the world financial markets', *Journal of the Japanese and International Economy*, **6**(4), 365-82.

Cohen, J. and Simmie, J. (1991) *Innovation and Technopolis Planning in Britain and France*, paper given at the joint ESRC-CNRS workshop, University of Bristol, December 18-20.

Comanor, W.S. and Scherer, F.M. (1969) 'Patent statistics as a measure of technical change', *Journal of Political Economy*, **77**, 392-8.

Comanor, W.S. and Wilson, T.A. (1967) 'Advertising, market structure and performance', *Review of Economics and Statistics*, **49**, 423-40.

Committee for Review of Export Market Development Assistance (1989) *Australian Exports: Performance, obstacles and issues of assistance*, AGPS, Canberra.

Corbo, V. and de Melo, J. (1983) *Technical Efficiency in a Highly Protected Economy: Preliminary results for the Chilean manufacturing sector: 1967*, Preliminary Working Paper, World Bank.

Corden, W.M. (1974) *Trade Policy and Economic Welfare*, Clarendon Press, Oxford.

Crafts, N.F.R. (1988) 'British economic growth before and after 1979; a review of the evidence', Centre for Economic Policy Research Discussion Paper, no. 292.

Crockett, G., Dawkins, P., Miller, P. and Mulvey, C. (1991) *The Impact of Unions on Workplace Productivity in Australia*, paper presented at the Twentieth Conference of Economists, Hobart.

CSO, *Annual Census of Production*, HMSO: London.

CSO (1992) *Economic Trends*, Annual Supplement, HMSO: London.

Daly, A., Hitchens, D.M.W.N. and Wagner, K. (1985) 'Productivity, machinery and skills in a sample of British and German manufacturing plants', *National Institute Economic Review*, No. 111, 48-61.

Danilin, V., Materov, I., Rosefielde, S. and Lovell, K. (1985) 'Measuring enterprise efficiency in the Soviet Union: A stochastic frontier analysis', *Economica*, **52**, 225-33.

Davies, S.W. and Caves, R.E. (1987) *Britain's Productivity Gap*, Cambridge University Press, Cambridge.

Davis, H.S. (1956) 'Economies of scale, expansion path and growth of plants', *Review of Economics and Statistics*, **50**, 293-310.

Dixit, A. (1992), 'Investment and hysteresis', *Journal of Economic Perspectives*, **6**, 107.

Dosi, G., Pavitt, K. and Soete, L. (1990) *The Economics of Technical Change and International Trade*, Harvester Wheatsheaf, Hemel Hempstead.

Fare, R., Grosskopf, S. and Lovell, C.A.K. (1985) *The Measurement of Efficiency of Production*, Kluwer-Nijhoff, Boston, MA.

Farrell, M.J. (1957) 'The measurement of productive efficiency', *Journal of the Royal Statistical Society*, Series A, **120**, part 3, p. 253-81.

Fecher, F. and Perelman, S. (1992) 'Productivity growth and technical efficiency in OECD industrial activities', in R.E. Caves (ed.), *Industrial Efficiency in Six Nations*, MIT Press, Cambridge, MA.

Førsund, F.R. and Hjalmarsson, L. (1974) 'On the measurement of productive efficiency', *Swedish Journal of Economics*, **76**, 141–54.

Førsund, F.R. and Hjalmarsson, L. (1979) 'Generalised Farrell measures of efficiency. An application to milk processing in Swedish dairy plants', *Economic Journal*, **89**, 294–315.

Førsund, F.R. and Hjalmarsson, L. (1983) 'Technical progress and structure, change in Norwegian primary aluminium industry', *Scandinavian Journal of Economics*, **85**, 113–26.

Førsund, F.R. and Hjalmarsson, L. (1987) *Analysis of Industrial Structure: A putty–clay approach*, The Industrial Institute of Economic and Social Research, Stockholm, Sweden.

Førsund, F.R. and Jansen, E.S. (1977) 'On estimating average and best practice homothetic production functions via cost-functions', *International Economic Review*, **18**, 463–76.

Førsund, F.R., Lovell, C.A.K. and Schmidt, P. (1980) 'A survey of frontier production functions and of their relationship to efficiency measurement', *Journal of Econometrics*, **13**, 5–25.

Freeman, R.B. and Medoff, J.L. (1984) *What Do Unions Do?*, Basic Books, New York.

Ganley, J.A. and Cubbin, J.S. (1992) '*Public Sector Efficiency Measurement: Applications of data envelopment analysis*', North-Holland, Amsterdam.

Gathon, H.-J. and Perelman, S. (1989) 'Etude comparative des performances des sociétés de chemins de fer' (with English summary), *Annals of Public and Co-operative Economy*, **60**(1), 61–80.

Goldratt, E.M. (1993) *The Goal*, Gower Press, Aldershot.

Grabowski, R., Kraft, S., Pasurka, C. and Aly, H.Y. (1990) 'A ray–homothetic production frontier and efficiency: Grain farms in Southern Illinois', *European Review of Agricultural Economics*, **17**, 435.

Green, A.J., Harris, C. and Mayes, D.G. (1989) *The Estimation of Technical Inefficiency of Manufacturing Industry, Applied Economics*.

Green, A.J. and Mayes, D.G. (1989) *Technical Efficiency in Manufacturing Industries*, mimeo, University of Exeter.

Green, A.J. and Mayes, D.G. (1990) *Sources of Technical Inefficiency in Manufacturing Industry*, National Institute Discussion Paper, No. 173.

Green, A.J. and Mayes, D.G. (1991) 'The measurement of technical inefficiency of UK manufacturing industry', *Economic Journal*, **11**, 523–38.

Greene, W.H. (1980) 'Maximum likelihood estimation of econometric frontier functions', *Journal of Econometrics*, **31**(1), 27–56.

Griliches, Z. (1987) 'R&D and productivity: measurement issues and econometric results', *Science*, **237**, 31.

Griliches, Z. (1990) 'Patent statistics as economic indicators: a survey', *Journal of Economic Literature*, **28**(4), 1661–707.

Griliches, Z. and Ringstad, V. (1971) *Economies of Scale and the Form of the Production Function: An econometric study of Norwegian manufacturing establishment data*, North-Holland, Amsterdam.

Grinyer, P., Mayes, D.G. and McKiernan, P. (1988) *Sharpbenders: The secrets of unleashing corporate potential*, Basil Blackwell, Oxford.

Haig, B. (1987) 'Industry productivity levels – are we in the world league?', in Bureau of Industry Economics (ed.), *Productivity Growth: The path to international competitiveness*, AGPS, Canberra.

Hammond, C. (1986) 'Estimating the statistical cost curve: an application of the stochastic frontier technique', *Applied Economics*, **18**, 971–84.

Hannah, L. and Kay, J. (1977) *Concentration in Modern Industry*, Macmillan, London.

Harris, C.M. (1988) *Technical Inefficiency of Australian Mmanufacturing industry*, Bureau of Industry Economics, occasional paper 4, Canberra.

Harris, C.M. (1991) *Enterprise Bargaining: Possible outcomes and policy issues*, Working Paper 72, Bureau of Industry Economics, Canberra.

Harris, C.M. (1992) 'Technical efficiency in Australia: Phase I', in R.E. Caves (ed.), *Industrial Efficiency in Six Nations*, MIT Press, Cambridge, MA.

Hart, P.E. (1971) 'Entropy and other measures of concentration', *Journal of the Royal Statistical Society*, **134**, Series A, 73–85.

Hart, P.E. (1980) 'Lognormality and the principle of transfers (the variance of logarithms and industrial concentration)', *Oxford Bulletin of Economics and Statistics*, **42**(3), 263–7.

Hart, P.E. (1993) *The Effects of '1992' on the Pharmaceuticals Industry in Britain and Germany*, National Institute Discussion Paper, Series 2, No. 8.

Hart, P.E. and Clarke, R. (1980) *Concentration in British industry, 1935–75: A study of the growth, causes and effects of concentration in British manufacturing industries*, National Institute Occasional paper, No. 32.

Hart, P.E. and Shipman, A. (1991) *Variation of Productivity within British and German Industries*, National Institute Discussion Paper, 203, August.

Hart, P.E. and Shipman, A. (1992) 'The variation of productivity within British and German industries', *Journal of Industrial Economics*, **40**, 417.

Hay, D.A. and Morris, D.J. (1981) *Industrial Economics: Theory and evidence*, Oxford University Press, Oxford.

Helm, D. and Yarrow, G. (1988) 'Regulation and utilities', *Oxford Review of Economic Policy*, **4**(2), i–xxxi.

Hendry, D.F. (1979) 'Predictive failure and economic modelling in macro-economics: the transactions demand for money', in P. Ormerod (ed.), *Economic Modelling*, Heinemann, London.

Huang, C.J. and Bagi, F.S. (1984) 'Technical efficiency on individual farms in northwest India', *Southern Economic Journal*, **51**, 108–16.

Industries Assistance Commission (1977) *Annual Report 1976–7*, Government Printing Service, Canberra.

Industries Assistance Commission (1978) *Annual Report 1977–8*, Government Printing Service, Canberra.

Industries Assistance Commission (1979) *Annual Report 1978–9*, Government Printing Service, Canberra.

Industries Assistance Commission (1980) *Trends in the Structure of Assistance to Manufacturing*, Government Printing Service, Canberra.

Industries Assistance Commission (1983) *Annual Report 1982–3*, Government Printing Service, Canberra.

International Mathematical and Statistical Libraries (1980) *Reference Manual*, Volume 3 (8th edn), International Mathematical and Statistical Libraries Inc.

Jarque, C.M. and Bera, A.K. (1980) 'Efficient tests for normality, homoscedasticity and serial independence of regression residuals', *Economic Letters*, **6**, 255–9.

Johnston, J. (1984) *Econometric Methods* (3rd edn), McGraw-Hill, New York.

Jondrow, J., Lovell, C.A.K., Materov, I.S. and Schmidt, P. (1982) 'On the estimation of technical inefficiency in the stochastic frontier production model', *Journal of Econometrics*, **19**, 233–74.

Kalirajan, K.P. (1990) 'On measuring economic efficiency', *Journal of Applied*

Econometrics, **5**, 75.

Krafcik, J.F. and MacDuffie, J.P. (1989) 'Explaining high performance manufacturing: the international assembly plant study', *International Motor Vehicle Program International Policy Forum* (May).

Lee, L.-F. (1983) 'On maximum likelihood estimation of stochastic frontier production models', *Journal of Econometrics*, **23**, 269–74.

Lee, L.-F. and Tyler, W.G. (1978) 'The stochastic frontier production function and average efficiency: An empirical analysis', *Journal of Econometrics*, **7**, 385–9.

Leibenstein, H. (1966) 'Allocative efficiency vs X-efficiency', *American Economic Review*, **56**, 392–415.

Leibenstein, H. (1969) 'Organizational or frictional equilibria, X-efficiency, and the rate of innovation', *Quarterly Journal of Economics*, **85**, 600–23.

Leibenstein, H. (1973) 'Competition and X-efficiency: Reply', *Journal of Political Economy*, **81**, 765–77.

Leibenstein, H. (1975) 'Aspects of the X-efficiency theory of the firm', *Bell Journal of Economics*, **6**, 580–606.

Leibenstein, H. (1977) 'X-efficiency, technical efficiency, and incomplete information use: A comment', *Economic Development and Cultural Change*, **25**, 311–16.

Leibenstein, H. (1978) 'X-inefficiency Xists – reply to an Xorcist', *American Economic Review*, **68**, 203–11.

Leibenstein, H. (1980) *Inflation, Income Distribution and X-efficiency Theory*, Croom Helm, London.

Levitt, M. and Joyce, M. (1986) *Measuring Output and Productivity in Government*, National Institute Discussion Paper, No. 108.

McAleer, M. (1984) 'Specification tests for separate models', in M.L. King and D.E.A. Giles (eds.), *Specification Analysis in the Linear Model*, Routledge and Kegan Paul, London.

McCalman, P. (1992) 'Accord type wage outcomes: A comparison with a decentralised system', *Australian Bulletin of Labour*, **18**, 46.

Machin, S. and Stewart, M. (1990) 'Unions and the financial performance of British private sector establishments', *Journal of Applied Econometrics*, **5**, 327–50.

Madge, A., Bennett, R. and Robertson, P. (1989) *Concentration in Australian Manufacturing*, Bureau of Industry Economics, Working Paper 57, Canberra.

Martin, B.L. (1994) 'The aims and effects of government leverage programs', Paper presented to the 1994 Industry Economics Conference, Australian National University, Canberra.

Martin, J.P. and Page, J.M., Jr. (1983) 'The impact of subsidies and X-efficiency in LDC industry: Theory and an empirical test', *Review of Economics and Statistics*, **65**, 608–17.

Mason, G., van Ark, B. and Wagner, K. (1993) *Productivity, Product Quality and Workforce Skills: Food processing in four European countries*, National Institute Discussion Paper, No. 34.

Mayes, D.G. (1983) *A Comparison of Labour Market Practices between Plants in the UK and Seven Foreign Countries*, National Institute Discussion Paper, March.

Mayes, D.G. (1990) 'The implications of closer European integration for Australia and New Zealand', *National Institute Economic Review*, No. 134, 110–17.

Mayes, D.G. (ed.) (1991) *The European Challenge: Industry's response to the 1992 programme*, Harvest Wheatsheaf, Hemel Hempstead.

Mayes, D.G. (1993) 'The implications of European integration for Australia', *EPAC Discussion Paper*, Canberra.

Mayes, D.G. and Ogiwara, Y. (1992) 'Transplanting Japanese success in the UK',

National Institute Economic Review, No. 142, 90–105.

Mayes, D.G. and Young, G. (1993) *Improving the Estimates of the UK Capital Stock*, Report for the Central Statistical Office, July, National Institute of Economic and Social Research.

Meeusen, W. and van den Broeck, J. (1977) 'Technical efficiency and dimension of the firm: Some results on the use of frontier production functions', *Empirical Economics*, **2**(2), 109–22.

Meller, P. (1976) 'Allocative frontiers for industrial establishments of different sizes' *Explorations in Economic Research* **3**, Summer, 379–407.

Metcalf, D. (1989) 'Trade unions and economic performance: the British evidence', *London School of Economics Quarterly*, **3**(1), 21–42.

Metcalf, D. (1990) *Industrial Relations and Economic Performance*, CEP Discussion Paper, No. 129.

Middlemas, K. (1983), *Industry, Unions and Government: Twenty-one years of NEDC*, Macmillan Press, London.

Mizon, G.H. (1977) 'Inferential procedures in non-linear models: An application in a UK industrial cross-section study of factor substitution and returns to scale', *Econometrica*, **45**, 1221–42.

Muellbauer, J. (1986) 'Productivity and competitiveness in British manufacturing', *Oxford Review of Economic Policy*, **2**(3), 1–25.

Nelson, R.R. (1991) 'Why do firms differ, and how does it matter?', *Strategic Management Journal*, **12**, 61–74.

Nerb, G. (1987) 'The completion of the internal market: A survey of European industry's perception of the likely effects', volume 3 of *Research on the Cost of Non-Europe*, Commission of the European Communities, Luxembourg/Brussels.

Nishimizu, D.M. and Page, J.M. (1989) 'Technical efficiency change: dimension of productivity change in Yugoslavia 1965–78', *Economic Journal*, **92**, 920–38.

Olson, J.A., Schmidt, P. and Waldman, D.M. (1980) 'A Monte Carlo study of estimators of stochastic frontier production functions', *Journal of Econometrics*, **13**, 67–82.

O'Mahony, M. (1992) 'Productivity levels in British and German manufacturing industry', *National Institute Economic Review*, No. 139, 46–63.

O'Mahony, M. and Oulton, N. (1989) 'Growth in multi-factor productivity in British industry, 1954–86', *National Institute Discussion Paper*, No. 182.

Oulton, N. (1987) 'Plant closures and the productivity miracle in manufacturing', *National Institute Economic Review*, No. 121.

Oulton, N. (1988) 'Productivity, investment and scrapping in UK manufacturing: A vintage capital approach', *National Institute Discussion Paper*, No. 148.

Oulton, N. (1990) 'Labour productivity in U.K. manufacturing in the 1970s and 1980s', *National Institute Economic Review*, No. 132.

Pagan, A.R. and Hall, A.D. (1983) 'Diagnostic tests as residual analysis', *Econometric Reviews*, **2**, 159–218.

Page, J.M., Jr. (1980) 'Technical efficiency and economic performance: Some evidence from Ghana', *Oxford Economic Papers*, **32**, 319–39.

Panic, M. and Rajan, A.H. (1971) *Product Changes in Industrial Countries' Trade: 1955–1968*, National Economic Development Office Monograph 2.

Parry, T.G. (1977) *Multinational Manufacturing Enterprises and Imperfect Competition*, Occasional Paper 1, Centre for Applied Economic Research, Melbourne.

Pitchford, J. (1990) *Australia's Foreign Debt – Myths and Realities*, Allen and Unwin, Sydney.

Pitt, M. and Lee, L.-F. (1981) 'The measurement and sources of technical inefficiency in the Indonesian weaving industry', *Journal of Development Economics*, **9**(1), 43–64.

Plowman, D.H. (1992) 'Industrial relations and the legacy of new protection', *Journal of Industrial Relations*, **34**, 48.

Political and Economic and Planning (1965) *'Thrusters and Sleepers: A study of attitudes in industrial management'*, Allen and Unwin, London.

Porter, M. (1990) *Competitiveness of Nations*, Macmillan, London.

Prais, S.J. (1981a) *The Evolution of Giant Firms in Great Britain, 1909–70*, Cambridge University Press, Cambridge.

Prais, S.J. (1981b) *Productivity and Industrial Structure*, Cambridge University Press, Cambridge.

Prais, S.J. *et al.* (1990) 'Productivity, education and training: Britain and other countries compared', *NIESR*, London.

Prais, S.J., Jarvis, V. and Wagner, K. (1989) 'Productivity and vocational skills in services in Britain and Germany: hotels', *National Institute Economic Review*, No. 30, 52–74.

Pratten, C.F. (1971) *Economies of Scale in Manufacturing Industry*, Cambridge University Press, Cambridge.

Pratten, C.F. (1988) 'A survey of the economies of scale', in *Research on the Cost of Non-Europe: Basic findings*, vol. 2, Commission of the European Communities, Luxembourg/Brussels.

Ramsey, J.B. (1969) 'Tests for specification errors in classical linear least squares analysis', *Journal of the Royal Statistical Society*, **B31**, 350–71.

Ray, G.F. (1984) *The Diffusion of Mature Technologies*, Cambridge University Press, Cambridge.

Rees, R. (1993) 'Collusive equilibrium in the great salt duopoly', *Economic Journal*, **103**(419), 833–48.

Richmond, J. (1974) 'Estimating the efficiency of production', *International Economic Review*, **15**, 515–21.

Rowthorn, R.E. and Wells, J.R. (1987) *De-industrialisation and Foreign Trade*, Cambridge University Press, Cambridge.

Roy, A. (1982) 'Labour productivity in 1980: An international comparison', *National Institute Economic Review*, No. 107.

Sargan, J.D. (1984) 'Wages and prices in the United Kingdom: A study in econometric methodology', in D.F. Hendry and K.F. Wallis (eds.), *Econometrics and Quantitative Econometrics*, Basil Blackwell, Oxford.

Scherer, F.M., Beckenstein, A., Kaufter, E. and Murphy, R.D. (1975) *The Economics of Multi-plant Operation: An international comparisons study*, Harvard University Press, Cambridge, MA.

Schmidt, P. (1976) 'On the statistical estimation of parametric frontier production functions', *Review of Economics and Statistics*, **58**(2), 238–9.

Schmidt, P. and Lin, T.-F. (1984) 'Simple tests of alternative specifications in stochastic frontier models', *Journal of Econometrics*, **24**, 349–61.

Schmidt, P. and Lovell, C.A.K. (1979) 'Estimating technical and allocative inefficiency relative to stochastic production and cost functions', *Journal of Econometrics*, **9**, 343–66.

Schmidt, P. and Sickles, R.C. (1984) 'Production frontiers and panel data', *Journal of Business and Economic Statistics*, **2**, 367–74.

Schumpeter, J. (1951) *Capitalism, Socialism and Democracy*, George Allen and Unwin, London.

Shen, T.Y. (1965) 'Economics of scale, expansion path, and growth of plants', *Review of Economics and Statistics*, **47**, 420–8.

Simon, H.A. (1959) 'Theories of decision making in economics and behavioral science', *American Economic Review*, **XLIX**(3), 253–83.

Stanford, J. (1992) 'Industrial policy in Australia', in J. Stanford (ed.), *Industrial Policy in Australia and Europe*, AGPS, Canberra.

Steedman, H. and Wagner, K. (1987) 'A second look at productivity, machinery and skills in Britain and Germany', *National Institute Economic Review*, No. 122.

Steedman, H. and Wagner, K. (1989) 'Productivity, machinery and skills: clothing manufacture in Britain and Germany', *National Institute Economic Review*, No. 128.

Stevenson, R.E. (1980) 'Likelihood functions for generalized stochastic frontier estimation', *Journal of Econometrics*, **13**, 57–66.

Stigler, G.J. (1976) 'The existence of X-efficiency', *American Economic Review*, **66**, 213–16.

Summers, R. and Heston, A. (1988) 'A new set of international comparisons of real product and price levels, estimates for 130 countries, 1950–85', *The Review of Income and Wealth*, Series 34, No. 1, March.

Telser, L.G. (1964) 'Advertising and competition', *Journal of Political Economy*, **72**, 537–62.

Thiry, B. and Tulkens, H. (1985) 'Productivité, efficacité et progrès technique', in H. Tulkens (ed.), *Efficacité et management*, Centre Interuniversitaire de Formation Permanente, Charleroi.

Timmer, C.P. (1971) 'Using a probabilistic frontier production function to measure technical inefficiency', *Journal of Political Economy*, **79**, 775–95.

Tirole, J. (1988) *The Theory of Industrial Organisation*, MIT Press, Cambridge, MA.

Torii, A. (1992a) 'Technical efficiency in Japanese industries', in R.E. Caves (ed.), *Industrial Efficiency in Six Nations*, MIT Press, Cambridge, MA.

Torii, A. (1992b) 'Dual structure' and 'Differences of efficiency between Japanese large and small enterprises', in R.E. Caves (ed.), *Industrial Efficiency in Six Nations*, MIT Press, Cambridge, MA.

Torii, A. (1993) *A Memorandum about Technical Efficiency and Business Cycles*, mimeo, Yokohama National University.

Torii, A. and Caves, R.E. (1992) 'Technical efficiency in Japanese and U.S. manufacturing industries', in R.E. Caves (ed.), *Industrial Efficiency in Six Nations*, MIT Press, Cambridge, MA.

Tulkens, H. (1989) *Efficacité et management*, Centre Interuniversitaire de Formation Permanente (CIFOP), Charleroi.

Tybout, J.R. (1990) 'Making noisy data sing: Estimating production technologies in developing countries', Georgetown University, Department of Economics, working paper, 90–16.

Tyler, W.G. (1979) 'Technical efficiency in production in a developing country: an empirical examination of the Brazilian plastics and steel industries', *Oxford Economic Papers*, **31**, 477–95.

Tyler, W.G. and Lee, L.-F. (1979) 'On estimating stochastic frontier production functions and efficiency: An empirical analysis with Colombian micro data', *Review of Economics and Statistics*, **61**, 436–8.

Uekusa, M. and Torii, A. (1985) 'Stochastic production functions: An application to Japanese manufacturing industry' (in Japanese), *Keizaigaku Ronsyu (Journal of Economics)*, **51**, 2–23.

van Ark, B. (1990a) 'Comparative levels of labour productivity in Dutch and British manufacturing', *National Institute Economic Review*, No. 131.

van Ark, B. (1990b) 'Manufacturing productivity levels in France and the UK', *National Institute Economic Review*, No. 133.

van Ark, B. (1992) 'Comparative productivity in British and American manufacturing', *National Institute Economic Review*, No. 142, 63–74.

Wenban-Smith, G. (1981) 'A study of the movements of productivity in individual industries in the U.K. 1968–79', *National Institute Economic Review*, No. 97.

Williamson, O.E. (1963) 'Managerial discretion and business behavior', *American Economic Review*, **53**, 575–90.

Yoo, S.M. (1992a) 'Technical efficiency in Korea', in R.E. Caves (ed.), *Industrial Efficiency in Six Nations*, MIT Press, Cambridge, MA.

Yoo, S.M. (1992b) 'Technical efficiency over time in Korea, 1978–88: Exploratory analysis', in R.E. Caves (ed.), *Industrial Efficiency in Six Nations*, MIT Press, Cambridge, MA.

Yotopoulos, P.A. and Lau, L. (1973) 'A test for relative economic efficiency', *American Economic Review*, **63**, 214–23.

Zellner, A., Kmenta, J. and Drèze, J. (1966) 'Specification and estimation of Cobb–Douglas production function models', *Econometrica*, **34**, 784–95.

Index

absolute efficiency, 24, 73, 95
adjustment, 23
  positive, 185
advertising, 120, 133–4
aerospace, 1
aggregate studies, 28
agriculture, 6
airlines, 6
allocative efficiency, 13, 14, 166
Annual Census of Production (ACOP),
  x, 8, 55, 62, 118, 126, 140, 146,
  186
APEC (Asia–Pacific Economic
  Council), 10
Asia, 2
asymptotic efficiency, 47
Australia, x, xi, 2–5, 79–80, 96–107,
  154–5
Australian
  Bureau of Statistics, 56, 66, 165
  Council of Trade Unions, 5
  Standard Industrial Classification
  (ASIC), 56, 72, 94
average technical
  efficiency (ATE), 51, 52, 69, 70,
  96–112, 163, 165, 168
  inefficiency (ATI), 52, 67, 69, 70, 73,
  82, 84–7, 96–114, 163, 165, 168

balance of payments, 3
Baldwin, John, xi
barriers to entry, 123, 132, 134
Bells whisky, 170
benchmarking, 156

best
  performance, 31
  practice, 3, 27, 185
Bramson, Michael, x
brand
  loyalty, 119, 172
  names, 133
Brazil, 159, 160
brewing, 79, 126
building materials, 73
Bureau of Industry Economics, x, xi, 5,
  7, 65, 157
bureaucracy, 21
Business Statistics Office, x, 56, 66

Canada, x, xi, 80, 131, 165–7, 168, 170–1,
  174–5
capital, 19, 39, 92, 94
  intensity, 139, 173
  stock, 19, 43, 60, 61, 62, 63, 94
cartels, 76, 122, 124
Caves, Richard, ix, x
cement, 76
Census and Statistics Act (1905), 7
Census of Manufacturing
  Establishments, 56
Central Statistical Office, 61, 186
change over time, 166–9, 179–80
chemical industry, 167
Chile, 159, 160, 176
clothing, 1, 4, 157, 183
  and footwear, 73
Colombia, 159, 160, 161
collinearity, 143